PENGUIN BOOKS

THE MEMORY GAME

'Packs a damn good punch . . . an ingenious storyline
with plenty of twist and pace' *Daily Telegraph*

' A treat – both intelligent and unputdownable'
Cosmopolitan

'A remarkable first novel . . . a thoroughly contemporary
thriller' *Independent*

'Haunting' Frances Fyfield, *Evening Standard*

'A beautifully crafted psychological thriller . . .
electrifying' *Harpers & Queen*

ABOUT THE AUTHOR

Nicci French is the pseudonym for the writing partnership of journalists Nicci Gerrard and Sean French. The couple are married and live in Suffolk.

There are now ten bestselling novels by Nicci French: *The Memory Game*, *The Safe House*, *Killing Me Softly*, *Beneath the Skin*, *The Red Room*, *Land of the Living*, *Secret Smile*, *Catch Me When I Fall*, *Losing You* and *Until It's Over* (the new hardback, published in May 2008).

The Memory Game

Nicci French

PENGUIN BOOKS

PENGUIN BOOKS

Published by the Penguin Group
Penguin Books Ltd, 80 Strand, London WC2R ORL, England
Penguin Group (USA) Inc., 375 Hudson Street, New York, New York 10014, USA
Penguin Group (Canada), 90 Eglinton Avenue East, Suite 700, Toronto, Ontario, Canada M4P 2Y3
(a division of Pearson Penguin Canada Inc.)
Penguin Ireland, 25 St Stephen's Green, Dublin 2, Ireland (a division of Penguin Books Ltd)
Penguin Group (Australia), 250 Camberwell Road, Camberwell,
Victoria 3124, Australia (a division of Pearson Australia Group Pty Ltd)
Penguin Books India Pvt Ltd, 11 Community Centre,
Panchsheel Park, New Delhi – 110 017, India
Penguin Group (NZ), 67 Apollo Drive, Rosedale, North Shore 0632, New Zealand
(a division of Pearson New Zealand Ltd)
Penguin Books (South Africa) (Pty) Ltd, 24 Sturdee Avenue,
Rosebank, Johannesburg 2196, South Africa

Penguin Books Ltd, Registered Offices: 80 Strand, London WC2R ORL, England

www.penguin.com

First published by William Heinemann 1997
First published in Penguin Books 1998
This edition published 2008
1

Permission to quote from *A Shropshire Lad* by A. E. Housman is given by The Society of
Authors as the literary representatives of the Estate of A. E. Housman.

Printed in England by Clays Ltd, St Ives plc

ISBN: 978-0-141-03413-3

To Edgar, Anna,
Hadley and Molly

One

I close my eyes. It's all there, inside my skull. Mist following the contours of the lawn. A shock of cold stinging in my nostrils. I have to make a conscious effort if I want to remember what else happened on the day we found the body; her body. The reek of wet, brown leaves.

As I made my way down the short slimy grass slope away from the house, I saw that the workmen were standing there ready. They were clutching mugs of tea and smoking and their warm, wet breath produced a cloud of vapour that rose up from their faces. They looked like an old bonfire that was being rained on. It was only October but this was early in the morning and as yet there was just the promise of sun, somewhere behind the clouds, over the copse on the far hill. I was wearing my overalls tucked a little too neatly into my wellingtons. The men, of course, were obstinately in the traditional rural proletarian costume of jeans, synthetic sweaters and dirty leather boots. They were stamping to keep warm and laughing at something I couldn't hear.

When they caught sight of me they felt silent. We'd all known each other for ever and now they were unsure how to react to me as their boss. It didn't bother *me*, though. I was used to men on building sites, even the miniature, domestic variety of building site like this one, my father-in-law's soggy patch of Shropshire, the Stead, as it was absurdly called, a self-mocking joke about rural squireship that had become serious over the years.

'Hello, Jim,' I said, holding out my hand. 'You couldn't resist coming yourself. I'm glad.'

Jim Weston was as much a part of the Stead as the treehouse or the cellar with its sweet smell of apples that lingered even at Easter. He was associated with almost every man-made object on the property: he had replaced and painted the window frames, spent searing August days stripped to the waist on the roof dealing out tiles. There would be a crisis, a growth on a wall, an electricity black-out, a flood, and Alan would summon Jim from Westbury. Jim would refuse, too busy, he would say. Then an hour later he would creak up the drive in his rickety van. He would contemplate the damage, tapping out his pipe and shaking his head sadly, and mutter something about modern rubbish. 'I'll see what I can do,' he would say. 'I'll try to patch something together.'

It was a matter of local folklore that Jim Weston never bought anything at list price and wouldn't buy anything at all if he could obtain it through favour or barter or through even murkier means in his own contribution to Shropshire's black economy.

When Jim had seen my plan for the new house, his face had fallen even further than usual, as if an architect's drawing was some newfangled invention for the benefit of mollycoddled fools like me from London who'd never got their hands dirty. I'd given a silent prayer of thanks that he'd never seen my original idea. This small house, an overflow space for the Stead, for all the children and grandchildren and ex-wives and so on that accumulate at the Martello gatherings, was the greatest offering I would ever make to the family, so I'd planned for them the dream house that I would have built for myself.

I had taken advantage of the relatively sheltered situation of the original site to conceive a structure of total clarity, nothing but beams, pipes, joists and plate glass, a functionalist dream: the most beautiful object I have ever drawn. I'd shown the plans to my soon-to-be-ex-husband, Claud, and he'd crinkled his brow and run his fingers through his thin brown hair and murmured something about it being really very interesting and well done, which meant nothing at all because this has been his reaction to virtually everything up to and including my announcement to him that I had decided that we should get divorced. I'd thought that his brother Theo at least might see what I was getting at. He'd commented that it looked like one of his old Meccano sets and I'd said, 'Yes, exactly, lovely, isn't it?', but he'd meant it as an insult. Then I had taken it into the presence of the Great Man himself, Alan Martello, my father-in-law, the patriarch of the Stead, and it had been a disaster.

'What's this? The metal frame? What about the thing that's going to be built around it? Can't you do a picture of that as well?'

'That *is* the building, Alan.'

He'd snorted through his grizzled beard. 'I don't want something that's going to have Swedish architecture critics buzzing round it. I want a place for living in. Take that piece of paper away and build it in Helsinki or somewhere far away like that and I'm sure a publicly funded committee will give you a prize. If we've got to have some bloody building in this garden – of which I'm far from being entirely convinced – then what we're going to have

3

is an English country house, with bricks or dry-stone walls or some decent local material.'

'This doesn't sound like the angry young Alan Martello,' I'd said sweetly. 'New styles of architecture, a change of heart, isn't that the sort of thing you've always been keen on?'

'I like *old* styles of architecture. I'm not young. And I'm not angry any more, except with you. Replace that structuralist horror with something I'll recognise as a house.'

It was Alan at his most gruff, charming, flirtatious and I was grateful that he'd felt able to yell at me in the old affectionate way while I'd been in the process of divorcing his son. So of course I'd gone away and put together a plan of impeccably rural appearance, complete with a rather amusing gambrel roof. It was designed in the sense that you design the contents of your shopping trolley as you walk around Sainsbury's. The prefabricated frame construction house was Norwegian, though manufactured in Malaysia. Alan would at least have been grateful to know that the extraction of the raw materials probably involved the destruction of a small patch of rain forest.

'What's this up here, Mrs Martello?' Jim Weston had asked, jabbing at the plan with his pipe.

'Please call me Jane, Jim. They're the ridge tiles, set in mortar.'

'Hmm.' He'd replaced his pipe firmly in his mouth. 'What do you want to go messing about with mortar for?'

'Jim, we can't argue about this now. It's all arranged. It's bought and paid for. We've just got to put it together.'

'Hmm,' he'd grunted.

'We excavate here, just a few feet down . . .'

'Just,' Jim had muttered.

4

'Then the footings, here and here, and then the hard core, then the damp-course and the damp proof membrane, then concrete and then the tiled ground floor on top of that. The rest is a matter of just joining it together.'

'Damp-course?' Jim had said dubiously.

'Yes, unfortunately there was a Public Health Act passed back in 1875, so I'm afraid we're stuck with that.'

Now, at the beginning of the first day of work, Jim looked more like something that was growing in the garden than a man who had come to supervise, or pretend to supervise, work in it. His face had been left outside in all weathers and had attained a complexion like the rear end of a toad. Hair sprouted from his nose and ears like moss on an ancient rock. He really was old now and his job consisted of telling his son and his nephew what to do. Their job consisted of ignoring what he said. I shook hands with them as well.

'What's this about *you* digging?' Jim asked suspiciously.

'Only a spadeful. I just said I'd like to dig the first spadeful, if that's all right. It's important to me.'

I've been an architect for nearly fifteen years now, and whenever I work on a building, I have a rule, which amounts almost to a superstition, that I must be there to see the first spade being dug into the ground. It's a moment of pure sensual pleasure, really, and I sometimes wish that I could do it myself with my own bare hands. After months, sometimes even years, of drawing up the plans and the specifications and obtaining tenders and calming the nerves of the client and bargaining with some functionary in the planning department, after all the compromises and the paper arguments, it's good to go outside and remind myself that it's all about dirt and brick

5

and fitting the pipes together so they don't crack in the winter.

Best of all are the ten- or fifteen-metre excavations which precede the really big buildings. You stand on the edge of a site somewhere in the City of London and peer down at a couple of thousand years of fragments of other people's lives. You'll see the suspicion of an ancient building, sometimes, and I've heard all the rumours of the contractors surreptitiously pouring concrete across an old Roman floor so that there's no nonsense about waiting for the archaeologists to give you the nod before the building goes up. We're constructing the spaces for our own lives on the squashed remnants of our forgotten predecessors and in a couple of hundred or a couple of thousand years they'll be building on top of our rusting joists and crumbling concrete. On top of our dead.

This was to be the smallest of holes, a scratching of the surface. John, Jim's son, handed me a spade. I'd measured the area out on the previous day and defined it with cord and now I walked into the middle of the rectangular space and pushed the blade into the ground and stood on it, forcing it into the turf.

'Mind your nails, girl,' said Jim behind me.

I pulled the handle of the spade down towards me. The turf crackled and split and a satisfying wedge of soil and clay appeared.

'Nice and soft,' I said.

'The boys'll just finish it off, then,' said Jim. 'If that's all right with you.'

A hand on my shoulder made me start. It was Theo. The Theo Martello in my mind is seventeen years old with shoulder-length hair parted in the middle, soft white translucent skin, full lips, with a prominent cupid's bow, that taste slightly of burnt tobacco. He is tall and thin and wears a long army-surplus greatcoat. I find his remembered figure hard to reconcile with this – oh my God – forty-something-year-old man standing in front of me with gaunt chiselled features, rough unshaven stubble, cropped greying hair, and hard lines around his eyes. He's middle-aged. *We're* middle-aged.

'We didn't see you last night,' he said. 'We arrived late.'

'I went to bed early. What're you doing up at this time?'

'I wanted to see you.'

He pulled me towards him and hugged me close for a long time. I held my favourite brother-in-law tightly.

'Oh, Theo,' I said, when he let me go. 'I'm sorry. I'm sorry about Claud.'

He smiled. 'Don't be. Just do what you have to do. It was brave of you to come up here and beard everyone in the family den. By the way, who *is* coming?'

'Everybody, of course. All the Martellos. And all the Cranes too, for what we're worth. Dad and my brother and his lot aren't here yet, but, by the time they arrive, I count that there'll be twenty-four guests. The Royal family may be collapsing, and we may have lost the meaning of Christmas, but the annual gathering for the Martello mushroom hunt goes on undiminished.'

Theo raised his eyebrows. The lines around his eyes and mouth creased in a smile. 'You mock.'

'No. I'm nervous, I suppose. God, Theo, do you remember, years ago, some ferry was sinking and a rescue boat pulled alongside and the women and children couldn't get across. So this man lay across between the two boats and the women and children walked across him.'

Theo laughed. 'You were the worn-out human bridge, were you?' he said.

'I felt like it sometimes. Or at least Claud and I were. The weak link that held the Cranes and the Martellos together.'

Theo's expression hardened. 'You flatter yourself, Jane. We're all linked. We're one family really. And anyway, if there's one link, it's the friendship between our fathers that started it, before we were born. Let's give them credit for that at least.' He smiled again. 'At best you were just a secondary link. A supporting mortice or whatever?'

I couldn't help giggling. 'Do I hear a technical term? What, pray, is a supporting mortice?'

'All right, all right, you're the builder. I never did wood-work. And I'm glad you came here, even if it meant running the gauntlet.'

'I had to supervise this, didn't I? Now I feel like I'm going to cry over my drawings and smudge them.'

We went through the French windows into the kitchen and collected mugs of coffee. From upstairs there was the sound of bodies stirring, cups clinking, lavatories flushing in the house behind us as we stepped back out.

'Shut the door behind you, for fuck's sake,' somebody yelled from inside. 'It's freezing.'

'Okay, okay, I'm just stepping outside.' It was Theo's brother, Jonah.

'Hello, Fred,' said Theo.

Jonah nodded in acknowledgement of the tired Martello joke. The point was that Jonah and his twin brother, Alfred, had been indistinguishable, as children at least. Theo had once told me that they had actually slept with each other's girlfriends (without the knowledge of the young women concerned), which I'd been too shocked to believe until I had seen the way they'd behaved in all other matters when they had grown up.

'The way to tell us apart, Theo,' said Jonah, 'is that Fred is the one with the red nose and without the sun tan.'

'Yes, I was going to comment on that, Jonah. Where was it this time?'

'Tucson, Arizona. A cosmetics conference.'

'Good?'

'There were some interesting possibilities floating around.' Jonah noticed Theo's smile. 'Now that everybody's teeth are so good we've got to think of other things to do with them.'

Theo bent over and sniffed the vapour floating up from Jonah's mug. 'Among them seems to have been the idea of toothpaste in the form of a hot drink,' he said.

'It's peppermint tea,' Jonah replied. 'I don't like starting the day with an unnatural stimulant.' Then he turned to me and his virtuous expression melted into a sort of sad smile. God, were they all going to smile like that at me this weekend? 'Jane, Jane,' he said, and hugged me in a gesture whose warmth was hampered slightly by having to balance the herbal tea in his mug at the same time. 'If there's anything I can do, just ask. That,' he continued, pointing down at the activity on the grass in front of us, 'that is a very positive step. It's a very good thing for you to have done that for all of us, for the family. I'm sure it's therapeutic as well.'

'Oh, yes, Jonah,' I responded, 'it was very relaxing in my time of need to consult with Alan and Claud and Theo and then redo everything and then go over it in sign language with Jim. I wish we'd stuck with my original plan.'

'Any carbuncle will be better than having to relive the

sort of night I spent in my room last night with Meredith and the kids, who didn't sleep for more than three minutes at a stretch for the entire night. And Fred plus the bits of his *famille* that aren't at boarding school were next door. As far as I can tell, the only couples to get a room to themselves were Alan and Martha and your son and his bit of fluff.'

This last was aimed at me.

'Alan *insisted* that Jerome and Hana have a room to themselves,' I protested. 'I think it gave him some sort of vicarious, predatory pleasure. I don't even know where my younger son ended up.'

'Or who with,' added Jonah. 'And far be it from me to breach the inviolable tradition which gives you Natalie's room to yourself. It sounds like a bedroom farce.'

I followed Jonah and Theo back into the kitchen but I didn't feel like food, or like joining what was now almost a throng of people fighting for access to the fridge or the stove. I could see no sign of either of my sons. Alan and Martha would exercise the privilege of the hosts and be down late, but almost everybody else seemed to be around. Claud, looking rumpled and pathetic after his night on the sofa, was stirring a large pan of eggs over the gas. Breakfast is the one meal of the day I've never been much interested in cooking, but since it is as much an organisational as a culinary matter, Claud has always excelled at it. He nodded amiably at me as he spooned the eggs out onto a large dish for Fred.

It was exactly a year since I had last seen the four brothers together in the same room. Here in their holiday clothes, their old jeans and sweaters or lumberjack shirts, they looked like students again, or even schoolboys, joshing each other and laughing. All except Claud who never quite got it right in casual clothes. He needed a uniform and strict rules. The twins, with their dark complexions and high cheekbones, would have looked more dissolutely sexy after an uncomfortable night on a couch. Claud needed eight hours' sleep and a well-cut suit to look his best, but his best was very good.

I stole a banana from the fruit bowl and escaped outside again with my coffee. The mist was dispersing in the hollows. The sky was blue now and it was barely eight o'clock. It was going to be a bright day, though very cold, and my overalls weren't quite warm enough.

I suppose that most of us have a landscape of the mind, the one that we see when we close our eyes, and this rolling patchwork of fields and woods was mine. Every tree, every path, every fence had associations which blended together in a mulch of memories from long summer weeks, and briefer weekends of snow or bare trees or new flowers, in which different years, even decades, were now indistinguishable.

The Stead was far from being an ancient house – the stone over the front door bore the inscription '1909 – P.R.F. de Beer', which was the name of the man who had had the house built – but it had always seemed old to us. The front door, though we never thought of it as that, was round the other side of the house and the drive led from it to the B8372 which went to Wales if you turned left and Birmingham if you turned right. But from where I was now standing, in front of Pullam Wood, I was looking across a small depression to the real front of the house, the doors that led to the living room and to the kitchen, and above them, the windows of Alan's and Martha's bedrooms and of the spare bedrooms, and above them, on a floor of its own, Alan's workroom, his sanctum, with its absurd little wooden spire on top. It was a large house, yet it seemed intimate; it was solid, yet the wooden floors were rickety and the walls thin as paper.

I reached the fringes of the wood – which I never go into – and turned to the right, away from Pullam Farm, and made my way around and down to where the men were tinkering with the digger. I heard a car arrive, Paul's unmistakable top-of-the-range Saab, splendid but not so excessively as to be too much of a betrayal of some political principle or other. Dad gingerly got out of the far side. He didn't notice me and shuffled over to the house. Then Erica appeared, also from the far side. She must have been sitting in the back seat and she was carrying little Rosie, asleep in an almost theatrical slumber. She bustled quickly inside. Paul caught sight of me and we waved at each other. There was no one left to wait for.

At ten o'clock not very sharp everybody gathered on the lawn for the great mushroom expedition, the inviolable tradition of the Martello autumn. The gathering of the extended family was so large that with a few pink coats and a pack of dogs, it would have looked like the local hunt. All those brothers and their families, and in the case of my brother, Paul, previous family and current family. I thought of one of those unreadable chapters of the Old Testament. Alan begat Theo and Claud and Jonah and Fred. And Chris begat Paul and Jane. I counted twenty people, not including me or Jim's workers, bustling around and chatting and not looking as if they were going any-where. The group was held up by the non-appearance of some of the younger generation, most notably Paul's three daughters by Peggy, his first wife. At about ten past, they finally strolled out, nonchalant, big-booted, long-haired, all in black, wearing one sarcastic expression that seemed to have been stretched across their three lovely faces. Because I was staying behind to oversee the building work, I stood slightly apart and was able to take in the whole scene. Christ, what a family. Everyone else was a mess of jeans and old sweaters but Alan and Martha were properly dressed. This was their day. Alan was wearing some ridiculously correct long jacket that would have kept him dry if he'd been standing under Niagara Falls. There was always the hint of theatrical camp about him, of the person who had been sent down to the costume department with instructions that he be kitted out as an ageing writer living the life of a country squire. He even had a staff that looked like the sort of thing that Errol Flynn used to battle with on fallen trees across streams. Martha looked lovely though: snow-white hair, slim as her granddaughters, and wearing much the same sort of black clothes, but not the Doc Martens. She wore a jacket that had been weathered on real walks and she carried the right sort of wicker basket for laying out mushrooms without mixing or decay. Almost everyone else had plastic shopping bags. I had once tried to explain to Martha that, contrary to legend, plastic bags were a good idea if you were going to eat the mushrooms on the same day, as we always did, because they softened them, made them go high, like game. But she hadn't listened.

Alan rapped his staff on the ground. I almost expected a peal of thunder.

'Forward,' he said.

It would have sounded ridiculous coming from anybody else.

It seemed to happen quickly after that. I went inside and

sat at the kitchen table waiting to be needed again outside. I half read the paper and did a few clues in the crossword and there was a tap on the window and I looked up and saw Jim's face through the glass of the kitchen door. I was going to shout some comment but his face was pale and alarmed. He just gestured me forward and I felt a moment's reluctance, not wanting to go.

As I came out of the door, Jim shuffled back towards the hole and I saw it was almost completed and I wondered if this was just a pedantic way of telling me about it. The men were grouped around the digger. The small group parted as I approached.

'We found something,' said one of them, Jim's nephew. He looked almost shifty.

I looked down at their feet. At first it didn't seem as if there were all that much to see. Toffee-textured clay soil, some broken tiles. What were they? Oh, yes, that's where the old barbecue must have been. That seemed a long time ago. And, shockingly white, there were some bones, jaggedly projecting from the soil. I looked at the men. Did they want me to take charge in some sort of way?

'Could it be an animal?' I said. Ridiculously. 'A buried pet?'

Jim slowly shook his head and knelt down. I didn't want to have to look.

'There's bits of clothes here,' he said. 'Little bits. And a buckle. It must be her, mustn't it? It must be their little girl, Natalie.'

I had to look. I had seen one dead body in my life. I had sat holding my mother's hand in the final moments of her years of pain. I had seen death wipe the expression from her face and her racked body had relaxed back into the bed. I had pressed my lips against her still-warm face. A day later I had touched it again in the funeral parlour, waxy and cold, her hair brushed, in her best clothes, with a small bag clutched pathetically in her left hand. And this was the body of Natalie, my dear, dear friend, after a quarter of a century, for ever sixteen. I knelt and made myself look closely at the bones. From the legs they must be, large and thick. There were traces of clothing, black, thickly grimed. I felt suddenly detached and curious. No flesh, of course. No sinews. The bones that had been detached from the ground were entirely separate. The soil in which they lay was darker than the rest. Would the hair have decayed? The skull was still buried. I remembered her lean body. Brown that summer. I remembered the mole on her right shoulder, and her long simian toes. How could I have forgotten her for so long?

'Someone had better call the police.'

'Yes, Jim, yes. I'll do that now. I don't suppose we ought to do any more digging. Is there a police station in Westbury?'

There wasn't. I looked in the phone book and I had to phone the police all the way off in Kirklow. I felt rather foolish saying to someone I didn't know that we'd found a body and that it was rather old, about twenty-five years, that I thought it was probably the body of Natalie Martello who had gone missing in the summer of 1969. But they took it seriously and in a short time two police cars arrived and then a civilian car and then later an ambulance, or rather a sort of ambulance that looked like an estate car. It seemed strange to have an ambulance to pick up bones that were so long dead they could have been put into a small cardboard box. One of the policemen asked me some halting questions on which I could hardly concentrate. The ambulance didn't take the bones away immediately. A flimsy kind of miniature marquee was raised over most of the hole. There was a light rain falling.

I didn't want to go and look at what they were doing but I couldn't leave the scene and I sat on a bank near the kitchen door and looked down at the tent and across at the wood beyond. I wondered if people would be coming back soon. I had my watch on but I couldn't remember what time they had left and I couldn't even remember how long mushroom hunts take as a rule, though I'd been on so many. I just sat on the bank and finally I saw a small group emerging from the trees. We always separated on these excursions and came back in our own time. They would be able to see the police cars and the incongruous tent but I couldn't see if they were surprised. I stood up to make my way towards them to explain what had happened but my eyes were suddenly wet and I couldn't see who they were. It could have been anybody.

Two

The knife slid through the spongy layers into the beige flesh. I peeled off some slimy skin, tossed an edible chunk of cep into a large bowl. Peggy came in with another bucket full of mushrooms; she smelt of the woods, the mulchy earth. Her khaki trousers were stained; she'd taken off her boots in the hall, and now padded in thick grey socks.

'Here you are,' she said.

With my fingertips, I gently lifted the yellow, gilled chanterelles lying like waxy flowers at the top, and sniffed at their curved trumpet shapes. Apricots.

'Who found these?' I asked.

'Theo, of course. Are you all right, Jane?'

'You mean about Claud?'

'No, about today.'

'I don't know.'

In the bucket there were warty, bulbous puffballs, horse mushrooms with a faint whiff of aniseed about them, and delicate white ink caps, fraying around their skirts. The kitchen smelt damply fungoid; wormy parasol mush-rooms blocked up the sink, tatters of woody stalks lay on the working surfaces. I wiped my hands, which were still trembling, down my apron and pushed back my hair. The kitchen was brightly lit, but nothing seemed quite real to me – not the horror in the garden, nor this parody of normality in the clutter of the Martello kitchen, heart of their large house. Were we all insane, a houseful of shocked people trapped in ritual? I was losing myself in activity.

'You did well,' I said to Paul, who was passing through the kitchen clutching dusty bottles of red wine to his chest.

'You should have seen them all: we could have picked twice as many. Some of them are useless though.'

He glanced at Peggy furtively on his way out. He looked harassed. We were each of us alone with our thoughts and private alarms. He had the additional burden of being stuck in a house with his ex-wife, current wife, and a sister who was divorcing his best friend. There was a necessity not to think too much.

I started chopping the mushrooms into thin slivers; the flesh was spongily resilient. I turned them and cut them smoothly along the grain. Pots bubbled. The effort of co-ordination soothed me. I opened the door of the oven and touched the oily red peppers with a fork; their skins were blistering. I drew in a deep breath.

'Jane? Claud told me to give you these.' My father held out three plump garlic bulbs. Turning to go – back to the crossword by the fire, probably – he suddenly said, 'It'll be all right, won't it?' and I saw that his eyes were puffy, as if he'd been weeping. I squeezed his shoulder.

'It'll be fine,' I said, meaninglessly.

I peeled six garlic cloves and crushed them into a large pan on the stove. Peggy, who was stooped over the sink, patiently stripping the spongy layers off the remaining ceps, sung a snatch of song under her breath and then said abruptly, 'I'm really sorry. It must have been horrible for you, finding it – her.'

'Yes,' I said. 'I suppose so. But no worse, really, than for everybody else.'

I didn't want to talk. I was saving up my emotions, I didn't want to expend them here, while making dinner. Not with Peggy, but she was unstoppable.

'You were all very brave. It's funny really: for the first time, I feel excluded from this family. You all know how to deal with each other.'

I turned to her and took her hand. 'Peggy,' I replied wearily, 'that's not true. You know that we never exclude anybody. We're the great extended family that starts with Alan and Martha and doesn't end anywhere.'

'I know all that, maybe it's just that I never knew Natalie.'

'It was a long time ago.'

'Yes,' said Peggy, 'a part of the great legendary idyllic Martello childhood. You all share that, don't you? It always reminds me . . .' She stopped as she caught sight of something out of the window. 'Look at them! I'll kill them! Why can't Paul deal with them? He *is* alleged to be their father.'

She hurtled from the room. Out of the window I could see her daughters standing conspiratorially behind a bush smoking cigarettes. They must have thought they were invisible. Peggy jogged noiselessly towards them, still shoeless. Jerome and Robert used to smoke in their bedroom, with the windows wide open, then come downstairs smelling of toothpaste, and I'd say nothing. I, too, was surreptitiously smoking, in the garden, late at night when I couldn't sleep for pondering about my life. Later, they'd learnt to smoke in my presence, even to offer one to me. I'd been itching for a cigarette all day, fidgeting on the edge of the hole, wandering round the garden, waiting for everybody to get back and learn what I had learnt. I stirred the pale yellowing garlic around the pan. A little manageable span of time, a way of measuring out the evening ahead.

'How are you doing, Mum? Do you mind being left to do all the cooking?'

Robert was standing over me, my tall, handsome son. His lank, dyed blond hair hung straight down over one pale eye. He was clothed in torn jeans, an old blue sweat-shirt that was worn almost grey and a checked shirt pulled roughly over it, cuffs unbuttoned, everything unbuttoned. His feet were bare. He looked good.

'It's all right. It helps me, in fact. Could you wash the lettuce?'

'Not as such,' said Robert, opening the fridge and peering inside. 'Is there anything I can eat?'

'No. What are all the others up to?' I asked.

'God, where shall I start.' He started counting theatri-cally and sarcastically on his fingers. 'Theo's playing chess with Grandpa Chris; Dad's basically co-ordinating the seating plan and delegating the laying of plates; Jonah and Alfred and Meredith have gone for a walk, probably to try to sneak a look into that tent thing; Hana and Jerry are in the bath, the same bath; and much, much more. I haven't seen Granny and Grandpa. They must be up in their room.'

There was a pause. Robert looked expectant. I tipped the mushrooms into the hot oil. He was waiting for something.

'Yes?' I said.

My knees felt wobbly and my stomach suddenly lurched. He cupped his hands over his mouth and began to speak as if through a megaphone; his voice blared

20

into the kitchen, bitter and angry. 'Hello, hello, is there anybody out there? This is Rob Martello speaking, a visitor from the real world. I'd like to announce that a body has been found on the premises. The only daughter of Mr and Mrs Alan Martello has been buried outside, about three feet from the back door and about two inches deep, for the last twenty-five years. The management regrets that as a result of this discovery, dinner may be served a minute or two late. We trust this will not interfere with your evening.'

I gave a tired laugh, I couldn't help it.

'Robert!' It was Claud. He had come in behind Robert but he was smiling too. 'I know it's awkward . . .' Claud began, but Robert immediately interrupted him.

'What? Awkward? The body of your sister dug up in the garden? Why should that be awkward? And anyway, it was a few hours ago now, wasn't it? And the police have taken the bones away. Perhaps Alan should have asked them to fill the hole in before they left, while they were at it. The way it is now, there's a chance that somebody may fall into it tomorrow morning and be reminded of it. On their way to another *fucking* mushroom hunt.'

Claud tried to look stern but failed and gave a resigned smile. 'You're right, Rob, we're probably not handling this very well but . . .'

'But appearances must be maintained. We don't want something like a dead body to get in the way of a great Martello weekend. Or else something serious might go wrong. You know, like serving the wrong wine with the wrong mushroom.'

Claud turned serious. 'Robert, stop this now. Natalie's disappearance happened before you were born, it's hard for you to understand. We gradually realised that Natalie was dead. Your grandmother – my mother – never really did. She always tried to believe that Natalie might have run away and that she would turn up one day.' Claud put his arm round Robert. He was tall enough to be able to do it. 'Today is bad for her – it's bad for all of us but it's especially bad for her – and we've all got to be strong and help her. If anything, it's good that this happened when we were together. We can support each other. And above all support Martha. There's lots to talk about, Robert. And not just about Natalie, about everything. And we will, I promise. But maybe today is just a time for us to be together. Remember that she hasn't officially been identified yet.'

'And isn't it good for us to eat together?' I said. 'Come here, my darling.' I pulled Robert to me and hugged him, hard. 'I feel silly only coming up to your chin.'

'So will you help me, Rob?' asked Claud.

'Yeah, yeah, Dad, all right,' said Robert. 'We can all be mature about this. Perhaps we should make a feature of the hole. Mum, could you redesign your cottage around the hole, the way you did with that tree once?'

'Is that a yes or a no?' Claud asked with that touch of steel he could suddenly bring into his voice.

Robert raised his hands in mock surrender. 'It's a yes. I'll be good,' he said, and backed out of the kitchen. Claud and I gave each other mirrored shrugs of helplessness. We were getting on better than we had when we'd been together. I realised that I had to guard against misleading nostalgia.

'Thanks,' I said. 'That was good.'

Claud leant over a bubbling casserole. 'That smells delicious,' he said. 'Like you said, we're still good friends, aren't we?'

'Don't.'

'I didn't mean anything.' He paused. 'I thought we'd eat at nine. Will that be all right for you?'

He looked me over. I was wearing tracksuit trousers and a man's shirt that had once belonged to Jerome. I had pulled on the first clothes I'd been able to lay hands on after my scalding shower. I'd wanted to wash everything away: the sweat of hard labour, the tears, the muddy soil that had held the body.

'That'll be fine, as long as I put the meat on now.'

I crumbled rosemary over the lamb and slid the joint into the oven. Then I turned up the heat under the haricot beans and poured rice into the mushroom pan, stirring vigorously. As always, Claud had lots to do but now he seemed unwilling to leave. He leant against the work surface and toyed with the remnant of a parasol mushroom that I had rejected.

'They think we're mad, you know.'

'Who?'

'The people around here. The only ones they'll eat are the ones that look exactly like the kind you get in boxes at the supermarket. But you can see what repels people, can't you? They're a little like flesh, don't you think? Not quite wholesome.' Claud picked up a field mushroom and stroked it with one finger. 'They have no chlorophyll, you see. They can't make their own carbon. They can only feed themselves on other organic material.'

'Isn't that what all plants do?'

'It sometimes worries me that you can say things like that,' he observed in the mournful tone that, I suddenly realised, I didn't have to bother about any more.

'How's Martha? Have you seen her?'

'Mother is being wonderful,' said Claud.

There was a tone of exclusion in his voice that chilled me and I was going to snap something back when Peggy stormed into the kitchen, her cheeks flushed, the soles of her woollen socks stained black from the garden. She picked up a tumbler and a bottle of whisky and marched out of the kitchen again.

'Peggy,' Claud called after her retreating back, 'remember we're eating in an hour or so and there'll be lots of wine.'

'Claud!' I hissed in rebuke but Peggy could take care of herself. I heard a snort that may have been a response as she thumped up the stairs. Claud turned back to me and said, very kindly, 'Are you all right, Jane? Is there anything I can do for you?'

Erica gusted into the kitchen, all perfume and purple nails and copper curls.

'Claud, there you are. Theo wants you to help him move some beds around upstairs. Jane, you angel, what can I do to help?'

She had already changed for dinner, her long slit skirt trailed the ground, her aubergine silk shirt swelled over her large breasts (well, bigger than mine), bangles clanked at her wrists and long ear-rings hung from emphatic lobes. She giggled and I remembered how much, in spite of everything, I liked Paul's young wife, who flowered so exotically beside poor Peggy's weary, ostentatious shabbiness.

'I've just seen Peggy's little girls sneaking into the out-house. Oh, to be fifteen and smoking in a shed again. Christ, what a weird foul day. Poor Natalie. I mean I assume it *is* Natalie, and not some archaeological relic. I suppose it must be, and you're all quite right to feel dreadful. My views about children dying have changed completely since Rosie, you know. Not that I was ever in favour of it, of course. I'd kill myself, I think. Frances was saying that she and Theo think it's probably a relief for Martha, but I wonder if that's true.'

She dipped her taloned fingers into a bowl of olives and popped a few absentmindedly into her avid red mouth.

Claud started methodically pulling corks from bottles, till eight of them stood in an open-mouthed row. I grated Parmesan cheese into the steaming pan of mushroom risotto and added a knob of soft unsalted butter, not from the fridge but from the larder, as butter ought to be. I'd always wanted a larder. Theo and his wife, Frances, walked past the window, tall and elegant. She was speaking animatedly, her eyes hard, but I couldn't make out the words and I couldn't see Theo's face. Then my brother-in-law turned his head and looked straight into my eyes. The years reeled back. He gave an embarrassed half-smile but Frances said something else. He turned his face back towards her and they walked on.

When I'm at the Stead I stay in the room I've had since I was a child. More like sisters than best friends, Natalie and I used to fight over who would have the bed nearest the window, and she'd usually win. It was her house, her bedroom, her bed. After she disappeared, I couldn't sleep where she had always slept. I would lie at the other side of the room, under the sloping roof, and hear the grandfather clock down the hall, and occasionally the hoot of the owls which nested in the woods. Sometimes I'd wake in the middle of the night and for a few seconds, until I had remembered all over again, I would see her shape under the blankets. Martha hadn't got rid of any of her things; she'd always been waiting for her to return. So every year, when we came here for our holidays, I'd have to put my clothes among Natalie's, mummified in polythene, which gradually became less and less familiar to me, until I realised they were the clothes of a young girl from whom I'd grown away without realising, into adulthood. One day they were gone.

Now I pulled back the curtains and looked out of the window at the garden, which was disappearing into night. Evening mist rose like smoke from the wet grass. The sky was nearly dark, but the horizon was pink. It'll be a nice day tomorrow, I thought to myself, as I stared out. Heaps of leaves lay in strange shapes round the lawn, waiting to be burnt. Away to the right I could see another, lower shape, the police canopy. Is there a company somewhere that manufactures tents for erecting over places where dead bodies have been found? There must be. It was very quiet. Paul's girls, down at the edge of the woods, sat in a conspiratorial triangle, now little more than a three-peaked shadow in the gloom. Voices floated up from downstairs, though I couldn't catch what they said. A pipe gurgled, there was a splashing in a drain outside, footsteps passed by my door and I imagined Jerome and beautiful Hana, pink as a prawn, scuttling down the corridor wrapped in towels. I thought I heard a quiet sob.

I opened my suitcase and lifted out a Victorian jacket, high at the neck and tight at the wrists, sexy-severe. Wearing it made me feel a bit more in control. I dabbed perfume behind my ears, and put on my ear-rings. I thought of Natalie that last summer, trying on purple lipstick, staring at herself steadily in the mirror, like a cat, with her blue eyes like my blue eyes. I thought of the pathetic bits of bone I'd seen in the clay this morning. What was I doing in this house, with Claud whom I was

26

divorcing, and his parents whom I was hurting, and his brother Theo, with whom I was exchanging knowing glances through the kitchen window, like a teenager?

'Jane, Hana, Martha and Alan.' It was Claud calling up the stairs. 'Come on everyone. I'm about to open the champagne.'

Three

Martha and Alan made their entrance like important guests. Alan came in on a crest of conversation, broad hands gesturing, belly hanging generously over his belt, beard untrimmed and grey hair touching his rather worn collar. But the tie was fashionably garish and his tweed jacket was unexceptionable. Always the bohemian who didn't care about clothes, but a *rich* bohemian. He hugged Frances, who happened to be standing near the door, and clapped Jerome heartily on the back. Jerome, his hair cut short in a Keanu Reeves crop, dressed in jeans and a black T-shirt, looked depressed and ill at ease. He was speaking only to Hana. She was also dressed entirely in black which emphasised her slavic features. Jerome glared at Alan who didn't notice.

'Here we all are then,' Alan cried, 'I'm dying for a drink.'

Beside him Martha looked pale, thinner than I'd remembered, her skin softening into old age. I could tell that she'd been crying steadily; she had that bright, fragile look about her. Jonah went and kissed her on the cheek: he was a beautiful man, I thought, dark-haired and blue-eyed. Why had I never found him or Fred attractive, the way I had Theo through that long hot summer? *The* summer. Perhaps each of them seemed one half of a man; I still thought of them as one word, Jonah-Fred, the twins.

And I still found their identical appearances a bit comic, or absurd. Their hair was receding a bit now, their beauty had begun to crack. They wouldn't age well, I thought. But even their separate wives, families, jobs, homes hadn't been able to carve out their separate personalities. I wondered if they still played jokes on people.

Claud started easing off the first champagne cork, and everyone stood with their glasses held forward expectantly. There was a murmuring in my ear. Peggy was standing beside me.

'I'm not sure that champagne is quite the thing in the circumstances,' she said.

I gave a shrug in response that could have meant anything. There was a harsh clinking. We all looked around. Alan was rapping his cigarette lighter against his champagne glass. Once he had all of our attention, he stepped into the middle of the room. There was a long pause and he looked reflective. If I had not known Alan, I might have been alarmed or embarrassed by this excessive silence. But I was reminded of a television programme I had seen about another megalomanic showman, Adolf Hitler, who had always begun his own great speeches with these lengthy, diffident pauses in order to secure the complete attention of his audience. When Alan spoke, his voice was at first so quiet that we all had to lean forward to hear what he said.

'You know how I like to welcome you all here with a joke or two, but this has become a different sort of occasion from what was planned. You may all be interested to know that I have just finished talking on the telephone to Detective Superintendent Clive Wilks, who is the head of the CID at Kirklow. He was being cautious, quite properly, but when I asked if the remains were consistent with them being of a sixteen-year-old girl, he said they were. Which, of course, is no surprise.' He gave a thin smile. 'And I'm afraid that Jane's wonderful house will have to be delayed for the moment.

'This mushrooming dinner is our tradition. It's very precious to me, the coming together of our two families and all their children and loved ones.' Here the group shifted uncomfortably. What was he going to say? 'But tonight's dinner is one that I will remember for the rest of my life. Twenty-five years ago our daughter Natalie disappeared. For some time we believed, or tried to believe,' this last with a glance at Martha, trembling on the edge of tears, 'that she had run away and would return to us. That hope faded, but it didn't die. Waiting for someone who never comes is a terrible thing, a terrible thing. Today, we have found her and at last we can properly mourn her death and celebrate her life. She can be laid to rest. I feel I should say something about her. Describe her, my only daughter. I don't know quite what to say.'

He was suddenly a sad old man at a loss. There was a boozy whisper in my ear.

'What a bloody showman. He's loving it, isn't he?'

It was Fred. He was already very drunk. I told him to hush.

'She was clever and beautiful and young; her life was just beginning.' I heard a stifled sob, but couldn't tell from whom it came. 'She was stubborn and she was bolshie.' Tears were rolling down Alan's cheeks now; he didn't bother to wipe them away but continued steadily. 'She never liked goodbyes – even when she was a tiny little girl, she would push me away if I tried to hug her outside school. She would never wave from a bus; she always used to look straight ahead. That was my girl, she never looked back. But we can say goodbye to her now.' Alan looked down at the glass in his hand, and then, more composed, he continued. 'This is a new era of our life,' he put an arm around Martha's narrow shoulders, held rigid against grief. 'Perhaps I can even write a proper book again,' he added, with a half-laugh. 'Anyway, I wanted to say to you that I am glad we are all here today. You all loved Natalie, and Natalie loved you.' He raised his champagne glass, bubbles winking in the firelight. 'I'd like to propose a toast. To Natalie.'

People looked at each other. Was this in good taste?

'To Natalie.'

Before I could get the champagne into my mouth, half of it was spilled as Fred emotionally clutched me to him.

'I'm sorry about your marriage, Jane,' he said thickly, 'and I'm sorry about your building. I've never seen one of your buildings and I was looking forward to sleeping in that one. But there'll always be a ghost in it now, won't there?'

'I wouldn't say that.'

'I would. I would say that,' said Fred. 'But the real question is this.' Here he paused so long that I thought he had finished. I would have moved away if he had not been clutching my sleeve. 'The question is, is it a happy ghost or a sad ghost?'

'I don't really know,' I said, looking for a means of escape.

'And what secrets does it have to tell?'

'Yes, but it's supper now,' I said and raised my voice. 'Supper, everybody.'

It was over. Pulpy rice with chewy-soft mushroom; pink

herby lamb; chocolate soufflés puffed at their rims. Candlelight softened everybody's faces; voices rose and fell like a rhythm. Even the young people, playing Boggle by the fire, spoke softly. Even Alan, twiddling the stem of his glass and declaiming on the state of the contemporary novel (rotten, of course, in his absence), didn't raise his voice. Fred had buttonholed me again and told me that Claud and I should both hire his wife, Lynn, to arrange our divorce, but his development of this scheme was interrupted when Lynn realised what was going on and took him up to bed.

'I must be pushed before I fall,' he said as Lynn sternly led him up the stairs.

'Is he all right?' I asked Lynn when she came back down, alone.

Lynn was a handsome assured woman, immaculately turned out in a dark velvet skirt and jacket.

'He's involved in a restructuring of the trust,' she said. 'It's been rather stressful.'

'Sackings?'

'Downsizing,' she said.

I hoped she would elaborate but she started offering sympathy and I lost interest. As soon as I could, I left Lynn and joined Jerome, who was still looking sullen, and Hana. He responded to my questions in monosyllables. I moved across to Theo who was staring into the fire. I touched him on the shoulder and he started.

'Sorry,' I said.

He turned but hardly seemed to see me.

'I'm thinking of the silliest things,' he said. 'When she was younger, eleven or twelve, we used to do cartwheels, in summer, when the grass was dry. The only way I could ever do cartwheels at all was to do them really quickly.

She used to laugh at me and say that my legs weren't high enough. She would do them and her skirt or dress would fall down, over her head sometimes, and we – I mean the boys – would laugh at her. But she could do them slowly, the way they're meant to be done. Down on your hands, then one leg slowly up, then the other leg following it, like two spokes in a wheel. Then down. They were perfect and we were too proud to tell her.'

'I don't think she minded,' I said. 'She always knew what she was good at.'

'And I remember when she used to sit reading, over there in the window seat, she always looked cross. That was what she looked like when she was concentrating. Cross. It was funny.'

I nodded, unable to speak. I wasn't ready for all this.

'You know that old cliché of coming back from school and finding your little sister has turned into a woman? It was a bit like that when she was fourteen, fifteen, sixteen. I'd come back from school in the holidays and she'd be going out with people she used to play with. And then Luke, remember?' I nodded. 'I felt strange about it. Not good, in a way. It was the first time in my life that it had occurred to me that we'd all be growing up. And that I'd see Natalie grown up and a mother and all that and I never did.'

He turned towards me. His eyes were wet. I took his hand.

'I remember that cross look,' I said softly. 'That awful summer when it rained all the time and she said she was going to learn how to juggle and she spent day after day with three of those bloody beanbags or whatever they were. She had that cross look and her tongue out of one corner of her mouth, day after day, and she did it.' I was just inches away from Theo now. We were murmuring to each other like lovers. 'I remember her lying in front of this fire. The flames in her eyes. I was next to her, right close up. And we'd giggle if anybody said anything to us. God, we must have been irritating.'

Theo smiled for the first time. 'You were.'

The spell was broken. Claud was in the background somewhere opening a bottle of port. The thick purple liquid gurgled softly into a trayful of glasses. He held up a hand and the murmur in the room ceased. 'To the cook,' he said, and smiled ruefully at me across the meal's debris. This dinner suddenly felt like a farewell. I wondered what would happen now, and I felt scared of the future.

'To Jane,' echoed everyone.

'To Alan and Martha,' added my father. I could tell from his voice, which slopped around its normally precise edges, that he was a bit drunk.

'And to Claud who's organised it all,' shouted Jonah above the hubbub.

'To Theo, who found the parasols,' said someone at the back.

The sweet and melancholy spell was broken.

'To us all,' said Alan.

'To us all.'

Four

My car didn't start at first. The morning was cold and the engine wheezed and died several times before coughing into life. I wound down the window. My sons were there, looking bleak. Robert was coming with me.

'Bye, Jerome, bye, Hana. Ring me when you get back to London. Drive carefully.'

Hana came up and kissed me through the window. I blew a kiss at Rosie, who pointed a finger at me which she then inserted into one nostril. Paul was loading an improbable amount of luggage into their car. I called to him. He waved. Alan and Martha stood side by side to see me off. I leant out and took Alan's hand and squeezed it.

'Alan,' I said, 'shall we meet next time you're in London?'

I felt awkward, as if I were asking if we could keep in touch. He ruffled my head as if I were still a teenager.

'Jane,' he said, 'you'll always be our daughter-in-law. Isn't that right, Martha?'

'Of course,' she said, hugging me.

She smelt so familiar: powder and yeast and wood-smoke. Martha had always managed to be gloriously sexy and reassuringly homely all at once. There were tears in her eyes as she kissed me, and for a moment I wanted nothing so much as to undo everything I had started: the separation from her son, the wretched plans for the cottage which had uncovered the remains of her daughter. Then she squeezed my hand.

'Actually, Jane, you're more a daughter than a daughter-in-law.' She hesitated, then added: 'Don't let me down, my dear.'

What did she mean? How could I let her down?

Claud came out of the house carrying a neat suitcase. He started to walk towards us, then stopped. He would be dignified about all this. He'll not give up, though, I thought as I looked at him: such a familiar figure. I knew where he'd bought his jeans, and in what order he'd packed his suitcase. I knew the music he'd put on in the car, and how he'd keep the needle just under seventy, and I guessed that when he got back to his small new flat in Primrose Hill, he would first of all phone me to make sure I'd arrived safely, and then pour a whisky and cook himself an omelette. Beside me, Robert sat quiet and tense. His pale, smooth face was quite blank. I put a hand on his for a moment, then lifted it to wave at Claud. He nodded.

'Goodbye Jane,' he called, and climbed into his compact car.

We left the Stead together, and for miles, as I drove through the Shropshire countryside, I could see Claud's small blue car and his dark head in my mirror. When we got to the motorway Robert put some loud music on, I put my foot on the accelerator, and we left Claud far behind.

Cigarettes are wonderful. Every morning I showered and went downstairs in a dressing-gown, where I ground some coffee beans, poured fresh orange into a glass, and lit up. I'd study my plans for my new project with a cigarette. I'd smoke whenever I lifted the phone. I'd smoke in the car –

God, how Claud would have hated that. I often smoked in the dark, at the end of a day, watching the glowing tip making lines in the air. I measured out my days in little tubes of nicotine. I smoked each morning when I thumbed through newspapers to see if there were any more references to the discovery of Natalie's body now that she had been identified, solely through her dental record. 'Tragic daughter of Angry Young Man,' said the *Guardian*. 'Martello Tragedy,' the *Mail*. Alan gave interviews, and they were usually accompanied by library pictures of him as a younger and more successful man.

I returned to London on the Sunday and at the end of that week I was phoned by an officer from Kirklow CID. They wanted to interview me purely as a matter of routine. No, I wouldn't have to come up to Kirklow, a couple of officers would be in London next week. I arranged a time and the following Tuesday morning at 11.30 sharp there were two detectives sitting in my front room. They were Detective Sergeant Helen Auster, who did all the talking, and Detective Constable Turnbull, a large man with red hair combed flat on his scalp, who sat with an open notebook not taking notes. I made us coffee and Turnbull and I smoked as well.

Auster was dressed in a businesslike grey flannel jacket and skirt. Her hair was light brown and she had startling yellow eyes, which seemed to be focused on something behind my head. She wore a wedding ring and she was young, almost ten years younger than me, I guessed. As we sipped our coffee, we exchanged trivial observations about how big London was. They didn't seem in a hurry to get down to business and I was the first to raise it.

'Are you doing the rounds of the family down here?'

Helen Auster smiled and looked at a notebook. 'We've

just come from your father, Mr Crane,' she said. She spoke in a light Birmingham accent. 'After lunch we're meeting Theodore Martello at his office on the Isle of Dogs, then we're going on to the BBC Television Centre to see your brother, Paul.'

'You'll spend most of your day in traffic,' I said sympathetically. 'Do you expect people to remember anything after all this time?'

'There are a few questions we have to ask.'

'Are you treating Natalie's death as murder?'

'It's a possibility.'

'Because she was buried, I suppose.'

'No, there is some evidence that is consistent with strangulation.'

'How can you possibly know that just from her bones?'

Auster and Turnbull exchanged glances.

'It's just a technical detail,' said Auster. 'Strangulation almost always fractures a bone called the hyoid bone which is at the base of the tongue. The hyoid bone of the deceased is fractured. But of course it's been in the ground for a long time.'

'Somebody must have buried the body,' I said.

'Yes,' said Auster.

'And that person must have killed her?'

'Maybe. At the moment we're just trying to collect information. As you probably know, it was assumed for some considerable time that Natalie Martello had run away from home. The last reported sighting was on the morning of 27 July 1969.'

'On the day after the big party, yes,' I interrupted.

'It was only months later that statements were taken and the inquiry didn't proceed very far. Natalie Martello remained registered as a missing person.'

There was a pause, which I leapt to fill as usual. 'I'm afraid the trail must have gone awfully cold by now. How are you going to find out anything?'

'What we're trying to say to people is, if you remember anything, however small, let us know.'

'Yes, of course.'

Auster looked down at her notebook once more. 'The last sighting of Natalie was by a local man, Gerald Francis Docherty. He saw her by the side of the river that runs along the northern edge of your parents-in-law's property. Obviously, we would like to hear of any later sightings.'

'I think we were asked this at the time. I didn't see her after the party.'

'Tell me about the party.'

'You must have heard about it from my dad. It was Alan and Martha's twentieth wedding anniversary. They'd been away on a cruise somewhere and my dad met them off the boat at Southampton on the day of the party and drove them straight up to Shropshire. The family had arranged a large celebration. There were lots of guests, and dozens of them stayed the night, in the house or in nearby houses. Lots of them slept on the floor, I think, in sleeping bags. I mainly remember the preparations. Claud and I had been running errands, I remember that – collecting various things, food, glasses. Natalie had too, I think. The party itself was on a lovely evening, very warm with that baked feeling you get at the end of a summer's day. We had a barbecue. Claud did that, with Paul helping him; why do men always do the barbecue, handle all the dead meat? Natalie was wearing a sleeveless black dress, I think. She always wore black that summer; I imitated her; so did Luke. That was her boyfriend, as you must know. They were very trendy; they were kind of skinny and sulky; they made me feel clumsy, rural, even though I was the one who lived in London. I'm rambling. What do you want me to tell you?'

Helen Auster looked a little blank and embarrassed. I don't think she really knew what she wanted me to tell her.

'Do you remember what Natalie was like at the party?'

'How do you mean?'

'Did she seem depressed? Angry? Exuberant?'

I felt my cheeks flush. When I thought of the party, it wasn't Natalie I remembered, it was Theo.

'I don't really remember seeing much of her. It was a very big party, you know. There were about a hundred people there.'

'I thought you were her closest friend.'

'I know, but it's hard to remember with parties, isn't it?'

'Yes,' said Helen Auster. 'What happened on the next day?'

'The party sort of continued, I think. Lots of the guests hung around, or returned. People went for walks and things, and then everyone started drinking champagne at midday.'

'Were all the family there for the party?'

'For the party itself, yes. Typically, having organised the whole thing, Claud left before dawn on the Sunday morning and went down to London with his best friend, Alec, to catch a flight to Bombay. He spent two months going round India with about twenty pounds in his pocket. Claud and I always meant to go there together. That seems unlikely now. I should explain that we're getting divorced.'

'I'm sorry.'

'That's all right. Brought it on myself. People were scattering throughout the day. I imagine it would be completely impossible to reconstruct who exactly was where at any one point on that day.'

'Except for Natalie, by the river, shortly before one o'clock. Was there any particular reason why she should be there?'

'None that I can think of. I mean, no particular reason, except it doesn't seem so odd that she should have been. I'm sorry, I don't think I'm being much help.'

'That's all right. Anyway, I gather that you were indirectly responsible for the body being found. Why were you building the cottage just there?'

I explained that I'd originally wanted to build the cottage – only then it wasn't going to be a cottage, but a structure – further down the hill, but had changed my plan when I'd found that a small tributary of the river flowed just beneath that area. Drainage would have been difficult and very expensive. I told her about the digging, and how we'd unearthed Natalie's bones.

'Why did you assume that it was Natalie?' she asked.

'I don't know,' I replied, slightly taken aback. 'I suppose it was just that Natalie disappeared, and I always thought she must be dead – though Martha would never believe that – so when there was a body next to the house, well . . .' I trailed off, then tried again. 'I've always thought that one day we would find Natalie's body. So in a way I've been waiting for that, and I think that perhaps we all have. But I never thought that, well, that she'd been killed. I assumed she'd had an accident or something. So finding her, it was awful, not just because it was her, but because somebody must have buried her. In fact, that's what I wanted to ask you about. Don't you think it's a peculiar place to bury

Natalie – in the garden, just a stone's throw from where she lived?'

Auster smiled across at her colleague. 'We were talking about that, weren't we, Stuart? It could be seen as a very clever place to hide a body. Most murderers aren't very good at hiding bodies. Remote areas of scrub or moorland might seem like a good idea, but they are places without much activity and it can be easy to see that digging has taken place. A garden is constantly being dug up.'

'But there are lots of people around in a garden,' I protested.

'Yes,' she said, with an obvious lack of interest. She clearly had no wish to sit debating theories with me. 'As I said, if you remember anything that might be significant, please get in touch.'

She looked at her watch and asked if there was a pub nearby. I said there was one at the end of the road and she asked if I would like to join them for a bite of lunch. I loathe pubs and I wasn't hungry but I said I'd have a drink. Turnbull said he wanted to go to Oxford Street on the way to the Isle of Dogs, so Helen Auster and I walked along the road to the Globe Arms, where she ordered a pint of bitter and a lasagne and I toyed with a tomato juice and smoked cigarettes. I began to take to Helen, as I now called her. She talked about being a female officer and the canteen culture, and about her husband who was a delivery coordinator in Shropshire for Sainsbury's. She asked me about my divorce and I confided a few banalities. When it was almost time to go, I returned to the case:

'It's all too late, isn't it?' I said. 'You're not going to be able to find anything out.'

'There are one or two possibilities, but it will be difficult.'

'It looks like you drew the short straw.'

'I thought so. Now I'm starting to think that the Martellos are an interesting family.'

Helen gave me a card and wrote her direct line on it. As we parted on the pavement on Highgate Road, I told her that she must get in touch the next time she was down in London and she promised to. Is it possible that I could become friends with a policewoman?

'Don't you think it's time you gave up smoking?'

Kim was sitting across the table from me; a candle on the paper tablecloth cast shadows on the pale triangle of her face. She skewered some swordfish with her fork, swilled it back with a gulp of wine.

'How many are you on now? Thirty a day?'

I had finished my meal – or rather, I had pushed it away, hardly touched, and was now sitting in a state of light-headed contentedness, blowing blue smoke over the debris of the table. I waved over the Italian waiter, and pointed at the empty wine bottle.

'Another of these please.'

I tapped the chimney of ash into the ashtray.

'More than thirty, I hope. I'm going to stop soon. Honestly. The trouble is, I do enjoy it so much. It doesn't make me feel ill or anything.'

The waiter came over, uncorked a bottle of amber wine and poured it into my glass to taste.

'I stopped quite easily before. I'll stop again.'

'Yesterday I saw the results of a woman I referred for a chest X-ray. She had a persistent cough and some mild chest pains. She'll be dead by this time next year. She's forty-four, with three teenage children.'

'Don't.'

'And how's your hostel coming on?'

'Don't.'

It wasn't coming on at all. It was a site marked on a piece of paper; a conversation in the office; a matter for meetings at the council offices; a subject for planning permission. At work, I had dozens of large sheets of graph paper on which I had blocked in my proposals: geometric designs, square by square, with sharpened pencils. I was just waiting for someone to tell me I could go ahead. Meanwhile, there was talk about consultation with local people. I didn't like the sound of that.

'Okay, let's not talk about the hostel,' said Kim. 'Let's talk about you. What are you doing with yourself now that you're alone?'

'I lit another cigarette, and poured another glass of wine.

'I've become a convenient single woman,' I said. 'I'm starting to find myself seated next to the divorced man at dinner parties. Does that happen to you much?'

Kim shrugged. 'Not any longer.'

'We don't usually have much to say to each other,' I continued. 'Then there are friends whom I haven't seen for ages, who suddenly ring me up, and they sound so sorry for me now that Claud and I have separated, and I can't help feeling some of them are quite pleased to be able to be sorry for me. But actually, I'm quite enjoying living on my own.' I was surprised by the firmness in my voice. 'I watch films on TV in the middle of the day, and go to exhibitions, and get in touch with people I'd let slip. I can be untidy. The house feels large, though. For ages, there have been four of us living there, and now there's just me. There are some rooms I never go into. I suppose I'll have to sell it one day.'

It wasn't just that the house felt large; it felt lonely. I spent as little time as possible there now, though in the past I had loved it when Claud and the boys had all gone out and left me alone. For nearly two decades I had gone out to work every weekday, and raced home to a large rackety house which was full of noise and mess and loud boys shouting for my attention. I'd vacuumed and ironed, and done the washing, and cooked, and as they'd grown older I'd ferried the boys back and forth from increasingly alarming social venues. I'd given dinner parties for colleagues – mine or Claud's. I'd gone to Christmas plays and summer sports days and cobbled together packed lunches from an empty fridge. I'd played Monopoly, which I hate, and chess, at which I always lose, dreaming all the while of a book by the fire. I'd made cakes for the school bring-and-buy. I'd baked late at night to make myself feel a good mother, especially after my own mother had died. I'd suffered loud records from the latest groups that had made me feel middle-aged when I was in my thirties. I'd overseen the acne and the sulks and the homework. I'd stayed in our bedroom when the boys had had parties. I'd sat, evening after evening, sipping a gin and tonic with Claud before supper. I'd woken up night after night with my head full of lists, woken up in the morning with a tired headache, gone to sleep in the evening knowing that my day was so full there was no room left for me.

Now there was no loud music, no sulks, no calls from a phone box at one a.m., 'Mum, I've missed my lift home, can you come and get me?' They'd all gone, and I could do whatever I chose: my time was my own, which was what I had always missed. But I didn't know how to deal with time, so I filled it up. I spent long hours in the office, often staying until eight o'clock in the evening. And then, as often as not, I went out. It's true that I was receiving lots of invitations from people who thought I might be in need of cheering up, or people who needed an extra female for their table. I went to films, sometimes illicitly in the middle of the day.

When I got home, I would drink a glass of wine, smoke a couple of cigarettes, and go to bed with a thriller. The long Victorian novels which I'd promised myself would have to wait. At weekends, I watched film matinées, and went for walks on the Heath. Were autumns always so damp?

One Sunday, I'd gone to Dad's house to cook lunch for him, and after we'd eaten I'd asked if I could look through the old photographs. I'd wanted to find pictures of Natalie, I didn't have a single one. Without realising it, Claud and I had erased her from our life. Now I wanted her back again. I leafed through old albums, looking for her image. Often she was only a blur at the edge of a picture; or a just-recognisable face in the group photos that we'd posed for each summer: eleven faces staring at the staring lens. There was Alan and Martha, young and glamorous and exuberant; Mum, always to one side and looking away – how she'd always hated having her photograph taken. After she died, Dad had searched for her perfect likeness among all the years of memorialising her – but always her head was turned towards something else. There were lots of Paul and me – tiny, with round tummies and bare legs, solemn at six or seven, awkward at thirteen – caught by the camera's eye and pasted down in Dad's book, with his looped script underneath. I found one of Natalie and myself at eight, standing hand in hand in front of the Stead, and staring at the camera. We looked quite similar then, though I was smiling anxiously and Natalie was glaring from under beetle brows. Natalie had rarely smiled, never to please. I'd taken away that photo, and another which must have been taken only a week or so before she died. She was wearing a sleeveless T-shirt and cut-off denims, and she was reading a book on the lawn at her house. Her lanky bare legs were tucked under her; a single lock of black hair fell over her pale face; she was absolutely absorbed. Had our last words been friendly, I wondered, or had we quarrelled? I couldn't remember.

What could I remember? I remember going with her to a party at Forston, near Kirklow, when we were about fourteen. I'd told her about a boy I'd been looking forward to seeing. What was he called? He had dark hair, parted in the middle. After a bit, Natalie had disappeared. Later, wandering about, I'd almost stumbled on Natalie and the boy with blond hair entwined on the floor. They were together for the whole party. It had seemed like for ever. Alan had picked us up at eleven o'clock in his Rover. I had sat in the back seat, crushed, and Natalie had slid over to me. Without a word she'd put her arms round me and held me close. I could smell his patchouli in her hair. Was I forgiving her or was she forgiving me?

One evening, the month after the discovery of the body, I'd been at a private view of an artist's paintings and I met William, a solicitor who had once been married to a woman with whom I had long since lost touch. He was a tall, blond man, handsome in a smooth, unfocused way. I remembered him as lean, but he now had a visible paunch. We strolled round the room together with our tall-stemmed glasses of sparkling wine, looking at large and derivatively painted canvases. The wine relaxed me. I told him about my marriage ending, and he asked what

47

had made me actually leave Claud. I didn't want to get into this.

'I suppose,' I answered slowly, 'that I couldn't bear to think that this was my life. It's hard to put into words.'

He told me that he had separated from his wife, Lucy, seven years before, and saw his daughter every other weekend. They had broken up because he had had an affair with a woman in his office.

'I don't know why I did it,' he said. 'It was like a madness, like a landslide which I was helpless to resist.'

I said that I had heard that excuse before and he gave a pained smile.

'God, Jane, I know. When Lucy left, I looked at the other woman and, of course, I didn't feel a flicker of desire for her: nothing. I destroyed my marriage and lost my only child.'

He stared at an orange splash (£750, according to the catalogue).

'I hate myself for it,' he said.

He didn't seem to hate himself so very much. He took me to a basement wine bar and ordered a bottle of dry white wine and some chicken sandwiches. He told me that he'd recognised me as soon as he'd seen me at the preview; that he'd always found me attractive. I was slightly drunk by now but at the same time eerily clear-headed. I thought to myself, I can get away with this. William was not a man who would leave much trace. I felt nervous though. I smoked, coiled my hair around my finger, chewed the dry salty chicken, drank some more. When we'd finished the bottle of wine, he asked me if I'd like another, and I heard myself saying: 'Why don't you come back to my house and have a drink there? It's just ten minutes in a taxi.'

At home, I drew all the curtains, put on some music, and even turned down the dimmer switch. I poured two glasses of wine, and sat on the sofa next to William. My mouth was dry and I could feel my pulse in my ears. William put a hand on my knee, and I stared down at the unfamiliar, broad fingers; out of the corner of my eye I saw the answering machine winking messages at me. I'd forgotten to ring my father. I turned towards William and we kissed. His breath was a bit sour. I felt his hand under my skirt and along my stockinged thigh, and I wondered how often he did this kind of thing. I pulled back and said, 'I'm out of practice; I've forgotten how to do this.' He shook his head and kissed me again.

'Where's the bedroom?' he whispered.

He took off his shoes and tucked his socks neatly into them. I took off my jacket, and started to undo the buttons on my shirt. He unbuckled his belt and stepped out of his trousers, which he folded neatly and laid on a chair. I felt a flash of dislike for him, but at the same time a muted desire. My flesh felt chilly when I took off my shirt; my body felt unused, awkward. I saw myself in the mirror as I unhooked my bra: there were faint stretch marks on my breasts, and the scar from the caesarean I'd had when I'd given birth to Jerome puckered my stomach. I'd lost weight since October; my arms looked thin and wrists bony. I turned back to William, who was now standing in his underpants.

'What do I do now?' I asked.

'Lie on the bed and let me look at you. You're lovely, you know.'

I pulled off my knickers and laid myself out on the large bed, closed my eyes. A mixture of excitement and embarrassed self-consciousness gripped me as William's hands began their slow journey up my body. I heard the telephone ring, then the answering machine switched on. The voice carried up the stairs quite clearly: 'Mum, hello it's me, Robert, on Thursday evening. I just wanted to make sure you were okay. Let me know what you're up to.' What *was* I up to? I wondered.

I didn't tell Kim much about William that evening, just mumbled that I'd had sex with someone other than Claud for the first time in twenty years and it had been all right, a bit nerve-racking.

'I kept expecting to hear the front door open, and Claud come in.'

'Did you enjoy it?' Kim was looking at me strangely.

'In a way. I mean, he was nice, I got pleasure. Kind of. But, well, I suppose that the next day I felt a bit odd about it. I still feel a bit odd, as if it happened to someone else.'

'Come on, Jane.' Kim got to her feet. 'I'm taking you home.'

I made coffee, and Kim made a fire. She'd always loved building fires, even when we were students. We'd shared a house in my second year at university, and Kim had often spent hours gazing into the flames, feeding them with wood, sometimes even with old essays, like a provincial version of *La Bohème*. As if she knew what I was thinking, Kim said:

'Do you realise, Jane, that we've known each other for more than half our lives?'

I tried to say something, then stopped. Kim crouched by my chair, took both my hands, and gazed at me.

'Look at me, Jane,' she said.

I stared into her intelligent grey eyes. She took a handkerchief from her pocket and wiped away the tears that were streaming down my cheeks.

'Your mascara's run everywhere,' she said. 'You're not going to attract men looking like that, unless you want to go out with a zebra.'

'I don't know why I'm crying,' I sobbed. There was a block of grief in my chest, my nose was snotty. 'I just feel so tired. Honestly, I'm just tired, Kim, it's been an emotional few weeks.'

'My darling Jane,' she said, 'listen to me now. You've stopped eating. You chain smoke. You drink more than usual. You work ten, twelve, hours a day. You can't sleep properly. You go out every night as if you're on the run. Look at yourself in a mirror: you're not tired, you're completely exhausted. You've left Claud, your boys have left you, you found Natalie's body lying in a hole. In the space of a few weeks, your whole life has turned upside-down, and it's more than you can bear, so don't try so hard to bear it. Don't be so brave. If you were one of my patients, I'd advise you to seek professional help.'

'What do you mean?'

'I think you'd benefit from counselling,' Kim said. 'You're in shock. It might help you to talk to someone.'

I blew my nose and wiped my face, and I lit another cigarette, then we sat with a pot of tea and some shortbread biscuits and played a game of chess, which I lost, of course. Then I cried again, great gulps of misery, and I wailed that I missed Claud, I missed my boys, I didn't know what to do with my life, and at last Kim put me into my bed like a child, and sat beside me until I fell asleep.

Five

She was younger than I expected. And she was a she. And it must have shown on my face.

'Is everything all right?' she asked.

'I'm sorry,' I said. 'I was probably expecting an old man with a white beard and a Viennese accent.'

'Do you mean a Jew?'

'No, I don't mean that.'

'Do you feel uncomfortable with a woman?'

'Well, I haven't even had a chance to sit down yet, Dr Prescott.'

Dr Prescott was at least six feet tall which lent force to what was already a most striking appearance. She was pale, almost transparent-skinned, with a long, thin artistic nose. Her wavy brown hair was deftly arranged so that only a few strands fluttered around her neck, giving her the appearance of a Brontë sister. A robustly healthy Brontë sister. A robustly healthy Brontë sister who power-dressed. I was stopping in on my way from Waitrose to the proposed hostel site and I felt faintly shamed by her crisp business suit. And then rather ashamed of being shamed. Did I expect female therapists to wear cheese-cloth and light joss sticks?

'Should I fill out a form or something?'

'Jane – is it all right if I call you Jane?' Dr Prescott shook my hand but then maintained her grip as if she were weighing it. 'Does it feel important to you to make this a formal occasion?'

'Is this part of the therapy?'

'How do you mean?'

I paused for a long time and breathed with slow deliberation. I was still standing up. My new analyst was still gripping my hand.

'I'm very sorry, Dr Prescott,' I said with elaborate calmness. 'I'm living rather a chaotic life at the moment. And a friend of mine, who is a doctor, and whom I trust more than anybody else in the world, has told me that she thinks I'm at a moment of crisis. And I'm having a rather chaotic day as well. I was at Waitrose when it opened and then I dashed home and unloaded everything, although, now I think of it, I haven't put the ice-cream in the freezer, and then I dashed over here. When I'm finished here I have to drive to the site of a building I've designed. I'm going to meet an assistant planning officer, and she is going to tell me that changes have to be made to my plan using money that doesn't have any prospect of being forthcoming and that's only the beginning of a project that is close to my heart and that's going to make me very miserable.

'Now I'm here in your office and I had some hopes that it would be something of a refuge from what I think of as my troubles. I suppose I thought we could begin by discussing what a course of therapy might be able to achieve for me. We could discuss ground rules, establish what sort of things we are going to talk about, that sort of thing. But just at this very moment I want to sit down and get going in some sort of sensible way.'

'Then sit down, Jane.'

Dr Prescott gestured towards the battered couch over

which an eastern-looking rug was draped. I quickly looked around the room. It was obvious that every detail had been planned. There was an armchair at the head of the couch. There was a Mark Rothko poster on the wall that would be invisible to the recumbent patient. On the window ledge behind the armchair there was a small abstract sculpture with a hole in it, carved in, I think, soapstone. The walls and the ceiling were painted a supposedly neutral white. There was nothing else.

'Should I sit or lie down?'

'Whichever you like.'

'It's a couch.'

'Whichever you feel like.'

I huffed and lay down on the couch and stared at the wood-chip paper, a product of a shoddy eighties' conversion. God knows what was under it. If she bought after '87, Dr Prescott was stuck with negative equity. She sat down behind my left shoulder.

'Can't we have a straightforward transaction about anything at all?'

'Why do you choose the term "transaction"?'

'No, no, no, no, no, I don't want to talk about why I chose the term "transaction". Dr Prescott, I feel that we've got off to the wrong sort of start. At this rate we're going to spend an hour without having reached "Good Morning".'

'What do you want to do?'

I felt a prickling in the corner of my eyes as if I was going to cry. 'I would like to smoke a cigarette. Is that all right?'

'I'm afraid it isn't.'

'Why are you afraid?'

'It's just an expression.'

I forced my neck rather painfully around so that I was able to meet Dr Prescott's eyes. 'Just an expression?'

She was unamused. 'Jane, what do you want?'

'I suppose I was expecting that you would ask what my problem was and I'd talk about what was on my mind, the pressures that I've been under, and we'd take things from there.'

'So talk.'

'Dr Prescott, can I ask you something?'

'You can say – or ask – anything you like.'

'Are you experienced at this? I'm in a ragged, vulnerable state. Perhaps we should talk about how I can feel confident about entrusting myself to you.'

'Why do you need to feel confident?'

'If I was dropping my car in to a garage to be repaired I would want to know that the mechanics were competent. I'd find out if the garage was any good. Before I give myself up to this therapeutic process I need to have some sense of what it's going to do for me.'

'Jane, this *is* the therapeutic process. In this room there is nothing outside the process. The way to feel confident about it is to trust it, give yourself up to it.'

They were all laughing around the table. It had seemed like a nightmare at the time but, as I described it, later that evening, it somehow mixed with the wine and the crème brulée and now the cheese, and it became a comic turn.

'I was feeling that I couldn't cope,' I continued, 'I was desperate for some sort of reassurance and I stumbled into this remedial class for deconstructionists. There was no way I was going to pin her down. Every time I asked a question she would be like Macavity the cat. She wouldn't be there. She'd have dodged to the side and she'd be saying that the real thing we ought to discuss is why I felt the need to ask that question. I would have needed a .45 Magnum to get her to tell me the time.'

This was the sort of therapy I needed. I was at Paul's and Erica's opulent house across in Westbourne Grove, the exotic bit of London I never felt really at home in. Around the table for dinner was Crispin, who was one of Paul's directors on his game show, *Surplus Value*, and his girlfriend, Claire. There was Gus, the obligatory eligible single man in whose direction I was being pushed. He was all right but I was much more attracted to the two other men, two Australian builders called Philip and Colin, either of whom would have been far better choices for my crying-for-help one-night stand than whateverhisname was, but unfortunately they were not only both gay, but living together. I wasn't particularly drawn to their technical expertise but they had benefited in other ways from their time in the sun moving heavy objects around.

'So you never managed to get through to her?' Paul asked.

'Yes, I did. In the end there was only one thing I could do: I stood up and said, "I'm going, and I mean that in the sense of walking out of the room and never coming back into it again." To which she replied, she really did, "What is it that you're trying to resist?" I suddenly saw myself trapped in this conversation for the rest of my life like someone being pulled into a whirlpool. So I'm sorry to say I finally told her to fuck off and stormed, it's the only word for it, I stormed out of the room.' I took a sip of wine and the most beautiful drag on a cigarette. 'And the next thing I knew, I found myself here telling you this story.'

'You should have thrown a bucket of water over her,' said Paul. 'She would have probably dissolved away into nothingness. Well done you, anyway.'

'But why *were* you so resistant?'

There was a complete silence around the table. It was Gus, the hitherto silent teacher.

'What?' I said.

'You didn't give it a chance,' he said. 'Your young therapist had a point. If one of my pupils starts to ask me about why we need to learn about history I just tell him to shut up. The very fact of him being so young and not knowing history means he wouldn't understand anything I told him. He can only answer the question by learning history.'

'Well fuck you too,' I said.

There was an awful silence but then Gus grinned and started to laugh which made it seem as if I had been witty rather than hysterically rude and a fairly good-natured argument about therapy ensued, with Erica and Gus guardedly in favour and Paul claiming that 'they' had proved that people who didn't go into therapy recovered more quickly from their neurotic symptoms than people who did. Crispin and his girlfriend were across the table whispering between themselves about something. I began to reach for people's bowls but Paul, who was sitting on my left, motioned to me to stay seated and spoke to me in an undertone.

'Are you all right?'

'I'm all right,' I said guardedly. 'Have you seen Claud?'

'Yes,' he said. 'I played squash with him this morning.'

'And?'

'He beat me three-one.'

'I don't mean that.'

'What do you want me to say? It's hard for him.' He thought for a moment and then visibly took the plunge. 'Jane, my darling, I shall say this just once. Or rather two or three things and I don't want you to say anything in reply. First, you're my sister and I love you and I will always trust anything you do. Claud is my best friend. Always has been, always will be. So it's a little complicated from my point of view but it's a minor problem. Second, I'm not going to say that Claud is a broken man, but the fact is that he's bemused, frankly, about what's happened to his life. He is genuinely baffled about why you suddenly broke up this dream marriage after twenty-one years.' Paul held up his hand to silence me. 'Please don't say anything. I'm not accusing you or criticising you in any way. I'm not saying it or thinking it. You never need to justify yourself to me. Third . . .' Now he paused and took my hand. I thought he might be about to cry, but when he spoke his voice was quite calm. 'The family – our two families, Natalie, and those summers – have meant so much to me that I can hardly put it into words. What was that poem, the one that Dennis Potter used for that film when the grown-ups all played children, *Blue Remembered Hills*? How does it go? Hang on.'

Paul got up from the table and clattered down the stairs so that the floor actually trembled beneath us. I sat at a bit of a loose end, isolated from the discussion going on around me. Gus was getting up to go. I felt a bit abject. We weren't going to be leaving together. We weren't even going to be exchanging phone numbers. He leant across the table and offered his hand:

'It was very nice to meet you, Jane,' he said.

'Yes,' I said. 'I'm sorry I said "fuck off" to you. I don't normally say things like that at dinner parties.'

'That makes it even worse,' he said, but rather cheer-fully. He was probably quite nice. Paul returned up the stairs, nodded at Gus who was going down, and spent too long rummaging through a book.

'Here we are,' he said. '"That is the land of lost content, I see it shining plain, The happy highways where I went And cannot come again." That's what I feel.'

'But you *can* come there again. You go there almost every summer. We've just been there.'

'Yes, but I mean childhood and things like that. That's what going back reminds you of. And finding Natalie, of course.'

He held my hand and I said nothing. It was Paul who broke the silence. 'Oh, and there was something else I wanted to say.' Suddenly he looked shifty. The noncha-lance seemed studied. 'That weekend, it made a huge impression on me. It seemed like one of those moments that changes your life. I thought I might make a film about the family.'

'Paul, are you serious?'

'Yes, I am. I started thinking about it when Alan made his speech. It's the right thing to do now. I feel that I've got to confront this.'

'You might have to – but do *we* have to confront it as well?'

'No, it'll be all right. It'll be a good film as well. I want to get behind the camera again, get back to making documentaries. It feels right.'

'Tired of making money, are you?' I asked teasingly. Paul never found this subject amusing.

'Look, *Surplus Value* runs itself now. Ask Crispin over there. It's a foolproof formula. It just needs a prod every now and then. I need a challenge.' He refilled his glass.

He had drunk too much this evening. He began to speak in a low voice that was almost a whisper. 'Finding Natalie is what did it. She meant so much to me. She still does. For me she represents a lost innocence, everything that slips through your fingers as you grow up, all the things you felt you ought to be and didn't live up to.'

'That's a lot to represent,' I said warily.

The last thing I wanted was an argument about who Natalie meant most to, but Paul just looked solemnly down into his glass. People started to move around the table and Crispin's girlfriend, Claire, sat down on my right. She grinned at me. She had a bob of dark hair, half-way between Louise Brooks and a Beatle, and a round face like a teddy bear, made rounder by her granny glasses.

'When's it due?' I asked.

'God, is it that obvious?'

'No, not really. I didn't dare say anything at first. One of the worst experiences of my life involved congratulating a woman on being pregnant and it turned out that she was just fat. But if the woman who looks a bit pregnant is also wearing loose-fitting dungarees and she doesn't drink or smoke anything for the entire evening, or touch the cheese, then I can take the risk of congratulating her.'

'Bloody hell, I didn't know I'd spent an evening sitting across the table from Sherlock Holmes. What else do you know about me?'

'Nothing. Except that you look very well.'

'I'm afraid you get a point deducted for that. I've been throwing up every day. I thought it was meant to stop after the first trimester.'

'There's no guarantee,' I grinned. 'A friend of mine

was suffering from morning sickness while she was in labour.'

'Thanks,' said Claire. 'That makes me feel *really* sick.' She edged a little closer. 'Look, I'm really sorry about this awful thing with your sister-in-law and everything else that's been happening with you. It must be terrible.'

'It's all right, but thank you.'

'And you were being very funny about that woman you saw but I thought she sounded horrid.'

'I don't know about that, but she isn't what I need just at the moment. I think you would need to be in perfect psychological health to cope with Dr Prescott.'

'You seem quite robust to me, Jane. You just need someone to talk to about it all. Look, you don't really know me, and please just ignore this if it's an irritation, but we do know this therapist who is the most lovely man. He might be just the sort of person you need.'

I must have looked doubtful because Claire became alarmed.

'Alex isn't a guru, or anything out on the fringe, Jane. He won't be doing things with crystals. He's a proper doctor, he's got letters after his name and all that. The main thing is that he's just great, a really nice guy. Let me give you his number. Which I haven't got of course. Crisp, love, have you got Alex Dermot-Brown's number?'

Crispin was deep in conversation with Paul about some technical matter and only heard the question when it was repeated.

'What for?'

'Don't you think he might be a good person for Jane to talk to?'

Crispin thought for a moment, then smiled. 'Yes, I suppose so. Be nice to him, though. He's an old friend.'

His Filofax was open on the table and he flicked through it and found the number.

'Here,' he gave me a slip of paper. 'Should your mission fail, Jane, we will of course deny any knowledge of you.'

Six

The following morning I wrote a letter to Rebecca Prescott enclosing a cheque for the session and saying that I had decided not to proceed. Then, feeling foolish, I rang the number that Crispin had given me. The phone was answered and somebody said something unintelligible.

'Hello, can I speak to Dr Alexander Dermot-Brown, please?'

More unintelligible speech.

'Hello, is your mummy or your daddy there?'

This achieved something at any rate as the gibberish became the comprehensible 'Dada, Dada'. The receiver was apparently snatched away from the first speaker who gave a high-pitched scream.

'Be quiet, Jack. Hello, is there anybody there?'

'Hello, I want to speak to Dr Alexander Dermot-Brown.'

'That's me.'

'You're a therapist.'

'Yes, I know.' There was a clatter in the background and Dermot-Brown shouted something. 'I'm sorry, you've caught us in the middle of breakfast.'

'Sorry, I'll try to be brief. I was given your number by Crispin Pitt and Claire um . . .'

'Claire Swenson, yes.'

'Could I come and talk to you?'

'All right.' He paused. 'What about twelve?'

'You mean today?'

'Yes. Somebody's gone on holiday. If that's not all right, it'll have to be next week some time. Or the week after that.'

'No, twelve will be fine.'

He gave me his address, in Camden Town, near the market. God, more disruption in the office. Not that it mattered all that much. 'Work' for me was the CFM office on the top floor of an old molasses warehouse overlooking the canal and the basin in Islington. The C – Lewis Carew – died of Aids in 1989. Now there was just me and the F, Duncan Fowler, and after the years of recession we were only just approaching a time where there was enough work for two of us. As long as I went to all the meetings concerning 'my' hostel and kept the paperwork up to date and popped into the office regularly then nothing much would go wrong.

I cycled over to the office anyway. I looked through the mail and chatted to our assistant, Gina (she's our secretary, really, but we call her our assistant to compensate for paying her so badly). Duncan came in at eleven looking as relaxed as ever. Duncan is a portly fellow, quite short, with a nearly bald head fringed with reddish curly hair and an almost excessively expansive beard. I told him about some new complications with the hostel, he told me about a housing co-op job which would earn us even less money. Still, it was nothing much to worry about. I have no mortgage, and the children are away being paid for mainly by Claud. Duncan has no mortgage and is divorced with no children and no alimony. We own our leasehold. As Duncan put it in the dark days of the early nineties, before we could go bankrupt, we would first have to get some work.

I told Duncan I was going to see my second therapist in two days and he laughed and gave me a hug and then I got on my bike. I was predisposed to like Alexander Dermot-Brown because I was able to get almost all the way from my office to his house by cycling along the canal. I just had to cross Upper Street and then I could make my way through the wastes of gasometers and railway land past the post office depot and leave the towpath when I got to Camden Lock. Just a couple of hundred yards or so later I was chaining the bike to the railings.

Alexander Dermot-Brown was wearing trainers, jeans and a thin, worn sweater with holes in the elbows through which a checked shirt was visible. He had a craggy jaw, almost like Clark Kent in the old comic strip, and he had wavy brown hair flecked with the first hints of grey and very dark eyes.

'Dr Dermot-Brown, I presume.'

He smiled and held his hand out. 'Jane Martello?'

We shook hands and he gestured me in and downstairs into the kitchen in the basement.

'Would you like some coffee?'

'Lovely, but oughtn't I to be going into a room and lying on a couch.'

'Well, we can probably find a couch somewhere in the house if you're desperate. I thought we should have a chat first and see what we think about things.'

With its ceramic floor and stained-wood panelling and cupboards, the kitchen would have seemed elegant if it had been empty. But there were toys on the floor, the walls were covered with posters, postcards and children's drawings stuck haphazardly with pins and tape and Blu Tack. The walls were scarcely less crowded than the notice board, a largeish area of cork tiling above one of the work surfaces, on which takeaway menus for local restaurants, invitations, notices from schools, snapshots were attached in what looked like a whole series of layers. Dermot-Brown saw me staring around.

'Sorry, I should have tidied up.'

'That's all right. But I thought analysts were meant to work in a neutral environment.'

'This *is* a neutral environment compared with my office.'

He took coffee beans from the freezer and ground them, tipped them into a large cafetière and poured in boiling water. He rummaged in a cupboard.

'I ought to give you some biscuits but all I can find are these Jaffa cakes. If I allow one for each child, that leaves one over. Would you like it?'

'That's all right. I'll just have coffee. Black, please.'

He poured coffee into two mugs and we sat down on opposite sides of the scrubbed-pine kitchen table. A smile was playing across his face as if the whole encounter seemed slightly comical to him, as if he was only pretending to be grown up.

'Now, Jane – is it okay if I call you Jane? And you must call me Alex – why do you think that you need therapy?'

I took a sip of coffee and felt the usual overwhelming desire. 'May I smoke?'

Alex smiled again. 'Well, Jane, one idea I have about therapy is that it's a sort of game and for it to work we both have to agree on some ground rules. One of them is that you don't smoke. I have small children in the house. It also guarantees you at least one benefit from your sessions, even if you achieve nothing else. The other benefit of the rule is that it's very easy for me to abide by because I don't smoke. There is a good chance that I'll be relaxed and in control while you're neurotically suffering from nicotine deprivation, and that's good as well, at least for me.'

'All right, I'll do without.'

'Good, now tell me about yourself.'

I took a deep breath and sketched out my situation, there, over the coffee, which he topped up, in that kitchen, my elbows on the rather sticky table. I told him about my separation and the discovery of Natalie's body. I talked a bit about the Martello family, this wonderful inclusive group that we were all meant to feel privileged to be connected to. I described my single life in London and its dissatisfactions, though I left out my sexual escapade. It took rather a long time and when I had finished Alex waited before responding. His first statement was an offer of more coffee. I felt a bit deflated.

'No, thanks. If I have too much it makes me all trembly.'

He ran his finger round the rim of his coffee mug in a slightly fidgety way. 'Jane, you haven't answered my question.'

'Yes, I have. I said I didn't want any more.'

Alex laughed. 'No, I mean, why do you feel you need therapy?'

'Isn't it obvious?'

'Not to me. Look, you're having to deal with life on your own after – what is it? – twenty-one years of marriage. Have you ever lived on your own?'

I shook my head.

'Welcome to the world of being single,' Alex said in an ironic tone. 'You know, I sometimes have a fantasy of what it would be like if I wasn't married and didn't have any children. I could suddenly decide in the evening to go out and see a movie or have a drink in a bar. Perhaps, occasionally, I meet a woman at a party and I think, if I were single, I could have an affair with her and it would be so exciting. But if I suddenly found myself single, it wouldn't be like that at all. Maybe I'd have an initial bit of euphoria. I might even have one or two sexual experiences. But I doubt whether it would be as much fun as I had anticipated. And then all the things I was used to, the reassurance of seeing people I know when I go home, all that would be gone. It would be hard.'

'I thought *I* was supposed to do all the talking.'

Alex laughed again. 'Who says? You've probably been reading too much Freud. I wouldn't pay too much attention to a man who psychoanalysed both himself and his own daughter if I were you. Anyway, not only do you have all that to deal with but you have a perfectly clear family tragedy as well. You have a perfect right to be unhappy for a while. Do you want me to wave a wand and take it away from you?'

'That sounds tempting.'

'Let me give you a very glib diagnosis, Jane, and it's on the house. I think you're a strong woman and you don't like to feel you can't cope, you don't want people to feel sorry for you. That's the problem. My comment is: life is painful. Allow yourself to give way to that. You could talk to me, of course, but you could also spend your money in other ways. You could have a weekly massage, have some nice meals in restaurants, go on holiday somewhere hot.'

It was my turn to laugh. 'Now that really *is* tempting.'

We were both smiling and there was a rather embarrassing pause. It was the sort of pause that in other circumstances I might have thought of dispelling by kissing Alex.

'Alex, I hate saying "but seriously?" . . . But seriously, I had this talk last night with my brother, who, incidentally, has got this deranged idea of making a film about the family, so you'll soon probably be able to learn all about my problems by watching BBC2, and Paul – that's my brother's name – was talking about our golden childhood. I've always had this image of our golden childhood as well but as he was talking in this nostalgic way there was something inside me that was saying no, no, no. Over the last few days I've been preoccupied with an image. It must be all to do with Natalie being found. But I've been thinking about my golden, golden childhood and a black hole in the middle of it, and I can't get a grip on it and I don't know what it is. Somehow it's there, always on the edge of vision but when I turn to look at it directly it's gone, gone to the edge again. I'm sorry, I'm probably not making sense. It hardly makes sense even to me. If you can imagine it, I'm listening to myself talking as a way of trying to understand. Perhaps what I'm asking is for you to trust me when I feel that there is something worth looking for behind all this.'

As I made this long, incoherent speech, I looked down at the table and when I finished looked up, almost scared of catching Alex's eyes. He was frowning, with a look of alert concentration that I hadn't seen before.

'You may be right,' he said, almost muttering it.

He took my mug and his and put them in the sink. Instead of returning to his chair he began to pace up and down. I didn't know whether I should say anything but decided not. Finally, he sat down again.

'You've probably got false ideas about the process of therapy. You may have seen films in which someone's psychological problem is dramatically solved. You may

69

have friends who are addicted to analysis and they talk to you about the wonderful insight it's given them into their problems and how much happier it's made them. It may have done, but if you've spent three hours a week for five years and twenty grand, then you've got a vested interest in its success.'

'Well, why . . .?'

Alex held up his hand to silence me. 'You do interest me, Jane. I think we could do something. However, I think we've both got to be clear about a few things first. This process isn't going to be like going to the doctor with an infection or a broken leg. You might ask me if I'm going to make you better and we might then have a boring philosophical discussion about whether I am going to do anything for you at all and what we mean by making you better.'

'I'm not looking for some easy answer.'

'I don't think you are. So let me be as clear as I possibly can about what may or may not happen. Let me give you a couple of warnings. You may feel, like many people do, that there could be nothing more pleasant than spending two or three hours a week having a good natter about your problems, getting them all off your chest. In my own experience this is hardly ever true. The process may be unpleasant in itself. How can I describe it?' Alex looked around the kitchen and grinned. 'The mess in this kitchen probably appals you. It certainly depresses me and infuriates my wife. So why don't we just clear it up? Well, although it looks dreadful we're actually used to it and we can find most things we need quite quickly. If I started to clear up, it would involve making everything even more chaotic for a while as I would have to empty all the cupboards as well. There would be a time when everything was worse, with the added fear that we might lose our nerve and leave it in that disastrous state. It would keep on seeming worse until just before the clean-up was completed. Even then, it wouldn't feel quite as comfortable as it did before. And although theoretically the new arrangement might be more functional, because it has been rationally arranged, in practice we would probably be unable to find things more often because we would still be used to the old irrationality. So, you see, I'm an advertisement for leaving well alone.

'You may not even achieve anything. I make no claim at all that after, I don't know, six months or a year, you will be happier or better able to deal with the practical problems in your life. You'll still be living in a world where people die and have irreconcilable conflicts. But I can guarantee at least something. Your life at the moment may seem like a collection of rough notes and impressions. Perhaps I can enable you to turn them into a narrative that will make sense to you. That may help you to take responsibility for your life, even, perhaps, to gain an increased control over it.

'That's something at any rate, and it's the least we can hope for. There are other possibilities as well. Let me give you one speculative example. I'm intrigued by the way you talk about your sister-in-law having been buried there, at the heart of the landscape of your childhood. That's a telling image. Some of us may have bodies in our minds, hidden, waiting to be discovered.'

'What do you mean?'

'Don't worry about it, it's just a thought, an image.'

'What about the practicalities? What do we actually do?'

'Good. Now it gets straightforward. I want to see you

twice a week for an hour which actually lasts fifty minutes. My fee is thirty-eight pounds a session, payable in advance at the beginning of each week. As I have said, it would be entirely understandable for you not to go into therapy at all. I can assure you almost a hundred per cent that without any therapy or treatment at all, you will be feeling substantially better in a year or so. The pain of your sister-in-law's reappearance will have receded and you will be used to your new life. If you do decide to go ahead, and I hope you do, then you have to make a commitment. By that I mean that the sessions are sacred, not to be missed because of work, illness, sexual opportunity, disenchant-ment, tiredness or anything. If you break your leg, come here on your way to A and E. Naturally, you are perfectly free to stop the therapy at any time, but I think you ought to make a private commitment to stick it out for something like four or five months at the very least. And also a mental promise that you'll give it a chance. I mean emotionally and intellectually. I know you're smart and that you've probably read Freud more recently than I have. If you come in here and start wanting to discuss transference, which I don't believe in anyway, then we'll both be wasting our time and you'll be wasting your money. There. Have I said everything?'

'Will it be like this?' I asked. 'Sitting in your kitchen, drinking coffee and chatting?'

'No. As you say, this is just a chat and we're deciding on the rules. When we begin we've got to, as it were, run out on the pitch and start to play. In my view, if this is going to work properly it has to be ritualised, it has to be something outside your normal social life. So, if you want to go ahead, then the next time you come it will be different. It will be in the room that is used for therapy.'

He used the word 'therapy' as if it were an unwieldy term that had been foisted on him. 'It won't be a social occasion. We won't be drinking coffee, we won't really be chatting. You'll lie on a couch, not because that is a psychoanalytic prop, but exactly because it shouldn't feel the way we are today, comfortable, getting on, looking face to face. Now, I'd like you to think about what you want to do, and then phone me.'

'I know what I want to do. I want to go ahead. If I'm not happy with what's going on, then I assure you I'll stop.'

Alex smiled and held out his hand.

'I suppose that's as much of a commitment as I'm going to get from you. All right, it's a deal.'

Seven

From signing divorce papers in triplicate at my solicitor's and rejecting the idea of marriage counselling, I cycled on a cold clear day north through London to the site of my hostel, the very thought of which already caused me a pang. The original idea had been for an entirely new building which would house fifteen Section 117s, that is, mentally ill patients discharged from hospital but still requiring some sort of supervision, if only to make sure they took their medication. I'd provided an elegant, functional and cheap design which, to my not very great surprise, had been rejected out of hand. If my career continued like this, I'd soon have designed as many unbuilt buildings as Piranesi, or Hitler. Plan B was to convert a building that had been a squat and had spent the last two years without a roof.

When I arrived, two men and one woman in suits were already standing outside. My friend, Jenny, from Social Services, was looking harassed, as usual. She introduced me to Mr Whittaker from Health and Mr Brady from Housing.

'How much time have you got?' I asked.

'About minus ten minutes,' said Jenny.

'All right, you get the quick tour. Things would be made easier, by the way, if I didn't see new faces every time I had a meeting.'

I took them up to where the roof wasn't and we worked our way down, all the way from the putative trussed rafters to the redeemed basement, sketching out the primary reconstruction, the basic repairs, the fire escape on the rear elevation and the deft adaptations I had made to the common spaces and passageways to give the house what amounted to an extra floor.

'There we are,' I said, as we stood on the front step, 'not only a work of genius and practicality but a work of genius and practicality that will virtually pay for itself.'

Mr Brady smiled uneasily. 'You may have a point there, and I only wish the auditors' calculations took your argument into consideration.'

'Don't worry, Mr Brady,' I said, 'we'll all be rewarded on Judgement Day.'

Mr Brady and Mr Whittaker exchanged glances. There's something disconcerting when planning officers start looking younger and better dressed than you do.

'Jane, it's an ingenious design. We're very pleased. There *is* one problem, which is that we're facing a fifteen per cent cut across the board, which we're having to enforce uniformly on all our projects, so we hope that you'll be able to incorporate that. Apart from that it's absolutely satisfactory.'

'What do you mean, "apart from that"? You've got a bargain basement scheme already. You accepted our tender.'

'Subject to, you know . . . et cetera et cetera.'

I took on my official tone. 'Mr Whittaker, you will surely confirm that this hostel will be a net saver of money once you stop fifteen people at a time going into bed-and-breakfasts or staying in long-term beds.'

'You know as well as I do, Jane, that that is theoretically true but irrelevant in our accounting terms.'

'Shall I just leave the roof off for the next fiscal year? After all, spring isn't all that far away. On the other hand, why bother with a house at all? Perhaps I could arrange for a skip to be delivered to the road outside. If there's any money left over, you could paint your new council logo on the side and the crazy people could stay in that. You could send their medication by mail. What do *you* say about this, Jenny?'

Jenny looked fraught. I realised I was behaving like one of her clients.

'Jane, this isn't helpful,' said Mr Brady. 'There's no point in trying to score points against us. We're all on the same side. The simple, hard fact is that the choice is not between producing a compromised version of your plan and your original. It's between the compromise and nothing, and even that may be a struggle. You should see what's happening in other departments. Tressell Primary School up the road may only be opening four days a week next term.'

'All right, I'll make the cuts and I'll also make sure that if I have a schizophrenic collapse while doing it, I'm safely out of the borough. So, when shall we four, or duly appointed representatives of we four, meet again?'

'I'll call your secretary, Jane,' said Mr Brady. 'Thank you for being so relatively reasonable.'

I got back on my bike and cycled as fast as I could until I felt the muscles in my thighs burning, mentally shedding little details and finesses of my hostel plan as I went.

My next unwelcome task on this day of unwelcome tasks was to visit my father, who wanted to show me some plans. I wasn't going to see him alone. I'd mentioned the invitation to Paul on the phone and he'd insisted on coming along, ostensibly to see how our father was, but I suspected that it had something to do with his film. At least I'd get a lift. I dropped the bike back at the house and waited for Paul to arrive, which gave me the excuse to smoke two cigarettes. Then we drove down to Stockwell with Paul constantly complaining that this was the very worst time to drive south and that we would have been quicker on the Northern Line and I replied that nothing at all is quicker on the Northern Line which resulted in a silence all the way to Blackfriars Bridge.

My father was born in 1925. He's sixty-nine. He's an old man. I know that intellectually, but don't usually feel it. After all, he was hardly older than I am now when *Sergeant Pepper* came out and that doesn't seem all that long ago to me. I was fifteen. I was almost not a virgin. He's always seemed the same age. But when Dad opened the door to Paul and me, I really did feel that a gap was opening up between us, that he looked frailer, greyer, stiffer around the shoulders, the liver spots on his hands were more shockingly prominent. But as I hugged him and looked more closely at him I saw that he was still handsome. He had more hair than his son, and it covered more of his head as well, and I brushed my hand through it, neatening it with what I hoped seemed like affection.

'Tea for you both?' he asked.

'You go and sit down and I'll make it,' I replied. 'I've brought a jar of lemon curd so if you've got any bread, we can have some of that on toast.'

Dad and Paul went into the living room, a cluttered space full of books and papers between four dark red walls. The kitchen, though, was more like a Quaker's meeting house, with rough plaster, whitewashed walls and uncomfortable wooden benches. A discordant note was introduced by the low-voltage spotlights in the ceiling, which in my experience are principally used for commercial premises and are entirely unsuitable for a kitchen, especially one which is as poorly wired as Dad's. Ever since I can remember, long before Mum died, Dad has been going to look at the wiring but the implications of what he might find have always been too alarming. Instead, he's forever adding to it. Everywhere you look, there is a spaghetti of flex tacked along the wall.

When I carried the tray of tea and toast into the living room, Dad was sitting in his armchair and Paul, perched on a footstool, was leaning conspiratorially towards him. The gloom in which they were plunged was a further product of Dad's lighting strategy dating from the mid-seventies, based on the concept that you don't light rooms, you light 'spaces'. The result was that the flexes were removed from the ceiling rose in every room in the house and horrible chrome lights were fixed in corners. The house was now made up of spaces of light and spaces of darkness and Dad and Paul were now sitting in one of the spaces of darkness. When I got close enough to see, I recognised the determined gleam in Paul's eyes: he was researching. There was even a notebook poking out of his jacket pocket.

'Has Paul mentioned he's going to do a documentary on the family, Dad?' I asked cheerfully, slamming the tray down.

Paul sat up and scowled. 'I was going to, Jane,' he said. 'Give me a chance.'

A trail of yellow worked its way down Dad's chin. 'Why?' he asked. 'What's so interesting about us?'

Paul took a deep breath and laid down his piece of toast.

78

'That's a very good question,' he said, and Dad looked faintly surprised. 'When I talk about my family – which, of course, is interesting to me – then I am also, for the viewer, in some ways allowing them a new way to think about their own family, their own childhood. Every family is different, and yet every family is similar.'

'Is that a quotation?' I muttered. Paul ignored me.

'When I talk about our family – you and Mum and Jane and me – and when I talk about the Martellos, because, of course, I can't leave them out, what are the things that I'll be addressing?' He wasn't waiting for a reply so I picked up his piece of toast and bit into it hungrily. I'd missed lunch. 'Nostalgia. Closeness and estrangement. Possessiveness and jealousy. The idyll of childhood. The pain of growing up. The hopes that parents have for children. The resentments that children feel about their parents. All these things and more can be explored through one family. I hope that you'll want to help me?'

'Enough of this nonsense,' Dad said. 'Drink your tea, Paul, I want to show Jane something. Come over here.'

He led me over to the desk in the corner. Drawings and large old books were piled high.

'How's your project going?' he asked.

'Which one?'

'I don't mean at the Stead. The hostel.'

'It's becoming a torment.'

'I'm sorry, Jane. Anything I can do to help?'

'Yes, kill everybody in the housing department.'

'It's half the job,' Dad said abstractedly. 'I asked you here with an ulterior motive. I thought you might cast an eye over this.'

'What is it?'

'This is going to be the project of my old age. I'm going to restore the interior of this house.'

'What to?'

'To the basic structural and decorative order of the interior as it was originally conceived in the mid-1880s. You can see I've done some preliminary drawings. The basic fabric is original anyway. The main work will be restoring the partition in this room and on the first floor.'

Paul was standing behind us now, looking over my shoulder. 'You mean you'll be blocking up the bits you knocked through in the sixties,' he said.

I gave Paul a kick but my father continued as if he hadn't heard.

'The cornices and some roses will need to be restored, of course, but fortunately we can take mouldings from those which survive.'

'I'm staggered,' I said. 'But isn't it going to be rather expensive?'

'I'm going to do it myself.'

'You're not.'

'I am. Pat Wheeler has said he'll help out.'

I didn't know what to say, but I didn't need to say anything because my father was talking animatedly. He shuffled through his preliminary drawings and specifications. He talked of sash pulleys, sealers and firebacks, plaster dabs, angle beads and door furniture. Le Corbusier had been born again as William Morris. Paul teasingly asked if he was going to have gas illumination and the central heating removed. My own feelings were mixed, not only because of the impracticality of the plan but because it seemed like a scheme in which my father was systematically removing himself from his own house. At the end of the reconstruction, if he ever reached the end, the interior would have been stripped of every innovation and ideal that my father had lived by. I mumbled something about respect for the past and my father gave a heavily sarcastic laugh.

'We all have different ways with our past. I hope I'm going to restore it and preserve it. Is that better than making a television documentary about it?' He gave a sharp look at Paul, whose face was reddening.

'I'm surprised to see you so starry-eyed about restoration,' Paul replied. 'You always used to write about buildings in their social context. What's the point of recreating a Victorian family house in the 1990s? Are you going to start riding around on a horse as well? My attitude to the past is to re-examine it in terms of today.'

'Natalie,' father said bluntly.

'What?' said Paul.

'You know what,' said father. 'Natalie's been dug out of the ground and you're turning it into a TV documentary, and you'll want us all to talk about how we feel about it, won't you? I suppose you'll want me to talk about your mother's death as well. Who else will contribute? Your two wives? Poor old abandoned Claud?' Now it was my turn to flush with anger and mortification. 'And what about Alan and Martha? Martha won't say much, she's always hugged her griefs close; but Alan – I can just see it – the angry old man looks back on his life and reviews it. He'll be good value all right. Is that what you want, Paul, a family of TV personalities?'

Paul looked shocked, but excited as well. He had caught a whiff of what his programme might be like. He replied in his best programme-proposal mode, 'The programme will be made with the utmost respect and integrity.'

Father turned his back on Paul and began talking about

opening and reconstructing a square pargeted brick flue. I wondered whether clay flue linings mightn't be better but he brushed me aside.

'I'm not giving up just because of an old man's need to strike poses. Have you ever heard anything as ridiculous as that half-arsed restoration? Has Dad gone senile?'

Paul sounded quite belligerent as he sat in the pub fidgeting with his half-pint glass, but I knew he was feeling guilty.

'Don't just blow smoke out of your nostrils at me, Jane. It's entirely legitimate for me to draw on my own experience for my work and my experience happens to consist of our two families. Just because *Surplus Value* is a hit, that doesn't mean I can't do anything but game shows.'

I was silent.

'Well, does it?'

I shrugged. 'It doesn't matter what *I* think. I'm not going to put up money for the film.'

'It's important to me. Since that weekend all I've thought about is Natalie. Making a film about her and us would be good for everyone. A way of coming to terms with what's happened.'

'Television therapy,' I said.

'Well, that's probably no worse than whatever it is that you're doing now. We're both just trying to help ourselves. What's so wrong with that?'

I laid my hand on his sleeve, and he shook it testily away.

'Paul,' I said, 'you want people to talk about their lives to you, but most of us don't know our lives. What you're doing is risky. You may trample all over people's memories and dreams at the very moment they're the most fragile. And these are people you've got to go on living with. I don't want Claud to tell the world how he feels about me. Television is so seductive: people tell things to the camera they'd never dream of telling their best friends.'

I stubbed out my cigarette and reached for my coat.

'It's just going to be an honest piece of film-making. I can promise you that I won't do anything that would be unworthy of Natalie's memory.'

'Save it for the *Radio Times*, Paul,' I snapped, and felt guilty and then didn't mind. We parted without saying goodbye.

Eight

My first session – my first *real* session – with Alex felt like the first day at a new school. I was nervous. I chose my clothes with unusual care and then felt insecure in them. Even Alex's house felt different to me, but then I wasn't taken down into the dark, warm, reassuringly messy kitchen but upstairs to a small back room on the first floor. I went in first while Alex went up another flight of stairs to fetch a notebook. I walked over to the window and put my hand on the cold glass. It overlooked a long narrow garden that led back to another long narrow garden proceeding from the house opposite, a mirror image of the one I was looking out of. Everything in the garden was pruned back hard in preparation for spring, which I felt as a rebuke to my own abandoned back yard. I was startled by the door closing behind me and turned round to find Alex.

'Please,' he said, 'lie down.'

I hadn't looked at the room properly, I had no sense of its contents or decoration or the carpet. I only saw the armchair and the couch beside it. I lay down on the couch and heard the strain of springs as Alex sat himself down behind me, beyond my vision.

'I don't know where I should begin,' I said tremulously.

'Why are you here? Start with that and go anywhere you want,' said Alex.

'Very well. At the beginning of September I told my husband, Claud, that I had decided we should separate and get divorced. It was very sudden and Claud and the whole family were terribly shocked.'

'What do you mean by the whole family?'

'I mean the whole extended family. Whenever I talk about "my" family, I'm not talking about the little Crane family but the big wonderful enviable Martello family.'

'You sound a little ironic.'

'Only a little bit. I may have reservations but I know it really *is* wonderful. We're all terribly lucky. That was the word my father always used. When he left the army and went up to Oxford just after the war, he met Alan on his very first day. Of course, we've all read *The Town Drain* now and we know what to expect so it's difficult to imagine what it must have been like for somebody like my dad – a scholarship boy all his life, very bright, very shy – arriving in Oxford, completely bemused and overawed and then meeting the prototype of Billy Belton. And if you think of the effect that he had on people just as the hero of a book, imagine him in person, incredibly funny, totally contemptuous of everything that you were meant to have respect for. They were almost in love at that time, I think.

'Within a couple of years Alan and my father had both got married and the two families were almost like one family. Alan got very rich when *The Town Drain* became a bestseller and was filmed and all that and he bought the house and the land up in Shropshire and that's where we spent our holidays. It was just the classic perfect place, and when you took people there they would be dazzled by this amazing family and the four handsome sons – and the beautiful daughter, of course. It was the centre of my life. Natalie was my sister and best friend. Theo was my first love. And it seemed natural, dynastic, when I married Claud.'

'Was Theo the older brother?'

'Claud is the oldest, then Theo, then Natalie, and Jonah and Alfred are the youngest. They're twins.'

'How did they react when you split up from Claud?'

'That's hard to say. One of the points of the weekend when Natalie's body was found was to show that I was still a part of the family.'

'Was it important for you to get their approval?'

'Not their *approval* exactly. I didn't want to be seen as smashing the family up.'

'Did people ask you why you'd done it?'

'Not really.'

'Well, why did you do it?'

'You know, I was thinking about this as I was cycling over here. I knew that I was going to have to give some sort of answer to that and I can't. Isn't that strange? Here I am, I'm forty-one years old and I married Claud when I was twenty, when I was still at university. I've thrown all that in the bin. And of course people have asked why. Claud was devastated and my sons were terribly upset and angry and they wanted a straightforward answer – to give them something to hold on to, I suppose – and I couldn't give it to them. It's not that I've got a reason which I wasn't telling them about. All I could have said is that I think I did something blindly and when I woke up out of a long sleep and looked around me, and when Jerome and Robert were grown up and away from home, I decided I had to get out. I'm sorry that was long and probably not very comprehensible.'

There was a long silence and I began to cry. I was furious with myself but I couldn't stop and the tears ran down my cheeks. I was surprised to feel Alex's hand on my shoulder.

'I'm sorry,' I burbled snottily. 'It's just that I feel terrible about what I've done and now I'm being stupid and weak. I apologise.'

Alex walked across the room and came back with a handful of tissues. 'Here,' he said.

I blew my nose and wiped my face. Alex surprised me by squatting down in front of me instead of returning to his chair. As the film of tears in my eyes dispersed, I could see that he was scrutinising me with great concentration.

'I'm going to say a couple of things to you,' he said. 'You already know that there's nothing wrong with crying in this room. In fact, you can do anything you want, so long as it doesn't stain the couch. There's something more important than that, as well. During all the time that you come and talk to me, I'm going to try to be as open and straightforward with you as I can be. I want to begin by telling you that I think you're not weak and that you shouldn't be feeling remorseful because you aren't able to give some easy motivation for why you left your husband. That takes courage. In fact, if you were giving me some glib reason for what you'd done, then our first plan would be to get rid of that and see what's behind it. You're not letting yourself off the hook and that's a positive sign. Now, are you feeling better?'

I sat up to blow my nose and scrunched the tissue up self-consciously and put it in my pocket. I nodded. Alex tapped my shoulder reassuringly and then began to stride up and down the room, as I could see was his habit when he was deep in thought. Apparently having made up his mind, he sat down in the chair once more.

'I'm certainly not going to start providing answers. That

will be your job. What I need to do is to keep some sense of the direction in which we should be moving. If you're unhappy with anywhere I try to push you, well, then you must say that, but I'd like you to trust me if you can. My first thought is that what you are telling me is that you haven't just ended your marriage but that you have cut yourself off from an important part of your past and your childhood. The impulse of many people in a situation such as yours would have been to escape from their family and it interests me that your own instinct was to return and look for their acceptance. I feel that what we must do is not so much talk of the details of your divorce but almost go away from them and back into this family. Do you agree with this?'

I gave a sniff. I felt composed again and able to speak. 'If that's what you think.'

'Because, Jane, one of the things I want to do for you is take the different forces that are overwhelming you and put them back under your control. One of the ways to do that is to look for the hidden patterns and see if we can recognise them. You've come to me, Jane, saying that you want to talk about your divorce, and that's important and we will deal with it, but one of the crucial problems is to decide what it is that you are asking for and I would like to suggest something. What I'm going to suggest is that it is no coincidence that your best friend, almost your twin, has been discovered buried in the ground, disinterred, dug up, and you have, for the first time in your life, decided to look for help, to dig up your own past, to disinter your own secret. Does that make sense to you, Jane?'

I was startled and a little disconcerted at first.

'I don't know. It was obviously a terrible shock to us

all. But that's just a tragic external event. I don't see what there is to talk about there.'

Alex was calm and unwavering. 'I'm interested by the words you use. It was a shock to "*us* all". Yet it was an "external" event. Was it really external? You know, I sometimes think that the areas that people don't want to talk about are often the best places to start. Your divorce is a matter of opinion, emotion, attitude. Natalie's death was a fact. Her discovery and disinterment are facts. I think that is where we should begin.'

I had always distrusted the therapeutic talk about emotion, its distrust for the reality of events and I was very impressed by Alex's practicality. I was won over by it.

'Yes, I agree. I think you're right.'

'Good, Jane. Talk to me about when Natalie disappeared.'

I settled myself back down on the couch. I pondered where to begin. 'It's awful but even though it was a terrible tragedy and every detail should be unforgettable, so much of it seems vague and long-ago. It was a quarter of a century ago, after all, in the summer of 1969. Natalie disappeared just after a big party out at the Stead – the Martello house in Shropshire. The party was to celebrate Alan's and his wife Martha's twentieth anniversary. Perhaps it was that there was nothing like a sudden event, the discovery of a body or something, which would have crystallised it all in my mind. What I vividly remember is that the last time Natalie was seen was on the day after the party, by a man from the village.' I paused. 'The odd thing is that I was there.'

'How do you mean?'

'Well, I wasn't exactly *there*, of course, but I was just near. I must have been the closest person to her, apart from the man who saw her, and then, maybe, the person who . . . well, you know.'

'The person who killed Natalie.'

'Yes. Maybe I should describe the place to you. Is that all right?'

'Of course.'

'Natalie was last seen by the Col, which is a small river or a large stream that runs along one boundary of the Martellos' land. There's a little path from Westbury, the local village, that crosses the Col and then goes through Alan's and Martha's land, and passes by the house. The man was walking along the path to deliver something to the Stead, or collect something, I can't remember, and he saw Natalie standing on the track by the water at the bottom of the slope of Cree's Top. He even waved at her, but she didn't notice him. That was the last time anybody saw Natalie alive.'

'Where were *you*?'

'On the other side of Cree's Top. It sounds like the summit of a mountain, or something, but really it's just a bit of raised ground that the stream winds around.'

I closed my eyes.

'I haven't been back there since that day, I could never bear the idea of it, I never even walk in that part of the grounds, but I can picture every detail. If Natalie had walked away from the bridge, along the track that goes beside the south side of the Col, Alan's and Martha's side, it would have taken her up the pebbly path through a few trees on the top and then she would have been able to look down at me. We were no more than two or three minutes' walk away from each other.'

'What were you doing there?'

'That is the one thing I do remember clearly. Every

detail. I was a moody sixteen-year-old girl. I don't think you would have liked me much. I was a bit in love and a bit forlorn and during that summer I was either with Natalie, though not so much as I had been, for various reasons; or with Theo; or on my own. That day, it was early afternoon, I was feeling particularly gloomy. So I took the sole existing manuscript copy of the love poems that I had been writing during the summer and I went down to the Col and lay there, right on the edge of the stream, against a boulder down at the beginning of the slope of Cree's Top. I sat there for a couple of hours reading through these poems and writing another one. Then, on an impulse, I tore the poems out of the book one by one, and screwed each one up so that it looked like a little white carnation and threw it into the stream and as I sat there I watched them float down the stream away from me until they were carried out of sight. Look, I don't think there's any point in going on about this.'

'Please, Jane, humour me.'

'If you say so. The problem I have with this process, what I distrust about it, is that I feel I'm being encouraged to indulge, maybe even increase, emotions that aren't particularly valid or positive.'

'What emotions?'

'I didn't mean any emotions in particular. But to take the situation I've just been describing. For years I felt this intense guilt that I could have done something to prevent what happened. I was so close and if things had been just a tiny bit different, if I had decided to walk over Cree's Top, it might never have happened, I might have been able to save Natalie. At the same time I always knew that that was ridiculous and that you could reason like that about almost anything.'

'You felt an intense guilt.'

'Yes.'

'Right, I think we'll stop there.'

Alex helped me up off the couch. 'I think you've done wonderfully,' he said.

I felt myself blush, the way I used to when I was singled out for praise at school and I felt a little cross at my own susceptibility.

Nine

There were bones among the bones. Natalie had been pregnant when she was strangled. The police told Alan and Martha, Alan called his sons, and Claud called me the day before the funeral. At first, I couldn't take in what his soothing voice was telling me. As always when Claud assumed his professionally calm manner, I became babblingly irrational. I could only think in unordered questions.

'How could she have been pregnant?'

'This is difficult for all of us, Jane.'

'Who could the father have been?'

Claud began to sound weary and impatient. 'Jane, I've only this minute heard, I know nothing more than you do.'

'The funeral isn't going ahead now, is it?'

'Yes, it is. The police have released the remains to us.'

'But aren't there examinations they can carry out? Couldn't they find out who the father is with DNA tests and things like that? You're a doctor, you must know.'

This was Claud's cue to assume his pedagogic tone. 'I'm sure the forensic scientists have retained specimens, Jane. But as far as I understand it, DNA profiling won't be possible. I believe that samples of blood or bodily fluid are required.'

'Can't you get DNA from bones?'

'Is this really the time, Jane? Bone cells have nuclei, so of course they contain DNA, but so far as I know it degrades in skeletons and if it has been buried in soil, the DNA strands don't just crumble, they also get contaminated. But this isn't my area. You must address your enquiries about this to the proper authorities, as they say.'

'It sounds hopeless,' I said.

'The situation is not good.'

Pregnant. I felt sick, and the feeling of foreboding that had been closing in on me felt like a fist around my pounding heart.

'Oh Christ, Claud, Claud. What are we all going to do?' I sat heavily on the old green easy chair by the phone and rocked to and fro slightly.

'Do?' he replied. 'We're going to stick together as a family, as we have always done, and we're going to get through this. I know it's hard for all of us, but we've just got to help each other. And it's hardest for Alan and Martha. It's very important to them that you should be at the funeral tomorrow.' His voice went soft. 'Don't desert us, Janie. We're in this together. You'll be there tomorrow, won't you?'

'Yes.'

I rang Helen Auster at her Kirklow direct line but she was too busy to say much. She said she'd be down in London in a few days and we could meet. What would I have asked her anyway?

The coffin was slim and the sky was grey. There were no leaves on the trees but there were bright flowers on the shiny new gravestones with their synthetic green gravel and picture postcard inscriptions. The beautiful old worn stones had no flowers. I looked up at the church. Northern

Romanesque, said a whisper in my ear. Claud, of course. If I had time afterwards, he told me, I must go and look at the Norman font. His voice was mercifully drowned out by bells.

Her grave was an open wound in the ground. Soon the parcel of bones would be lowered into it, the mud flung over it. In a year, grass would have grown over the scar. It would become a site to visit occasionally, to lay flowers upon. At Christmas we would come with holly, and in the spring we would gather daffodils and blossom. Eventually, the grave would no longer look new and livid. It would merge into the melancholy landscape and children would play beside it. The small band of Sunday worshippers would walk by it unseeing. One day, there would be no one left to visit the place where Natalie lay. Strangers would pause beside the gravestone and run their fingers along the gouged dates, and say: she died young.

When I saw Martha I thought my heart would break. She had aged ten years in the space of a few weeks. Her face was old with grief, her hair a colour beyond white. She stood quite straight in the icy wind and did not weep. I wondered if she had any tears left now. She didn't believe in God, but I knew she would come every week to sit by her daughter's grave. For the first time, I wondered how many years she had left. She'd always seemed immortal to me, and now she seemed frail and worn. Alan, too, looked ravaged. I thought he seemed suddenly smaller, hunched over in his greatcoat, clutching his stick. The four sons stood tall and still, handsome in their dark suits. The rest of us – wives and ex-wives, grandchildren and friends – stood back. Jerome ('Got a class') and Robert ('Nah, don't like funerals') had not come, but Hana, unexpectedly, had turned up at my door at seven in the morning, dressed in a long mauve skirt and clutching a bacon sandwich, a Thermos flask and a bunch of jewel-like anemones.

'Just say, if you don't want me to come,' she'd said, but I did want her to come. I was glad that she stood beside me holding my hand, with the air turning her nose red and her absurd clothes flapping in the wind. A few feet away, a middle-aged man with a vaguely familiar face – beaky and intent – blew his nose loudly into a large handkerchief. There was no other sound. No birds sang.

Into the chill air, the vicar awkwardly delivered his words of death and resurrection. The coffin with its pitiful double burden was lowered into its space. Martha stepped forward very slowly and dropped a single yellow rose onto the top of it. There was a low sob from behind me. No one else made a sound. Martha moved back and took Alan's hand; they didn't look at each other but gazed steadily at the hole in the ground which even now was being filled in. Claud stepped forward with a bunch of flowers, and one by one we followed him. Soon the raw earth was quite hidden by a heap of vivid colours. The family's wound was exuberantly patched.

The Stead looked different to my aching, itchy eyes. When I was a child I thought it the most welcoming house in the world. I remembered it as a place one came home to after long walks in the dusk: glimmering stone, the glow from the windows, wisps of smoke from the chimney, all prom-ising warmth inside. Now, I thought it looked abandoned. The windows were dark. There were weeds around the front door. The weeping willow that hung over the driveway looked dank and untidy.

Jane Martello, the flying caterer, had brought meringues, plump scones with unsalted butter and the jam I'd made the year before, and a Madeira cake. The night before the funeral, I'd baked until the early hours: the kitchen had been full of the smell of vanilla essence and lemon zest. As the cake had risen in the oven, I'd called Claud again.

'Who'll be there?' I'd asked.

'I'm not sure,' he said, and mentioned a few names.

'Luke! Will *Luke* be there?'

'Well, why not, Jane?' Claud had replied a bit tetchily, and looking at the kitchen clock I'd realised that it was well past midnight: I'd probably woken him.

'But Luke was her boyfriend. Natalie was pregnant and Luke was her boyfriend.'

'Goodnight, Sherlock, I'll see you tomorrow.'

As I arranged my spread on the long oak table in the Stead's kitchen, I realised that the man who'd blown his nose was Luke. In a few minutes he'd arrive with all the others and we'd chat politely. The sharp graveside grief would dissolve into the boredom of sandwiches and dull talk. We should all have left separately, carried away our bereavement and dread and lived with it a bit. I slid the scones into the oven to warm them, and Hana arrived carrying the meringues. We didn't say anything: she'd always known how to be silent.

'Jane, my dear. Hana.' It was Alan, but Alan without any bombast. His beard looked clumsily cut, or was it just unbrushed. I'd never let Claud grow a beard. 'Martha's gone upstairs, but she'll be down in a minute. Can I do anything?'

'No, Alan. Nothing.'

'In that case, I'll – ' he waved a hand vaguely, and shuffled out.

I left Hana sorting plates, and went into the garden. Even before I lit a cigarette, my breath curled into the air. I could see groups of people straggling up the drive. I couldn't quite face them yet and I wandered through the side gate and round the front to miss them. My food could stand in for me for a little while.

'So what are you doing now?'

This was just what I had feared. I looked at a respectable man in a sombre suit, badly pressed and not very clean. He probably wore it to work occasionally. But what I really saw was a slim boy with round metal glasses, a shock of long dark hair kissing Natalie, consuming her, cradling the back of her head in two tender hands. Natalie's bit of rough. He seemed unaccountably thrown by the question.

'I'm a teacher,' he said. 'In Sparkhill. A secondary school.'

Luke was thin and tall. He stooped over me as he talked, and with his long nose he looked a bit like a melancholy bird. But his eyes were sharp. Automatically, I said what I always said to teachers, about it being the most worthwhile profession and all that. Blah blah blah.

'I'll give you our address,' he said, 'and you can write off for our brochure.' A glimmer of the old abrasive Luke, but his heart wasn't in it. 'Look, Jane, can we talk?'

He grabbed me by the elbow and steered me through the groups of people to the door.

'That's better,' he said, talking in a rushed whisper, as if he was in a hurry and might be overheard. He looked over my shoulder as he spoke to me, the way people do at parties when they're looking for someone more interesting. 'I heard – Theo told me – that Natalie was killed. Well, surprise, surprise. But then he said she

98

was pregnant. And then I realised that I wasn't exactly being welcomed back into the fold after all these years. Martha couldn't even say hello to me. Theo, everyone, they all think it was me.'

'Think it was you what?'

I felt hard and merciless. All the angles of his face collapsed and he drew out his handkerchief again. I had an abrupt and brief memory of him sobbing as a boy, but it evaded me. I reflected that of all the men in Natalie's life, he was the first I had actually seen weeping over her.

'I loved her. I know I was only a stupid teenager, but I loved her. She was so sweet and so – so – *ruthless*.'

'How do you know you didn't get her pregnant?' I asked, collecting the adjectives he'd just used and storing them away for later.

He wasn't crying now. He was looking hard into my eyes. 'We didn't,' he said. 'She wouldn't. There must have been somebody else.'

'Who? When?'

'How should I know? I promise you I've been trying to think of anything, anything at all. Once, God knows where it was, we were kissing, I was kissing Natalie. She had this beautiful golden down on her cheeks, even though she was so dark. I remember it on my lips. And I started touching her, caressing her, and she just pushed me away and said: "You're just a kid, you know." I was a whole year older than her. I couldn't believe it, but that's the sort of thing she did. You know. You knew her better than anyone.'

I didn't want to be having this conversation.

'Okay, so why tell me about it?'

'But do you believe me?'

'Who cares what I believe?'

99

'I do,' Luke said and then muttered something I couldn't hear. He made a visible effort to compose himself. 'That's it, isn't it? You're all closing ranks. I can see it's convenient for you.'

I turned and left him.

'You're making it easy for yourselves, you know,' he said.

I ignored him.

Ten

'Here, these are all yours.'

I started dumping records in cardboard boxes. When Claud and I had met, he had had an extraordinary collection of LPs, arranged alphabetically within their various subject categories. I had had five; two of them were by Miles Davis and the other three by Neil Young, all too scratched to play on Claud's deck. He'd had them as well, anyway. He'd bought music all the way through our marriage: classical, jazz, soul, punk. He was endlessly enthusiastic, endlessly tolerant. When Jerome or Robert had wanted to rebel they'd brought back the latest noise: house, techno, grunge, I'd never known which was which, and I'd obliged them by being ignorant and horrified. But Claud had learnt to like it all. He'd played rap songs about policemen being murdered that had shocked even Robert. He'd pontificated on the importance of extending the right to free speech to someone like Iced Tea, or whatever his name was.

Claud had played Guns 'n' Roses to me appreciatively, while his sons had watched him sulkily, and I had contemplated a cover illustration featuring a woman apparently being abused by a robot. Whenever his brothers had come round, they'd thumbed through the collection, pulling out this memory, or that, an appalling fifteen-minute drum solo that would apparently supply a Proustian recollection of some long-lost party or some poor deluded girl.

'And these.' I stacked CDs in neat piles beside the boxes. Claud gazed at me, wet-eyed. I did not respond. 'I've gone through most of the books, but of course you should go through them as well, just to be sure. There are some it's a bit hard to decide about. I've put them all together on this shelf.'

'James Morris's *Venice*.' Claud's voice was wistful. 'Do you remember our time there?'

I did. It was in February, damp and misty and almost empty. We'd walked miles along grey paths, ignoring the sweet stench of the waters, exclaiming over the green peeling facades of ancient palazzi, wandering into churches where opulent art bloomed. We'd made love on hard wooden beds with bolsters, to the creak of shutters.

'*Mushrooms of Europe, Decline and Fall of the Roman Empire*, Auden, Hardy's poems, *Birds of Great Britain*.' Claud was flicking his finger along the shelf. '*One is Fun*, I suppose I should take that. This one must be mine.' He pulled out a slim Shell guide to England's country churches, and added it to his box. 'We can give the shared books to the boys. That seems appropriate, somehow. And now can I have a drink?'

'They don't read books. We haven't done the pictures, or the china; quite a lot of the furniture is yours.'

'Jane, can I have a drink? Don't be in such a hurry to clear every last trace of me out of the house.'

We sat at the kitchen table, and I poured two glasses of something cheap and red. I lit a cigarette, sucking the smoke cancerously deep into my lungs. At first we chatted about the boys, then about Natalie – and, surprisingly, this was contemplative and relaxed. I'd heard too many expressions of nostalgic affection. Claud talked about her mischief, her teasing, her capacity for finding out secrets, for making alliances. This was the real Natalie, not the girl who was safely dead and idealised. I'd forgotten about this Natalie. It revived my sense of her. Claud and I exchanged remembered moments and refilled our wine glasses. It was hard to reconstruct the sequence of events, but she hadn't been so much with Luke in those final weeks. She had become bored with him and kept him at a distance to his rage and bafflement. He used to phone up and call round and end up talking to me or to Martha.

We talked about the famous party and my own hazy memories of the day after and Claud's absolutely precise memory of the Air India flight to Bombay with Alec and the two months spent bumming around with nothing but – can it really have been just twenty pounds? Dust and dope and dysentery. I'd always meant to go. As we spoke, I remembered that Claud and I had planned to recreate his journey one day (in a more salubrious style) and I hoped he wouldn't mention this. I fiddled with a small antique dish on the table. It was made by somebody famous, very expensive: one of us had given it to the other, but I could no longer remember who.

This wasn't a good idea. Claud raised his glass and grinned at me wryly and I felt a hopeless, reminiscent stab of desire for this man. Before we'd separated, we'd often got on best when we were in other people's company. I'd watch him across a room, and see him being charming, or watch an attractive woman clutch his arm or laugh at something he'd said that I couldn't quite hear, and I'd realise how fortunate I was. Most of my friends adored him, and envied me for his good looks, his attentiveness to me, his fidelity. He never noticed when women flirted with him, or worse, which made him all the more disarming. I realised we were stuck in a lurching silence. I could see what was coming.

'I know I shouldn't say this,' Claud began, and I knew he was delivering a prepared speech, 'but this, all this,' he gestured at the chaos around us, 'it seems so wrong. One minute you were talking about our problems, and the next I found myself in a bedsit somewhere and I think we should try again.' There was a terrible bright eagerness in his voice now. 'I hate to say it but perhaps we could go to counselling.'

I couldn't help being touched: Claud had always had a contempt for any kind of psychotherapeutic process.

'No, Claud.' I forced myself to stop, not to expand into an explanation with which he could argue.

'But you're not happy,' he insisted. 'Look at you: you're chain-smoking, you've got all thin and pale. You know you've made a mistake.'

'I've never said I was making myself happy,' I said. 'But I've got to live with what I've chosen.'

'What did I do wrong? What did I do to you to make you want to choose *this*?' More gestures. At the room. At me.

'Nothing. I don't want to talk about this. It won't do any good.'

'Is it something else, something you're not saying?' he asked desperately. 'Is it Theo? There, I've said it. Have I not measured up to your starry-eyed view of him?'

'Don't, Claud, you're being ridiculous.'

'There are things that I could tell you about Theo, things he's done . . .'

'I don't think there are, Claud. And anyway, it has nothing to do with us.'

Suddenly he seemed to slump. 'Sorry,' he said, 'I'm so sorry but I miss you terribly.' He leant his head in his hands and gazed through the cage of his fingers.

Sitting at the kitchen table with Claud, the way we'd sat for so many years, watching tears dribble through his hands and not moving to comfort him, I couldn't remember why I'd ever broken up our marriage. I felt no connection with that anger, that whirling frustration, panic and sense of time dripping away. All I wanted was peace, friendship, routine, home. I'd built my life up brick by brick, then one day last September I'd pulled it down on top of me. I felt old and tired and defeated. For a moment, I thought I would go and kneel by Claud's chair and hug him until he stopped quietly crying and bury my head in his lap, and feel his hands stroking my hair, and know myself forgiven. But I did nothing and the moment passed. After a minute or two he stood up.

'I'll come for these things another time.'

I still had the dish under my fingers. 'What about this?' I handed it to Claud.

'This? It's ours.' He took it in two hands, and without any evident emotion or even a change of expression he snapped it in two and handed me one of the pieces. I was too shocked to move or even to speak but I saw that he had cut one of his fingers quite badly.

'I'll just take these.'

He put the fragment of china into one of the boxes. I opened the door for him, and a gust of rain blew into the house.

'You disappoint me, Jane,' he said. I could only shrug.

In the bedroom, I took off my jeans and grey cardigan, unhooked my ear-rings, brushed out my hair, and pulled on a dressing-gown. I had a thought. I went to the bathroom and rubbed soap around one of my fingers. I pulled hard and the ring slipped over the knuckle. I rinsed it and took it to my study, Jerome's old bedroom, now cluttered with easels and sheets of graph paper and unanswered correspondence. I opened a small drawer in my desk, where I kept the wrist-tags the boys had worn in hospital when they were born, the champagne cork with FINALS written on it in biro, my mother's last letter to me, wonky with pain, and the recently acquired photographs of Natalie. I put the ring in there, and closed the drawer. Then I went to bed and lay for a long time, waiting for oblivion.

Eleven

'Does it shock you?'

'It shocks me most dreadfully,' I said. 'I don't think I could even tell you the way it makes me feel.'

'Tell me,' said Alex.

I giggled. 'Yes, that's what I'm here for, isn't it? I'm sorry, I was speaking in clichés. I was just automatically saying the sort of thing you're meant to say about big emotions. That they're inexpressible. It's all too expressible. I suppose I feel cheated, except cheated is too small a word, because it shows that there was another side of Natalie that I didn't know. I can put it even more clearly than that. We had a childish friendship, Natalie and I, that was almost like a game. We told each other that we were best friends and sisters. There were so many boys around, and we were the two girls. We used to talk about everything, especially at night-time, in her bedroom. That summer, in 1969, it began to be a bit different. We'd had things with boys before but her relationship with Luke seemed different, something I couldn't share. And at the same time I was really smitten by Theo.'

'Tell me about Theo.'

'What do you mean? Then or now?'

'Whatever.'

'Theo's still great. I love him. If you were to meet him today, I can guarantee you'd take to him. He's tall and quite striking and balding now, but he's bald like an artist, not like a bank manager with strands of hair combed across his head.'

'That's interesting,' said Alex laughing. 'We must explore your aversion to bank managers.'

'I *like* my bank manager,' I insisted. 'He's been very nice to me, however much I've provoked him.'

Despite the bleak news, this session with Alex was more relaxed. I was conscious of a friendly, even a flirtatious, atmosphere. I felt liberated. I knew I was allowed to say anything I wanted.

'Anyway, Theo isn't a bank manager and he isn't an artist either. He's in some vague in-between area and it's extremely difficult to pin him down to exactly what he does do. He's a consultant about the management of information. Yes, you may well ask. He's a businessman with some company based in Zurich and he's also an academic with visiting professorships all over the place. It's all very modern and post-managerial and very highly paid and all a bit abstract and philosophical and he's always off to a conference in Toronto or superintending a merger in some schloss in Bavaria. People like me who live in one place and work nearby seem unimaginably old-fashioned. He's dazzling, as he always was.

'I had hardly seen Theo for a couple of years before that summer of '69. He had been away at school and I had been going out with this young man who not only had a motorbike but he could take it to pieces and put it back together and there were no bits left over and that was impressive in its way, but we all gradually got together at the Stead at the end of July for Alan's and Martha's party and I was knocked out by Theo. He was six-two with long hair and he was in the sixth form doing about twelve science A levels but he was also reading Rimbaud and Baudelaire in the original and he could play the guitar, I mean really play it, not just strum but play individual notes so as to make moody Leonard Cohen sort of music and I was completely his. In a spiritual sense, for the most part.

'Sorry, I got carried away. The point I was trying to make is that this was the summer that Natalie and I grew up in a way. The estrangement, to the degree that there was an estrangement, represented the fact that we became separate people, that we developed our own independent, private lives. How can I describe it? There was one moment I remember, about a week before she disappeared. I was in the nearby town, Kirklow, probably buying something for the anniversary party. I saw a group of young people sitting outside a pub in the square, drinking and smoking. Natalie was one of them. Her hair was swept back off her face, she was laughing at something someone had said and as she laughed she looked round and caught my eye. She half smiled at me and looked away, and I realised I wasn't allowed to go over and join them. Looking back at that summer, I think that the pain of the terrible tragedy of Natalie's death was heightened because it coincided with the moment that I was forced to stop being a child and go into all the confusion of being an adult.'

After I finished there was a vast silence which I felt no impulse to break. I didn't feel afraid now of these hiatuses.

'Well, that's that then,' said Alex and I was shocked by his sarcastic, flippant tone.

'What do you mean, "that's that"?' I asked.

'That's extremely neat, Jane. You've sewn it all together. You've managed to face up to Natalie's death and link it together with a positive development in your own life. She died, you grew up and became an architect. There we are. Analysis over. Congratulations.'

I felt crushed.

'Why are you being so sarcastic, Alex? That's horrible.'

'Do you like reading, Jane?'

'What are you talking about?'

'I bet you like reading novels. I bet that when you go on holiday you read a novel every day.'

'I don't, actually. I'm quite a slow reader.'

'Have you ever wanted to *write* a novel?'

'Are you making fun of me, Alex? Just say what you want to say and don't piss around with me.'

'No, honestly, Jane, I think it's something you ought to consider. I bet you'd be good at it. Only don't do it here with me. You're an intelligent woman, Jane, and what you've just told me is not at all an implausible arrangement of your experience. That's what you're good at. I'm sure that you could come into my office tomorrow and deliver another version of your life and interpret it in another, different way and that would be convincing as well. If you were perfectly happy with your life and everything was going nicely then you could be contented with that. That's the sort of thing that most of us do, though most of us probably aren't as good at it as you are. You invent neat interpretations of your life in the way that an octopus squirts out a cloud of ink and scuttles away behind it. Am I being unfair, Jane?'

I felt terribly disoriented, as if I'd drifted loose.

'I don't know. I don't know what to say.'

Alex moved forward into my line of sight and knelt next to me. He looked more amused than disapproving.

'You know what, Jane? I suspect that you've got your

Penguin editions of Freud at home and though you've promised yourself that one day you'll read it all, you've never quite got around to it, but you've dipped into it here and there. And you've read one or two books about therapy as well. One of the things you've learnt is that analysis is about talk and about interpretation. It's not very concerned with facts and things, only with the value we place on them. Is that about right?'

'I don't know about that,' I protested. I didn't want to give in to him. He was so sure.

'I want you to forget about all that,' Alex continued. 'I want to cure you – for a while, at least – of your considerable skill at turning your life into a pattern. I want you to grab hold of the things in your life, the things that really happened. We'll leave the interpretation until later, shall we?'

'I'm surprised that you think there are facts separate from interpretations, Doctor.'

'And I know that you don't really believe that. I can bullshit with the best of them and if that's what you want we can sit here and play games for a couple of hours a week and split hairs about the meaning of meaning. Do you want that?'

'No, I don't.'

'So far, you've given me the standard coming-of-age-in-the-summer-of-love story.' He stood up and moved back to his chair. 'Tell me some of the awkward, unpleasant things that were going on.'

'Isn't it enough that Natalie was pregnant and then murdered? Do you need any more unpleasantness?'

'But Jane, you're giving me an account of this wonderfully idyllic summer spent with the family that everybody adored. Where's the context for murder?'

'Why should there be a context? She may have been killed by somebody who had nothing to do with the family, someone we've never even heard of.'

'What are your thoughts on that, Jane?'

'You mean *emotions*?'

'No, thoughts. Ideas.'

I paused for quite a long time. 'I've only got one, really. Maybe I'm just being stupid – that's probably what the policewoman I talked to thought – but I keep bumping up against the obvious, the problem of where Natalie was found. Since her body stayed hidden for twenty-five years, and then was only stumbled on by accident, it was clearly an almost perfect hiding place but it's so peculiar. I don't know anything about murderers or what they do with their victims but I imagine that they bury them in remote forests or leave them on moorlands or in ditches. Natalie was last seen by the river. She could have just been thrown in there. But she was buried under our noses on the day after a huge party when the whole area was full of people. It doesn't make any sense to me, but the one thing I am sure of is that it wasn't some passing vagrant who attacked her and then buried her virtually on our front doorstep.'

'So? What else have you got to say to me? There must be something,' Alex insisted.

'Oh, I don't know. It was all such a long time ago. I feel that even by talking about some of these things you give them more importance than they really deserve.'

'Test me.'

I gripped the couch, my fingers like claws.

'There were problems, like all families have. In some ways ours may have been more accentuated because we were so close and saw so much of each other.'

'Spare me all the excuses, just tell me.'

'There were silly things. You've got to realise the ages we were because we were still young enough for these little differences to matter a lot. Natalie was just sixteen and Paul was eighteen and about to go to Cambridge and he was absolutely obsessed with her.'

'Did they have any sort of relationship?'

'Natalie completely rebuffed him. It's hard to imagine now, but Paul was a very shy teenager, aggressively shy really, and he'd never had any sort of girlfriend before. I could almost see him plucking up his courage to make a move towards Natalie and once or twice, late at night, he tried to do things like put his arm round her and she was quite brutal about it.'

'Unnecessarily brutal?'

'I don't know. How can one judge these things? If I am allowed to do a bit of interpretation, I remember that it sometimes seemed as if part of the attraction of Luke for Natalie was as a way of causing pain to Paul. And when she drifted apart from Luke, she played with Paul as a way of tormenting Luke.'

'How did *you* feel about it?'

'You mean, watching my older brother being humiliated by my best friend. I was upset, perhaps less than I should have been. Embarrassed mainly. And maybe I was a bit jealous; everyone, well boys at least, always noticed Natalie. She'd seem so indifferent to them, though of course she wasn't, and she didn't wear make-up like the rest of us did, and she didn't laugh at their jokes, and she didn't flirt except in an ironic kind of way. She often seemed contemptuous in fact, but it never mattered. Paul was out of his depth with her. But look, adolescence is all red in tooth and claw, isn't it? I'm already making it sound a bigger deal than it really was.'

'What did Paul feel?'

'He has never talked about it, except as part of his golden youth which he is now going to turn into a television documentary.'

'Do you think that is what he really feels?'

'It may be what he feels now. I don't believe he can have enjoyed it much at the time, at least not during that summer.'

'Is that it?'

'Yes.'

I could hear an impatient sigh behind me.

'Jane, you've tossed me a bone. But that isn't the real thing you were going to tell me.'

I was reminded of standing on a very high diving board as a child and the only way I dared to dive was to throw myself from it without preparation or forethought.

'The difficult thing that summer – it was often difficult but it was especially difficult then – was Alan's infidelity.'

'Yes?'

Well, what did it matter?

'It's not exactly the world's best-kept secret that Alan has been unfaithful to Martha as a matter of habit. It's the old dreary cliché. Alan loves Martha and is utterly dependent on her. But he's had lots of affairs for virtually the whole of their marriage, as far as I can make out. I suppose he would have been like that anyway but when *The Town Drain* happened and Alan became famous, then the young and available literary women needed beating off with a stick.'

'Did Martha know about these affairs?'

'I think she did in theory. It wasn't flagrant. It just went on and on. The affairs weren't talked about. They weren't important, I think that was the basic cover story.'

'Did she mind about them?'

'I think people always do, don't you? Martha is a wise woman and I suppose she saw from the beginning what Alan was like and realised that nothing could be done to change it. But maybe she was too wise and not bloody-minded enough. I'm sure she always suffered a great deal.'

'Did you all know about it?'

'Not really. In retrospect, there were things that only became clear once we cottoned on. It may be hard for you to understand, but there are ways in which you can know and not know things at the same time. Do you see what I mean?'

'Absolutely.'

'Anyway, the truth about Alan's behaviour became unavoidable. To cut the whole sordid story short, we discovered that the summer before Alan had been sleeping with a girl who was a friend of Natalie's and mine. She was the same age as we were. She was called Chrissie Pilkington and she was a daughter of a local family, good friends of the Martellos, and she was at school with Natalie. It was awful.'

'How did you discover?'

'She told Natalie. Natalie told *me*. It was an odd thing, really, because we had this intense afternoon talking about it. I think I was more shocked than Natalie – she didn't seem surprised, but she did seem, well, *disgusted*, I suppose. She was very cruel about him, about his beery breath and his paunch. I remember the way she imitated him being drunk. But then, after that, she never mentioned the subject again, and I didn't either. I think that I knew it was forbidden.'

'Did you say anything to Alan? Or to Martha?'

'No, it never seemed the right time, really. But I told

Theo. I guess that most of us younger lot must have known.'

'What happened? What did you feel about all this?'

'What happened? I don't know, really, it sort of got lost in the chaos of Natalie's disappearance. These things never lasted a long time for Alan and he probably used the awfulness over the disappearance as a way of making a break.'

'And what did you feel about it?'

'Different things. I always have where Alan is concerned. Sometimes I think he's just an awful exploitative shit who would do anything, so long as it was what he wanted to do at a particular moment. And sometimes I think he's just pathetic and weak and should be looked after or put up with. And sometimes I even think about him the way that people who don't actually know him personally think about him: good old incorrigible Alan, a bit outrageous and flamboyant, but there's nobody else quite like him and we're lucky to have him. When I'm feeling close to Martha I feel most hostile, but then she's probably quite stoical about it all.'

I was silent. My mind was a blank. I felt exhausted by it all. Alex was thinking too.

'Sorry for being rude, Jane,' he said.

'You were a bit.'

He stood up and hauled his chair round so that I could see it. It was on castors. I could see the indentations in the carpet where it had stood. Was this the first time it had ever been moved?

'Jane, we're almost finished and I know you must be exhausted but I'd like us to try something. I had it in mind for later sessions, but it might just be worth a crack now.'

'What?'

'Bear with me for a moment, Jane. I want this process to be steered by you. I want to follow the clues that you leave for me. Now, we'll be talking about lots of things, I hope, but I have this feeling that the black hole at the centre of it all is the day that Natalie disappeared, this conjunction, or near-conjunction, when you almost met.'

'Yes. Well?'

'It's something I want to return to.'

'I'm not sure there is anything more to go back to. It was a very long time ago.'

'Yes, I realise that. But let's try something. It'll be good for you anyway. Let's try a sort of exercise. I'd like you to lie back, really lie back, close your eyes and I'd like you to relax every bit of your body, starting with your feet and your legs, your body, down your arms and finally through your face and head. Does that feel good?'

'Mmm.'

Alex's voice was now almost like a hum in the background, like the buzzing of bees outside a window.

'Now, Jane, without opening your eyes, I would like you to imagine that scene by the river on the day when Natalie disappeared. I don't want you to describe it, I don't want you to look at it. I'd like you to imagine yourself back there, sitting by the river. Put yourself back there. Can you do that?'

'Yes.'

'You're sitting down, aren't you, with the hill behind your back?'

'Yes.'

'Describe it to me.'

'I can feel the stone of Cree's Top behind my back. On my right is the wood. The wood that's between the river and the Stead. The River Col is on my left. I can see it flowing away from me. I can tell because of the pieces of paper I scrunch up and throw in. They drift away from me and then just as they drift round the bend they start to bobble across the little rapids, well, just shallow water across stones really, then they're out of sight.'

'What is the weather like?'

'Hot, really hot. Mid-afternoon. I'm in the shade under a line of elms which are on my right forming the edge of the wood. The stone behind me feels cool.'

'Do you do anything?'

My mind went blank, I stuttered something.

'That's all right, Jane, open your eyes. We'll leave it there.'

I started to raise myself up.

'By the way,' he said, 'am I supposed to know why Alan Martello's novel is called *The Town Drain*? Is it a quotation or something?'

'Haven't you read it?'

'It's on my list.'

'I thought everybody had read it. The title comes from something that the Reverend Spooner is supposed to have said to one of his undergraduates. It goes something like, "You have hissed all my mystery lectures and tasted a whole worm. You must leave by the town drain." You know, the down train is the train from Oxford to London.'

'I suppose the joke works if you've read the book.'

'It's not really a joke, it's meant to stand for an anti-Brideshead sort of disenchantment.'

'Well, thank you for the lecturette, Jane. Perhaps I should be paying *you* something.'

I raised an eyebrow.

'Now that really *is* a joke,' Alex added hastily.

Twelve

When we were little – eight or nine years old – Natalie and I used to lie in bed at night and discuss what we were going to be when we grew up. I can see her now, hugging her knees through her nightie. We were both going to be beautiful and adored and have lots of children. We would always be friends, and visit each other's large houses in the country. Everything was possible. It never occurred to me, when I said I was going to be a singer, that my singing voice sounded like a bullfrog's croak. An off-key croak. My mother used to play me notes on the scuffed upright piano that Dad sold after she died, and I would try to sing them back to her. When the look of encouragement on her thin face didn't waver, but remained there like a bright flag signalling patience, I knew that I hadn't succeeded. I relinquished the idea of being a singer, and started selecting things I was good at: drawing, writing, numbers. What could you do with numbers? Before I was ten, I knew I wanted to be an architect, like my dad. I made models from old cardboard boxes, and drew impossible plans on graph paper stolen from my father's desk. I made futuristic apartment blocks from empty match boxes. It became my territory, the place no one else invaded.

Natalie said she wanted to be a ballet dancer at first; then an actor; then a television announcer. She wanted to be seen, looked at. As she grew older, she spent hours watching herself in mirrors, staring at her pale face, being her own audience. It didn't seem like vanity so much as a cool self-assessment that was unnerving to someone like me. For me, mirrors were sources of rebuke or occasional consolation.

I thought of Natalie as I chose my clothes for the day. Detective Sergeant Auster was coming to see me at my office. Then I was having lunch with Paul. Would I mind, he asked me casually, if there was a research assistant there as well? His proposal had been accepted, the TV documentary was going ahead, the commissioning editor was right behind him and had already pencilled a slot into the spring schedule. I pulled a black waistcoat over a burgundy silk shirt, zipped up slim-fitting black trousers, and rummaged around for my black boots. Yes, I did mind. A panic had assailed me since finding out about Natalie's pregnancy. Sometimes I could hardly breathe. I rode my bike along the London roads and thought, 'No one seeing me would know that I'm living inside a fug of dread.' I was in disguise.

When, standing in her hallway, I had told Kim about the pregnancy, her eyes had filled with tears. 'Poor kid,' she'd said, and her reflexive compassion had startled and shamed me. I had been trying to solve a technical problem. Had I really considered my childhood friend? Had I tried to imagine what she must have gone through? Kim interrupted my reverie.

'There was a time when I was trying to get pregnant, you know. When I was with Francis.'

'I didn't know that.'

'It seemed like a good idea. Nothing happened. We tried a few things, both had some tests which were inconclusive.

Anyway, he's married now with two daughters. You've got to laugh, haven't you?'

'Why didn't you tell me, Kim?'

'I'm telling you now. It was important for me to tell you about it. I want you to know that you can lean on me because you can trust me to lean on you.'

'But you didn't lean on me.'

'Don't be silly, Jane, I've always depended on you.'

We hugged and I left her standing in the doorway with her funny sheepish grin on her face, but I felt dissatisfied by our talk. I thought back over our friendship of weekends away, lunches, cups of tea in greasy spoons, long walks. Was Kim right? I wondered if our relationship had con-sisted of me seeking support and Kim giving it to me. Even her revelation, long after its importance had passed, seemed a sop to me to encourage me to depend on her. As I cycled along the canal towpath I constructed a version of our relationship in which I was always the fallible, needy one and Kim was always the resilient free spirit. Was this what even the closest friendships were like? One who gave and one who received?

Helen Auster was alone this time. She came up the stairs to our office looking touchingly ill at ease, panting at the length of the climb and the weight of her bulky shoulder bag. We shook hands and then I led her across to my desk. She was immediately impressed by the view and I pointed out the wharf below, by the canal, showed her the direction I cycled back, then took her across to the other side to show her the tower over on the Isle of Dogs which, I told her, had somehow single-handedly managed to make the skyline of London look frivolous.

'I like it,' she said.

I poured us both a coffee and we sat at my desk.

'What do you want to talk about?' I asked. 'Talking to the police always makes me feel guilty.'

'I don't think this meeting will be anything like that,' said Helen.

'It must be difficult to start up a murder inquiry again after a gap of twenty-five years.'

'Between you and me,' said Helen, 'we're starting from scratch. The CID back then went on considering Natalie to be a runaway. And so,' she gave her bulging case a pat, 'we're doing it now.'

She unzipped her case and removed a slim file. She handed me two lots of paper, each stapled together.

'These are two lists of names,' she said. 'The first is of people who were present at the party for Alan and Martha Martello on Saturday 26 July, 1969. The second is of people who were present – I mean staying at the house or in the vicinity or just visiting for the day – on the following day, the Sunday, when Natalie was last seen.'

I looked through the names. There were pages of them.

'This is extraordinary,' I said. 'How did you get all these names? Was there a guest list?'

'No, we've been talking to various members of the family. The most help was from Theodore Martello. I've seen him a few times now. He's got the most amazing memory.' Was she blushing?

'He certainly has. There are names here I've completely forgotten. I don't think I've seen William Fagles since the party. It says here that the Courtneys now live in Toronto. They were the parents of one of Natalie's best friends. Can I have copies of these lists?'

'These are your copies. If you could just have a look through, it may jog your memory. You'll see that some of the guests are only identified by their first names and you may be able to complete them. You may think of some others as well.'

'Well, for a start, the Gordon here must be Gordon Brooks. He used to be a friend of the twins.'

'I haven't gone through the list with them yet. But just write it in.'

'It sounds a terribly dull process.'

'It's more exciting than what some of the other officers are doing, I can tell you.'

'Have you talked to Alan yet?'

'Yes, of course,' Helen said. 'Let me show you what I'm reading.'

She reached into her case and pulled out a bright new Penguin edition of *The Town Drain*.

'Are you enjoying it?'

'It's wonderful. Not that I know very much about literature . . . but I think it's terribly funny. Alan Martello's so grand now, it's hard to imagine him writing something that's so . . . well, disrespectful.'

'I don't think he's really all that grand.'

'He was quite stern with me when I asked him what he was writing at the moment. You're quite a family, aren't you?'

'People have always seemed to think so. If you're going to read all the books written by members of the family, you'll need to take a sabbatical. For a start, there are all the children's books that Martha has illustrated. They're quite wonderful, some of them. All the time that Alan was noisily, theatrically blocked with his writing, Martha was steadily and quietly working away.'

'I think I'll stick with Alan Martello for the moment. Are the rest of his books good?'

'There is only one other novel, and a couple of short story collections. Nothing that comes near to matching up to *The Town Drain*. But don't dare tell him I said so.'

We chatted for a few minutes about other things. Helen asked me about architecture and I asked her why she'd joined the police. She told me that she'd studied physics at university and then had had a vision of a life spent in a research laboratory and had suddenly rebelled against it. I liked her for that. She drank the last of her coffee.

'I think I'd better go,' she said. 'Once you've looked through that, we could meet again, if you like. I'm down in London quite a lot at the moment.'

'Doesn't your husband mind?'

'He works harder than I do.'

I walked with Helen to the top of the stairs. I had to say something. 'Helen, twenty-five years is a long time. Is there any point to this?'

'Of course.'

'I thought you might be able to do a DNA test on the . . . you know, the baby, but Claud says you can't after all that time.'

Helen smiled. 'That's right.'

'So there's no forensic evidence.'

'There are one or two other possibilities. No substitute for good old-fashioned police work, though. As our Chief keeps telling us. Goodbye, Jane, see you soon.'

My father was refusing to have anything at all to do with the programme. Paul had begged and blustered, and even sent Erica round – bearing bulbs for Dad's garden as her excuse – to put the case on his behalf. Yet it never occurred to me to turn Paul down.

I biked hurriedly through the damp air that was

becoming thin drizzle to the Soho restaurant that Paul had selected. His research assistant was a young woman called Bella – very tall and skinny, with a halo of red hair and large, kohl-rimmed eyes that she kept fixed adoringly on Paul. She smoked acrid cigarettes lighting each one off the one before, drank mineral water and picked at a side salad.

Over poached eggs, I asked Paul who else he was seeing. 'You know Dad's not talking to me?' I nodded. 'But Alan's being marvellous. I've already had two sessions with him. My God, he can talk. He's grown his beard and hair longer, you know, and he's looking gaunt and wild. He quoted poetry at me, and talked a lot about the weakest being the strongest, or something like that, and when he described our summers together it was like hearing a novel being read out.'

I pulled a face. 'He's spent the last couple of decades in pubs and restaurants like this, talking his novel away.'

Paul, dipping brown bread into his egg yolk and gulping red wine, took no notice.

'He wouldn't really talk much about Natalie, but he gave me some photographs. Martha didn't exactly say she wouldn't talk to me, but when I turned on the tape recorder and asked her questions, she just sort of smiled at me – this really sad, wispy smile – and shook her head. She doesn't look a happy woman, Jane.'

'She's ill,' I said, and then asked, 'What about the others?'

'They'll all talk. Everybody wants to be on television. Theo considers himself real tele-guru material. Alfred and Jonah seem all set. Claud is being helpful.' He glanced sideways at me and Bella also looked at me with curiosity.

'It's going to be interesting, Jane. And big too, I think. We'll be like the Waltons.'

'I think I will have some of that wine,' I said. 'What are you going to ask me then?' Bella leant forward and clicked on the tape recorder.

'Is that all right?' she asked, but it was a rhetorical question. This was TV. What could I have against it?

It's strange, alarming really, how we will talk to a tape recorder and a potential audience of anonymous unthreatening millions, the way we won't, can't, talk to a friend or a lover. Or a brother. Paul asked me about my memories of the Stead ('Just tell me them at random, as they occur to you,' he said), and as the spools on the recorder whirled, and Bella's pen scratched busily in her notebook, I plucked forth memories I hadn't known I'd kept. Croquet on the lawn; wild games of tag; expeditions through the woods with Claud being the leader, secret midnight feasts with food pilfered from the Stead's generous larder, the dribbly, slack-mouthed retriever the Martellos used to have (was Candy his name?), who would jump clumsily into the stream for sticks; raspberries under a green net that we would pick on hot afternoons; jam-making days (gooseberry, blackberry, strawberry, loganberry, damson, plum), stinging sunburn when we would rub lotion into each other's shoulders; loud lunches when we'd all show off and Alan would egg us on. I remembered early mornings, when the dew was still on the grass, and long evenings, when the grown-ups were eating their supper and we could hear the chink of knives on plates, the murmur of conversation, and we would pull wellingtons on over bare legs and run down the garden to the swing in the great copper beech tree. In these memories, we children moved as one group, the adults were always in the background, and it was always sunny. It wasn't really what Paul wanted.

'It's interesting,' said Paul, 'that you're only remembering when you were very little. What about later, when you were a teenager?'

Suddenly the wine turned sour in my mouth. Why was I going along with this? I wanted to stop it. 'Do you want to talk about the summer when Natalie disappeared? Is that what you're focusing on?'

'Talk about it if you like.'

'I remember your pain, Paul. I remember watching your humiliation by Natalie and wondering what to do about it and . . .'

'What are you going on about?' said Paul sharply, and Bella clicked off the tape recorder and laid down her pen. 'What do you think you're doing, Jane?'

'What do you mean?'

'Don't play the innocent with me like that. You know what I mean. You're deliberately destroying the memory, aren't you? Well, aren't you?'

'No,' I replied. I pushed away my plate, sipped some more wine and lit a cigarette. I felt a bit more in control now, not so seduced by the gentle golden light of my imagined past. 'Are you going to ignore your crush on Natalie and her cruelty towards you? It was complicated, wasn't it? There was you and Natalie, and then Natalie and Luke, and me and Theo, and then me and Claud, and there were the twins who were so odd really, playing silly jokes, and there was Alan fucking girls while Martha cooked our meals and put plasters on our knees, and there was Mum being unhappy, and who knows what Dad felt about the whole thing?

'And then I remember' – I couldn't stop now, words

were spilling out of me – 'I remember that when I was sixteen and you were eighteen, Natalie disappeared. You see this as the end of our innocence. It may be good television. Do you really believe it?'

At some point, Paul had switched on the recorder again. I could see that he was torn between personal confusion and professional interest. I was delivering the goods, all right. Then I said something terrible. The words were out of my mouth, and lying between us like a sword, before I'd even thought them:

'When did *you* last see Natalie, Paul?'

To my surprise, Paul didn't react with hostility. He looked at me for a few seconds, considering me, and then rolled a pellet of bread between his fingers, before leaning towards the recorder and speaking directly into it:

'I can't remember. It was a long time ago.'

We had coffee and Bella and I smoked another cigarette: Paul sat between two bluish clouds of smoke and asked me other questions, but the real interview was over. Soon I put on my leather jacket, kissed Paul on the cheek, nodded at Bella and left. London was grey and shabby in the wet wind, and bits of paper lay over the pavements. A woman and her child asked me for money and I gave them five pounds and she asked me for ten. Wretched world.

Thirteen

'There's a little bit of Alan that's enjoying all of this.'

I was cooking supper for Kim, who'd arrived from her surgery looking exhausted and clutching two bottles of wine and some squishy packets of cheese. The potatoes were mashed, a green salad was prepared, there were fresh flowers on the table: I had someone to cook for. Kim had taken off her shoes and was padding round the kitchen in a dazed fashion, lifting up pan lids, peering into my fridge. I'd been to the supermarket on my way home from work and the fridge was satisfyingly full: tomatoes that looked suspiciously off-red, fennel bulbs, some lettuce with a funny name, a slab of Parmesan, tubs of yoghurt, fresh pasta, a packet of smoked salmon. I had resolved to be good. No more of those dinners that only had to be lit and inhaled. Most mornings, I went swimming on my way into work; most evenings, I prepared myself a proper meal.

'How do you mean?'

She pulled a cork and poured us a glass of wine each. I took a gulp, then threw some chopped onions into a pan and started to pull the snotty slime out of a squid with my finger.

'Well, I suppose he's devastated. But did you see that interview in the *Guardian*? Honestly! And Paul just rang me and told me that he's just been photographed for one of the women's mags. They're doing a big feature on famous people whose children have died.'

'There are no problems,' said Kim sardonically, 'only opportunities.'

'That's what you tell your patients, is it? Then the biggest opportunity of all is this thing at the ICA tomorrow evening, part of their "Angry Old Men" season; Alan Martello in conversation with Lizzie Judd. You know, the academic who made her name with that book called *Sitting Uncomfortably*, that attack on C. S. Lewis and Roald Dahl and other children's writers that got into the newspapers. She's a carnivore.'

'Are you going along?'

'Of course. It's like a bullfight, isn't it? People say you should see at least one in your life. I don't know whether Alan will be in his chivalrous gentleman mode or his shocking truth-teller mode, but both will be disastrous.'

'Don't worry, Jane, people will have a good time. It'll be like a modern version of bear baiting, just the sort of thing Alan enjoys.'

'It won't be much fun for the daughter-in-law of the bear.'

Kim had met a man, I learnt over squid. His name was Andreas. He was six years younger than her and a musician. He was small and handsome and sentimental, and their first date had lasted for an entire weekend, broken off only when Kim had been called out of bed to make home visits. I'd always envied Kim's sex life; the variety, the excitement, the sheer numbers. One of her more interesting qualities as a friend was her willingness to talk about what she actually did in bed with these men. I had always had so little with which to reciprocate. I ventured a feeble question about whether it might turn out to be serious and she waved me away as she always did.

'Do you miss Claud?' she asked over cheese.

What could I say? I knew that Kim wouldn't hold my confusion against me.

'I miss a bit of my life, but, then again, I wanted to be free of that old intimacy. Maybe I'm a bit scared by what I've done but I'm excited as well somehow.' I paused to gather my thoughts. 'I feel that something huge is going on in my life, but that I'm in the wrong place at the moment. I almost wish I could tag along with the police, be involved. I feel like I've got to do something to find out how Natalie died. I need to know what happened.'

'But it must have been that old boyfriend, mustn't it?'

'You mean Luke?'

'Yes, and the police have got him.'

'They're talking to him.'

'There you are then. Luke got her pregnant, they had some row, he killed her, maybe by mistake. And buried her.'

'In Alan's and Martha's garden. Right by the house.'

'People don't do logical things when they've killed somebody. Did I ever tell you about the patient of mine who killed his wife? He dismembered the body and sent the bits off to branches of Barclays Bank all over the world.'

'That sounds quite clever.'

'Except that he put his address on the customs declaration.'

'Why?'

'His psychiatrist said that he wanted to be caught.'

'Is that story true?'

'Of course it is. Anyway, I don't see that the improbability lets Luke off the hook any more than anybody else. Somebody must have buried her there.'

'Yes,' I admitted. 'It makes everyone less likely.'

They always say that if you started public hangings again, they would attract hordes. The ICA was packed out. The audience was mostly young. Television cameras were being set up near the stage, and a large man wearing round wire-framed glasses like Bertolt Brecht's was wandering around the stage with a clipboard. I squeezed along the row towards the two empty seats in the middle. Theo still hadn't arrived. The man sitting in the seat next to mine was almost invisible in a large tweed overcoat. I stepped on his foot and tripped over a plastic bag on the floor.

'Sorry,' I said irritably, and he nodded briefly, before going back to his ceiling-gazing.

Theo arrived. In his black suit, carrying a briefcase, he looked formal and out of place. He kissed me on the cheek, and whispered:

'I've just been with Alan. He's drunk.'

'Drunk?' I squawked.

'Arseholed.'

'What do you mean, he's *drunk*? He's due on stage in about one minute.'

'He can still talk,' Theo said. 'Ms Judd will have a hard time stopping him.'

I moaned. Why had I come?

A minute or two after eight, Lizzie Judd walked purposefully onto the stage, a severely beautiful woman in a slim grey suit. Her blonde hair was swept back from her face, she wore no jewellery or make-up, and she wasn't carrying any notes. She sat down in one of the two chairs, and poured herself a glass of water. Then Alan bounded onto the stage, as if he were making an entrance on a chat show.

'What is he wearing, Theo?' I whispered.

I knew the answer. A velvet smoking jacket he some-times wore in the evening at home. On his grizzled head was a black fedora. He reminded me of a Toulouse-Lautrec poster I had had on the wall of one of my student bedsits. I felt a rush of emotion for this undignified, truculent old man. Not many people clapped, though the man beside me was one of them. Alan sat heavily on the empty chair next to Lizzie Judd. He had a large tumbler in his hand three-quarters full of something whisky-coloured. He sipped from it and his eyes swept the hall.

Lizzie Judd expressed her ('and I'm sure the audience's') sympathy over the discovery of Natalie's body. She gave a brisk account of *The Town Drain* ('anti-romantic . . . tradition of comic realism . . . lower-middle class . . . essentially male'). She referred to the, much less well-known, successors in a sentence, and concluded that the long publishing silence was doubtless something we would get on to later.

'Mr Martello,' Lizzie Judd began.

'Call me Alan,' Alan interrupted.

'All right, Alan. John Updike has said that there is no need to write funny novels. What would you say to that?'

'Who's John Updike?' Alan said.

Lizzie Judd looked a little startled.

'I'm sorry?'

'Is he American?'

'Yes, he is.'

'Well then.'

'Is that your answer?'

Alan was lying back in his chair when she said this (I

noticed that his socks were different colours). He sat up slowly, sipped some whisky, and leant towards his interrogator.

'Look, Lizzie, I wrote a fucking good novel. A *fucking* good novel. Have you got a copy of it here? No?' He turned to the audience. 'Has anybody got one?' There was no response. 'All of you, open your copies of *The Town Drain* at the copyright page and you'll see that it has been reprinted year after year after year. It seems to make people laugh. Why should I care what some po-faced American says?'

Lizzie Judd was icily calm.

'Perhaps we should move on,' she said. 'Your novels have recently received some feminist criticisms.'

Alan snorted.

'I'm sorry?' she asked.

'No, it's all right, go on.'

'It has been said that women feature in your work either as shrews or as big-breasted objects of the sexual attention of your heroes. Even some of your admirers have said that, forty-five years on, the sexism of your novels remains a problem.'

Alan took a large gulp of whisky, which prevented him from speaking for a surprisingly long time.

'Why should that be a problem?' he asked after his final swallow. 'I'm glad that they still seem sexy. Is there anything wrong with finding large-breasted women sexy? Jolly good thing.'

I put my head into my hands. There was a suppressed giggle beside me. Not from Theo, from the man on my other side.

Alan had paused, apparently enjoying the embarrassed silence. Judd remained expectantly silent.

'I was only joking, Lizzie. I'm not supposed to talk about things like breasts, am I? It's not allowed. Are you saying I hate women, Lizzie, love?'

'Why should you think I'm saying that?'

'That's what people like you say. Are we talking about me or are we talking about my books, Lizzie? I love women. I like fucking. Or at least I used to, when I could manage it. Is that what you want to hear? Now, shall we talk about my book?'

My head was between my knees now and I began to consider blocking my ears. I heard a shuffling sound. Was he standing up?

'I wrote that novel from my heart.' A fist banged against a chest. Hugely amplified by the radio microphone he was wearing, it sounded like a battering ram against a castle gate. 'And I wrote it when I was very young, and I don't give a fuck about people who use the book to argue about what Alan Martello thinks about women. I'm bored, bored, fucking bored with discussions which say that one novel is better than another because it's *nicer*.'

There was an agitated murmur in the audience. I looked up to find myself at the centre of a forest of raised arms. Lizzie Judd pointed at a young woman sitting to one side.

'Would you say then that morality has nothing to do with literary merit?'

'Oh fuck off,' Alan said. 'This isn't the Oxford fucking Union, is it? I thought we were here to talk about my books. Or are we going to talk about sex? Lizzie, do you want to tell us what you do in bed and with whom, if anyone?'

There were shouts now from different parts of the auditorium. Lizzie Judd remained calm as she called for quiet like a tennis umpire.

'Mr Martello, do you want to continue with this discussion?'

Alan raised his glass, as if in a bizarrely inappropriate attempt at a toast.

'*I'm* all right,' he said.

Hands waved in the air. A pale and slender young man stood up, his scarf was wrapped around his neck so many times I could hardly see his face.

'I'm a man too, Mr Martello,' he said.

'Yes?' said Alan dubiously.

'But I'm not of your generation,' the man continued in a quavering voice. 'I think women have often been damaged by the affection you say you have for them, by the predatory sexuality that you portray with approval. Is the world ever going to change if people like you, with a voice that others listen to, maintain your chauvinism dressed up as the writer's freedom?'

Murmurs of agreement rippled round the theatre. The TV lights shone hotly down. Alan was sweating; Lizzie Judd looked immaculately cool.

'You pompous pillock,' said Alan, slurring his words now. 'If women are relying on you to defend them, they must be in trouble. You're just encouraging them to be victims. Crying harassment and rape and all that at the drop of a hat. Bloody hell.'

A female cry of 'Bastard' came from the back of the auditorium. Lizzie Judd remained alarmingly cool.

'This is your position on the issue of rape, is it, Mr Martello?'

Alan finished his whisky, and put his glass down, slightly missing the table so that it fell and shattered on the stage.

'Don't mind that,' he said. 'Balls! Women like strong men and a bit of violence. Only complain afterwards.

Make 'em feel better to complain. Don't like to admit they like rutting like sows. I've never heard a woman complain. We're not supposed to say that, are we? Not politically correct, is it?'

'This is your position as a respected novelist, is it?' Lizzie Judd asked, showing some signs of alarm at what she was unleashing.

'I'm not a fucking respected novelist,' Alan shouted thickly. 'I haven't finished a fucking novel for thirty years. But yes, we're not social workers. We work in a world where ordinary men are killers, where women want to be fucked or want to be raped and don't know the difference. It's the world of the fucking imagination.'

'Some people might say that there is a continuum between the abusive fantasies that are dramatised in fiction such as yours and the actual violence suffered by women.'

Alan stood up unsteadily.

'You want to see a continuum? I'll show you a fucking continuum.'

Like a toppling tree he fell down on Lizzie Judd, put a hand on her breast and kissed her noisily on her startled mouth. Her microphone must have been close to her face because the smacking kiss echoed loudly around the auditorium. I had several impressions simultaneously. Cameras rolling. Shouts from the crowd. People jumping up and running forward. Alan being pulled off Lizzie Judd. He shook somebody off and began to shout:

'You think I don't know about rape? My daughter was raped and murdered and the man who did it has been released. He claimed his fucking right to silence, he wouldn't answer any questions and the police let the rapist and murderer go. Now you can fucking crucify me.'

Alan continued to shout unintelligibly and flap around

until he was restrained by several members of the audience that now filled much of the stage. Theo ran forward and fought his way through the crowd to his father. Lizzie Judd was being helped to her feet, her hair in disarray, her face smeared with lipstick. She was holding her eye. I alone stayed in my chair. I felt incapable of movement.

'Jesus Christ,' I said aloud. 'What a complete fucking disaster.'

'It wasn't so bad.'

I looked round, startled. It was the man next to me.

'Hang on a minute. I've just watched my father-in-law defend rape and assault a famous feminist in front of a paying audience. That's bad enough for me.'

'I was just trying to say . . .'

'Just go away.'

He went and I was left alone.

Fourteen

Neville Chamberlain Comprehensive School in Sparkhill. A disaster in grey concrete. Probably no more than twenty years old, already stained with moisture, like underarm sweat. An East German police interrogation centre dropped into a world of towerblocks, crouching red-brick houses and bypasses. I'd left home in the dark and now, as I parked outside, it was still before eight. No one was about.

The steamed-up, rapidly cooling interior of the car was depressing. I had nothing to read except an *A-Z*, so I crossed the road to a tiny café opposite the main school gate. I ordered a mug of mahogany-coloured tea, fried egg, bacon and grilled tomato. Almost all the tables were occupied by men in donkey jackets and the air was smoky and steamy. I looked at the front page of the *Sun* being read by the man opposite me. I wondered if there would be anything in the press about Alan's fiasco.

By twenty past eight I was back outside on the pavement, walking up and down to keep warm. Ten minutes later I saw him, on a bicycle. He was wrapped in a large coat, heavy gloves, helmet, but Luke's pale, thin face was unmistakable. As he approached the gate, he swung his right leg deftly back over the bike and rode the final few yards standing on the left pedal, swinging between the groups of pupils who were gathering. I had to run across the road to intercept him. I called his name and he turned his head. He didn't seem surprised and just gave a slightly sarcastic smile. He pulled off his helmet and ran a gloved hand through his long hair which was streaked with grey.

'Don't you have a job to go to?'

During the drive up, my mind had buzzed with things I wanted to learn from Luke. Now that I was here, it was difficult to think of what to ask.

'Can we talk?' I said.

'What are you doing here? What do you want?'

'I mean, can we talk *privately*?'

A vein throbbed in his temple. He flushed deeply and I thought he was going to shout at me, but then he looked around and made an obvious effort at self-control.

'Come with me,' he said. 'I can give you five minutes.'

Luke chained his bike to a stand and led me through a heavy swing door. We walked noisily down a school corridor whose grey aridity was relieved by paintings and collages on the walls.

'Have you seen the papers today?' he asked, without turning his head.

'No.'

'I could sue Alan, you know.'

'You might lose.'

Luke responded with a curt laugh and led me into a room that was so small that when we both sat down we were almost touching each other. We were surrounded by shelves with bright new exercise books and sheaves of drawing paper.

'Well?' he said.

'Did you co-operate with the police?'

Luke laughed again, in apparent relief.

'That's it?' he said. 'You haven't got anything, have you?'

'Well, did you?'

'I've been questioned by the police, my name has been in the papers. I'm afraid that I'm not very interested in talking to you about this. Look, I don't know what it is you're trying to discover, but if you're trying to prove something out of some girlish fantasy about Nat, just forget it.'

'If it wasn't your baby, whose could it possibly have been?'

Luke hardly seemed to be listening to me.

'I always liked you, Jane. The others, Nat's brothers, they looked down on me. I used to feel in my innocence that you didn't.'

'I was scared of you,' I replied. 'You seemed so sophisticated.'

'I was a year older.'

'Luke, give me some reason to believe it wasn't you?'

'Why should I?' He looked at his watch. 'Your five minutes are up. I hope I haven't been of help to you. I'll leave you to find your own way out.'

I sat in my car for a few minutes, then drove slowly towards the motorway until I saw a payphone. I rang Helen Auster in Kirklow and asked if I could meet her, now, as soon as I could get to her. She sounded puzzled but agreed. The day brightened as I drove west from Birmingham and as I entered Shropshire and drove along the top of the hills, my spirits lifted slightly. Kirklow police station was a large modern building just off the central market place. Helen met me at the front desk, wearing a long coat, and suggested we go for a walk. As we talked we strolled around the beautiful soft-stone buildings that made up the centre of the town. It was very cold and I wasn't sure why I was there.

'Are you all right?' Helen asked.

'I've just been to see Luke McCann,' I said.

'Where?'

'At his school in Sparkhill.'

'Why did you do that?'

'Have you seen the papers? Have you seen what happened with Alan at the ICA?'

Helen smiled thinly. Her pale skin was flushed in the cold and her cheeks were reddening.

'Yes, I saw that.'

'It was awful, but I think Alan is right and I feel desperate about it.'

'You mean about Luke.'

'Yes,' I said. 'That's why I went and confronted Luke. I didn't really know what I was going to say but he seemed shaken.'

'Isn't that understandable?'

'Look, Helen, I know that there's no scientific way of showing that Luke was the father of Natalie's baby but I've been racking my brains about what you could do to establish a connection. I thought I could go through the party list with you and identify all the people who might have known Luke. He might have said something to them. Have you talked to his parents? They might have something to say.'

Helen looked around.

'Let's go in here,' she said, and steered me into an empty tea room where we both ordered coffee. When it arrived, we sipped it for a moment in silence, cradling our chilled hands round the cups. Helen looked enquiringly at me.

'Who told you that it was impossible to connect Luke to the foetus?'

'Claud. He said that you wouldn't be able to do DNA fingerprinting because the DNA would have decayed and got contaminated.'

Helen gave a brief smile.

'Yes, he's right. One of the bases of the DNA oxidises and the strands crumble. And the DNA that was extracted from the recovered bones was 99 per cent contaminated.'

'I don't know what you're talking about.'

'It doesn't matter. DNA fingerprinting is no use for this case but there is another technique that's called polymerase chain reaction.'

'What's that when it's at home?'

'It's a way of amplifying very small amounts of human residue. Of course, the DNA strands are still broken up but there are a great many repeats in the DNA sequence. And these little repeat sequences are characteristic and they are inherited.'

'What does that mean?'

'It means that Luke McCann wasn't the father of Natalie's baby.'

I felt my cheeks flush.

'I'm terribly sorry, Helen. I've been stupid.'

'No, Jane, it was quite understandable. Mr McCann was never arrested or even questioned under caution. So he wasn't officially released, and so we didn't announce the results of the test. In the light of subsequent events, we've decided to issue a statement this afternoon.'

'Is the test reliable?'

'Yes.'

'God, Luke should have just said. It was my fault, though.'

We drank our coffee. Helen insisted on paying for herself. Then we walked across the square towards the police station. We halted outside and I prepared to say goodbye. Helen hesitated and spoke a little haltingly:

'You and Theodore Martello, you went out together, didn't you, that summer?'

'That's one way of putting it.'

'Why did it, I mean, how did it end?'

'Unhappily.'

'He talks about you a lot, Jane.'

'How would you know?'

'Oh, you know, when I've talked to him. I told you before, I've talked to him quite a lot. On and off.'

She looked awkward but eager, and a thought – a rather terrible thought – flashed across my mind. I stared at her, and she flushed a bright, hot red. But she didn't look away. I knew, and she knew that I knew; I wanted to say something, to warn her or tell her not to be foolish. But then, with a grimace, she turned rather clumsily and left me. I had a spare half hour on my parking ticket and used it walking around the centre of Kirklow, entirely heedless of my surroundings.

Fifteen

I found my life slipping – almost pleasurably – into a routine. The solid banks between which all the appointments and obligations and habits flowed were provided by the sessions with Alex Dermot-Brown. They had become as regular and unthinking as sleeping and eating. The morning bike rides along the canal, the weaving through the market to his house were now automatic. The visits accumulated in my memory and became comfortingly indistinguishable.

Session by session, I worked my way through what seemed to me to be everything about my life. I talked about my adolescence and Paul and my parents, but of course the story kept coming back to the Martellos, almost as if the Martellos constituted my story. They had always seemed to be at the centre of what was best about it. I described for Alex the childhood summer games. Other people had nostalgic, mythologised views of their early years: our shared childhood really was golden. I talked of my closeness with Natalie and Theo, and a great deal about Claud, as if I was trying to remake the relationship in my own mind, perhaps in a way that would justify my having left him.

It was hard to tell it as a narrative because our marriage hadn't so much broken up as faded away. I couldn't fasten on to any obvious reasons. There was no infidelity, certainly no violence, not even any obvious neglect. That wasn't Claud's style. In lots of ways I admired Claud more than I ever had. As I turned him into words, there in Alex's back room, I felt that I was in danger of making him seem almost irresistible, and of appearing to be talking myself out of what I had already done.

Claud had been in his mid-thirties when he got his consultancy at St David's and he'd turned out to be wonderful at the new responsibilities, all the committee work. Really wonderful. Apart from surgery, gynaecology is historically the area of medicine most dominated by men and Claud and I had always had subdued conflicts about the issue. But, as he might have said but never did, what could he have done as a senior registrar except make futile gestures and thwart his own career? Doctors who make trouble when they are young are the ones who somehow miss out on promotion. When Claud did become a consultant, this all changed. Of course, being Claud, it all seemed dour and unspectacular and it took time, most notably for his opponents, to see what was going on. What Claud was doing was instituting a committee on the role of female gynaecologists in the profession. When people cottoned on there was a real storm. There was a court case, there was an editorial in the *Daily Telegraph* or somewhere, but Claud was a match for them all.

When we were children, it was always Claud who knew what wire went where on the plug, and what time the last train left and all the things nobody else bothered about, and he showed the same grasp of detail at the hospital. Other people huffed and puffed while Claud didn't say very much at all, but at the crucial moment it was always Claud who had talked to the right people on the committee beforehand or who had somehow got the agenda immovably fixed according to some arcane rule that nobody else knew about. The result was that during the past seven years, every single gynaecological appointment at St David's had gone to a woman. He was a hero. And it was clever as well, because he had caught the mood that wasn't yet prevailing. He had got the bandwagon moving before jumping on it.

The odd thing was that Claud never once came to me and said 'I told you so'. He never explained to me that he had been keeping his powder dry all those years so that it could be used when it would be effective. I wish he had, but he was always rational and modest about his achievements, insisting that gynaecology had been wasting its resources and that he was only doing what was efficient. Besides, he said, under the new contract system, the female gynaecologists were more co-operative and flexible. Maybe Claud is the sort of person who accomplishes major reform, an instinctive conservative who admits change in order to save as much of the old system as he can. Maybe. But, in the evenings, there was no detectable difference between the Claud who had swung an entire department behind his proposals against all the odds and a Claud who had failed. This detachment served him brilliantly over the years but it came to repel me.

Claud's triumphs were part of what settled my feelings about him. If I felt nothing for him after what he had achieved, then our marriage really must be in trouble, I reasoned. How does a marriage go wrong? I almost wish I could say that I had caught him in bed with his secretary or one of his adoring female house officers. Claud would never have been unfaithful to me and I knew he would be a loyal husband until one of us died, if only because he had been witnessed signing a document to that effect in a registry office on 28 May 1973. It was all just little things and the lack of little things.

Sex, of course. See under 'Lack of'. When we were first married we had a passionate sex life and Claud was rather elegantly good at it. I don't just mean tactile manipulation but that he seemed to have the whole thing worked out. More than any man I'd ever slept with (a fairly small number, who could be counted on the fingers of two hands) Claud saw sex not just as an impulse but as a part of affection, friendship, humour, tenderness, consideration. I adored it and him.

For most of my teens, Claud had been what Jerome and Robert used to call a dork. He started wearing glasses when he was about three years old and he was always the serious one, without the charisma that Theo and later the twins displayed so effortlessly. He was dogged, painstaking but never the star. Then, in the awful year or so after Natalie disappeared, when it looked as if the Martello family might be broken up by the pain, we became close. That was dogged as well. Claud set out to charm me and his efforts were so transparent, but they worked. To like somebody is one of the good ways of making that person like you but it can just as easily have the opposite effect. Claud got it right. There was nothing sexual for a long time. I was going out with various boys and Claud became a good friend. We used to write to each other when he was away at medical school, long and interesting letters, and I was surprised to find myself telling him things that I kept from other people. We made no demands on each other, we didn't show off, and so when I was in my first year at university I was slightly startled to realise that he was my best friend. He started going out with a girl called

Carol Arnott – the first proper girlfriend he had ever had, as he told me and told absolutely nobody else – and I was curious to find myself a little jealous.

It was 1971 and I remember it best in terms of clothes: crushed velvet, flares, cheesecloth blouses with dropped cuffs like a medieval minstrel, shades of purple that I wouldn't dare wear again until the early nineties. I was eighteen and Claud was twenty and I coolly set out to steal him from poor Carol, which I managed with no difficulty at all. Our first night together was in the narrowest of single beds in a bedsit in Finsbury Park which Claud shared with two other medical students. In a process so smooth that it must have seemed inevitable, we managed to decide to get married, which we did at the end of my second year. I wonder if we felt that we were healing the breach in the family. By 1975 I had Jerome and Robert and while still children ourselves we had to be grown up and juggle the childcare with our training and our careers. As I look back on it, I see two decades of frenzy and panic culminating in an autumn afternoon when I drove Robert up for his first term at college. I had a moment to think and the first thought that entered my head was the absolute conviction that I had to leave Claud. No debate, no counselling, no trial separation, just a line drawn under my life.

There. That was what I presented Alex with. That was where I now was, bemused, tearful, out of control. What would he make of it? Although I was anxious to guard myself against it, I already caught myself caring about Alex's judgement on what I said. Perhaps I was even trying to impress him. I became curious about his life. I noticed his clothing, the differences from day to day. I liked the metal-rimmed spectacles he sometimes wore, always with an air of casualness as if they had been tossed on, and the long hair which he constantly pushed off his forehead with his hands. Sometimes he was strict with me. He surprised me by disapproving of my detective work.

'I thought you wanted me to deal with facts,' I protested, a little hurt.

'That's right,' said Alex, 'but the facts that we're interested in at the moment are the ones that are inside your own head. There's plenty of work there, hard work. We need to distinguish between the things you're telling me that are true and those that aren't. Then there are the things that are true and are not true that you *aren't* telling me. That will be more difficult.'

'There's nothing I'm telling you that isn't true. What are you talking about?'

'I'm talking about this golden childhood stuff. Look, Jane, I told you from the start that I would try to be frank about the way my thinking was going, so maybe I should talk a bit about the way I'm feeling at the moment.' Alex paused for thought. He always gave the impression of immense deliberation before speaking, not like me, gabbling away. He made thinking seem almost like a matter of engineering, a practical skill. 'You've been saying two contradictory things to me, Jane. You're clinging on to the happy childhood as if it were a talisman against something. At the same time you've been talking of this body that was buried at the heart of it. Now *I* might just say that the two were independent. Somebody can come from the outside and murder a member of the happiest of families. The world is full of cruel bad luck like that. But that's not what *you* say. It's *you* who insists that this is impossible.'

'What are you saying, Alex? What do you want me to do?'

'You're trying to hold up two heavy weights and you won't be able to manage it. You have to let one side go, Jane, and face up to the consequences. You have to think about your family.'

This was one of those moments in the sessions when I felt like a hunted animal. I would find some bit of cover somewhere and feel safe, then Alex would track me down and drive me out into the open again. I described the image to Alex and he laughed and laughed.

'I'm not sure I'm happy with the idea of you being a beautiful fox while I'm some brutal red-faced squire on a horse. But if it means that I can stop you skulking in some false paradise then I suppose I can live with it. Now, over to you. Even if it's only an experiment, Jane, I want you to strip away your picture-book account of your family. Start thinking of it as a family in which a murder could happen, and let's see where that gets us.'

'What are you talking about? What do you mean, "a family in which murder could happen"?'

When Alex replied, I detected a harder tone which I had never heard from him before.

'I've just been listening to you, Jane. You must take responsibility for what you say to me.'

'I haven't talked about any murderer in the family.' I felt a sour, sick taste in the back of my mouth.

Alex remained firm. 'It was you, not me, who talked of the oddity of where Natalie's body was found.'

'Yes, well it *was* odd, wasn't it?'

'What did you mean by that if you weren't implicating your family in some way?'

'I wasn't.'

'All right, calm down.'

'I'm perfectly calm.'

'No, what I mean is that even if the idea is a shock, you should treat it as an experiment.'

'What do you mean, an experiment?'

'It's simple, Jane. Sometimes these ideas in therapy can be treated like hypotheses. Imagine, if you can, that you didn't come from this ultra-perfect family that everybody admired and wanted to join. Imagine it was a dangerous family.'

Had I been wanting Alex to say this to me, to say this *for* me? I made a token attempt to protest but Alex interrupted me and continued.

'I'm not asking you to make accusations or be disloyal. It's just a way of re-orienting yourself, to allow yourself a new freedom.'

It was one of those moments when I craved a cigarette as a means of thinking clearly. Instead, I told Alex about my evening at the ICA and the colossal, shaming, harrowing awfulness of Alan's behaviour. When you are the daughter-in-law of Alan Martello, a good deal of your work is done. He's been famous since his twenties and, independently of his own efforts, he has been a free-floating symbol. A youthful radicalism was pinned on him once, now this has been replaced with an equally odd anarchic conservatism. He has been at various times, often at the same time, a little Englander, a satirist, a class warrior, a liberator, a reactionary, a professional iconoclast, a conformist, a rebel, a bore, a sexist exploiter. I sometimes wonder what I would make of him if I were encountering him for the first time, but I've always adored him in a mixed-up way. I've seen him put himself in the most indefensible positions, I've witnessed or heard of behaviour that I totally deplored, he has heedlessly hurt people, especially my beloved Martha, but I've been on his side. He was the person who presided over that wonderful Martello household, his vitality fuelled it, he was the centre of it all, its symbol. Was it just because of that that I couldn't reject him? Even at the ICA, in the middle of all the shambles, I felt a perverse loyalty but that time it really did feel perverse.

Alex hardly followed up the things that I expected would interest him. Sometimes it seemed almost a matter of pride, as if he had to demonstrate his independence. He listened with concentration to the account of my wavering attitude towards Alan but then he went back yet again to my memories, or non-memories, of the river bank on the afternoon when Natalie was last seen. This time I actually showed some impatience. He was insistent.

'I'll follow you in whatever you want to talk about,' he said. 'But I would like you to indulge my interest in this. Something you said to me very early on interested me. You said, "I was there."'

'I don't remember if I used those exact words, but it's not such a big deal. All I meant was that I was on the river bank close to where Natalie was last seen. You can't read all that much into it.'

'I'm not reading anything into it. I'm listening to you. That's what you pay me for. "I was there. I was there." An interesting choice of words, don't you think?'

'Not really.'

'I think it is.'

Alex got up and paced around the room as he always did when he was being theatrically excited. Being behind me and out of sight wasn't enough at moments like these. He wanted to be higher than I was, to dominate me.

'You're being woolly, just because we're dealing with words and emotions. You wouldn't be like this in your work, would you? If you had a plan of a house twenty metres wide and a site fifteen metres wide, you wouldn't just go ahead and build the building and hope that it would somehow work out along the way. You would redesign the building to fit the space. It may be that all we need to do is iron out the discrepancies in what you've said to me. You've said that you come from a perfect happy family and yet one of the family was killed and you say it couldn't have been someone from outside. How can we make those statements fit together? You tell me that you were there, and yet you weren't there. How can that make sense? Were you in reality *not* there, or do we have to get you there?'

'What do you mean, "get me there"?'

'You have come to me with a story with strange dark holes in it, with walls that need to be breached. Let's strike a bargain, Jane. I'm going to stop being a bully, I promise. We'll talk about the things you want to talk about, for the time being at any rate. However' – he held up a finger – 'there will be one exception. I want us to stay with this scene by the river, I want you to go back into it, to inhabit it, to explore it.'

'Alex, I've told you everything I can possibly remember about that afternoon.'

'Yes, I know. And you're doing well, perhaps better than you realise. What I want you to do now is stop trying to remember. You can free yourself from all that. I'd like to try to repeat the exercise we did the other day.'

So we went through that process. I closed my eyes and relaxed and Alex talked soothingly to me and I tried to put myself back by the river, leaning against the stone, there on that summer afternoon. I was better at it now. The first time the scene had appeared like one of those supposedly three-dimensional photographs. They give an illusion of depth but it's not a depth you can put your hand into. This was different. I could yield to it. I was in a space I could walk through, a world in which I could lose myself. Alex's voice seemed to come from outside. I described to him what I experienced. I was sitting down, my back resting on the dry mossy stone at the foot of Cree's Top, the river on my left flowing away, the last screwed up pieces of paper floating round the curve ahead of me. The elms on the edge of the wood on my right.

Alex's voice from outside my world asked me if I could stand up and I could without any difficulty. He asked me if I could turn round. Yes, I could. I told him that the river was now on my right flowing towards me and away behind me, the elms and the wood were on my left. Now I was looking up the little hill of Cree's Top. Alex's voice told me that he didn't want me to move or to do anything. All he wanted to know was, could I see the path? Of course I could. There were thick bushes by the side, and it occasionally disappeared from view as it snaked its way up the slope, but I could see almost all of it. Very good, said Alex. All he wanted me to do now, he said, was to turn round once more and sit down in my original position. No problem. Very good, he said. Very good.

Sixteen

Days were up and down, but I surprised myself by coping. Take a typical example, a sunny Monday morning early in December. It was one of those days that occur every so often on which women are encouraged to bring a schoolgirl to work with them in order, supposedly, to make their jobs seem less alarming. I couldn't help feeling that anybody who contemplated my working life would suddenly find herself attracted to the kitchen and nursery, but I decided I must make the gesture. So I rang up Peggy, whom I always felt I never rang up quite often enough. Evidently, Emily, the middle girl of Paul's previous family (she's almost sixteen), was slowest in thinking up a plausible excuse and she was offered up to me for the day.

Just after nine o'clock in the morning she slouched down her garden path, Peggy waving unnoticed behind her. She was dressed in black like a Greek widow, though with the rings through her nose she was unlikely to be mistaken for one. She sat in the passenger seat, switched *Start the Week* off and we headed east from Kentish Town. I asked after Peggy and Emily grunted something and asked about Robert. I muttered a non-committal pleasantry and said he seemed to be getting on well with his new girlfriend. I feel protective about my nieces where my predatory youngest son is concerned and I've talked to him, and to Jerome as well, about their duty to look after their younger cousins. I was edgy, mainly because I would normally have been smoking but Emily would have probably wanted to join me and so I had decided in advance to give up for a morning.

I love my sons but when they were growing up the house did sometimes feel like a sports changing room. Perhaps in reaction to this I have always felt a special pang of affection for the three bolshy Crane girls. I sometimes worried that I might try too hard with them and put them off me but as we stopped and started along York Way, Emily chatted with what – for her, at least – was remarkable fluency. I asked her if she had heard anything about Paul's documentary. Emily rolled her eyes, as she did in response to almost anything to do with her father.

'Silly man,' she said.

I felt obliged to be soothing.

'No, Emily, I'm sure it'll be very interesting.'

'You *want* to be on telly, do you, with everybody knowing about your family?'

'No, not really.'

'We're all refusing to be in it. Dad got really cross. Cath called him a voyeur.'

'Well, at least Paul must be pleased to hear her using a French word. If only she'd called him an auteur.'

We giggled together. We arrived, late as always, at the hostel where there were two council employees waiting, neither of whom I'd met before. Pandora Webb, an inter-mediate treatment officer. And Carolyn Salkin, a disability officer. In a wheelchair. At the foot of the steep concrete steps leading to the front door. Carolyn's hair was cut very short, giving her the air of a fierce sprite. She was the sort of person I would have taken to immediately if I had met her anywhere but in front of my precious project. She came bluntly to the point.

'There is evidently no wheelchair access in your plans, Ms Martello.'

'Please call me Jane,' I panted. 'And this is my niece, Emily.'

'There's no wheelchair access, Jane.'

'The issue was never really raised,' I replied, incredibly feebly, but it was Monday morning and I was feeling self-conscious in front of my niece.

'I'm raising it now.'

I needed to go away and think this through but it didn't seem possible.

'As far as the brief went, this is a hostel where highly independent recently discharged people can stay briefly with light supervision. I agree, Carolyn, that ideally every building should have full wheelchair access but with my alterations this is now a narrow four-storey house. Surely it would be better if wheelchair-bound patients, or, indeed, employees, were directed to premises that would be more suitable.'

The two women exchanged glances. They looked ironic, contemptuous. Pandora was clearly not on my side, but she was obviously happy to leave the talking to Carolyn.

'Jane,' Carolyn said, 'I didn't come here to debate disabled politics on the pavement. And I'm not bargaining. I'm simply here to make sure you understand the council's policy on access in new buildings. You should have been told about this already.'

'What needs doing?' I asked wearily. 'I mean specifically.'

'I'd show you myself if I could get into the premises,'

said Carolyn icily. 'You'll have to arrange an appointment with another member of my department.'

'Who funds the extra equipment?'

'Who funds the fire escape, Jane?' Carolyn asked sarcastically. 'Who funds the double-glazing?'

I felt a small stab of rage at her unfairness.

'If I were Miës van der Rohe, you wouldn't be forcing me to put ramps across every angle.'

'I would if he were designing a building in this borough,' said Carolyn.

'Who's Miës van der thingy?' asked Emily, when we were back in the car.

'He's probably the main reason I became an architect. His buildings were based on complete mathematical clarity, straight lines, metal and glass. His greatest building was for an exhibition in Barcelona in the twenties. The building was so pure in form that Miës wouldn't even allow a wall where pictures could be hung because that would have violated its perfection.'

'That's not much good for an exhibition,' Emily protested.

'No,' I admitted. 'I don't think he would have had any more success with this hostel than I have. When I went into architecture, we still thought it might be a way of transforming people's lives. That doesn't seem particularly fashionable at the moment.'

'What are you going to do?'

'I think I'm too old to retrain as a civil liberties lawyer.'

'No, I mean with the hostel.'

'Oh, the usual. Put some things in, take some things out. Lose a little bit more of my original inspiration. I haven't lost hope entirely. Slashing my budget is partly their way of showing that they still intend this hostel to get built.'

We drove back to my office and I introduced Emily to Duncan and he showed her how to move his drawing board up and down. I dictated a couple of letters which it would have been quicker to type myself. We made coffee and I told Emily a bit about the profession and what I could remember of the training and we gossiped and then I drove her back to Kentish Town a little after lunch. I went in with her and had a cup of coffee with Peggy. She was always worried about things. She was worried about Paul's documentary, with which she was refusing to have anything at all to do. She was worried about Martha, and I couldn't think of anything to say about that. She was worried about Alan making a complete fool of himself, but I told her that that wasn't worth bothering about. And she was even a little worried about *me*. Paul had told her about my therapy and she wanted to discuss it with me.

'As you know, I had years of therapy after Paul walked out,' she told me. 'After about two years, I plucked up courage and looked around and my analyst was asleep.'

'Yes, you've told me about that, Peggy,' I said. 'I think it's quite common.'

'It was a waste of money all the same. I decided that pills would be cheaper and more convenient. I was prescribed Prozac, I got through my crisis and I took the girls to Kos. I worked out that the holiday cost less than three months' therapy. Admittedly, when I was there I felt that I'd need about three years' therapy to recover, the way that the girls behaved with all those waiters buzzing around them like bees round a honey pot.'

'What are you saying, Peggy? Do you think I'm wasting my time?'

'No, it's just that I suppose I'm surprised. You were always the strong one. Also, now you mustn't get offended by this, I don't understand what you're doing. You were the one who suddenly decided to break up with Claud. He was shattered, he's desperate about it. Now you're feeling bad about it and looking for help. Not only that, Paul tells me you're going around stirring things up about Natalie. I don't understand what you're doing, Jane, I really don't.'

I felt an acid ache of rage in my stomach and I wanted to shout at Peggy or hit her but I've never been any good at Mediterranean displays of emotion, much as I've always envied them. And I felt that Peggy was right, in a way. I responded with icy calm.

'Maybe I don't understand what I'm doing myself, Peggy. Maybe that's what I'm trying to find out.'

The cocktail glass in the freezer, and the jug and the spoon. The gin of course should be there for at least a couple of days so that it pours viscous. For that reason, something like Gordon's Export Gin, the one with the yellow label that you get in duty free, is essential. Anything weaker, like the Gordon's domestic in the green bottle, and it will freeze, defeating the point. A few drops, perhaps a teaspoon, not more, of dry vermouth, then a slosh of gin into the jug which is so cold you can scarcely hold the handle. The briefest of stirs. A fat slice of lemon peel, twisted to release some of the oil, into the frosty glass, then submerge it in the harsh, icy liquid. If there is any liquid left in the jug, it can be returned to the freezer for the second glass.

Later that evening I snapped the polythene off a new packet of cigarettes and rinsed the ashtray in the sink. I opened a tin of black olives and tipped them into a small ramekin. They were pitted. I didn't want to have to concentrate on anything this evening. I took them, along with my dry martini, so cold that it seemed to be steaming like a witch's potion, and sat in front of the television. I switched it to a channel at random and watched without paying attention.

The drink took effect almost from the first sip and a pleasant numb sensation sank through me. I do some of my best thinking while sitting in the audience at an orchestral concert or wandering round a gallery ostensibly looking at pictures or, as here, half drunk, half watching a TV programme. I had been shaken by what Peggy had said. I am a person who likes to be visibly in the right, I really want to do the right thing, and I realised that I must seem – to Peggy and others – like a person self-indulgently doing the wrong thing. I was relying on Duncan's good nature when I neglected my work. I was relying on my sessions with Alex Dermot-Brown to relieve me of the responsibility for the decision I had made. I was carrying out some halfbaked investigation into the Martello family . . . Why? As revenge? I had things to do, and there were things I was looking for. But I didn't know what they were. Would it be better to drop it all and return to my life and make a go of it there with the stoicism that I'd always prided myself on?

I went to the freezer and emptied the remains of the drink into my glass, which was now wet and warm. I stopped thinking and the television programme began to take shape, like a picture coming into focus. A woman – rather striking, except that her eyebrows were drawn too fine – was talking about the family as the basis of society.

'Just as a leaky house is better than no house,' she said, 'an imperfect marriage is better than a broken marriage. The single most destructive social issue of our time is the feckless and selfish behaviour of parents who place their own convenience before the future of their children.'

There was loud applause.

'Fuck off,' I yelled at the screen.

'Sir Giles,' said the chairman.

Sir Giles was a man in a grey suit.

'Jill Cavendish is quite right,' he said, 'and we should none of us be ashamed to say quite categorically that this is a moral issue. And if our church leaders are not willing to give guidance on this, then it is time for us, the politicians, to act. As we know, there are young teenage girls who are quite deliberately becoming pregnant as a quick, easy way of getting a council flat. They are deliberately choosing a life on the dole at the expense of the rest of us. As a result, whole generations of children are growing up without moral guidance, without a father to guide them. No wonder these children turn to crime.

'I think, ladies and gentlemen, it is time for the ordinary men and women of this country to stand up and say to the socialists, "This is what you have brought us to. This is the logical result of your policies, of the disregard for morality and the family that we saw in the 1960s." They tell us to understand the plight of these feckless women. If you ask me, we should understand a little less and punish a little more. When I was a boy, a young girl knew that if she got pregnant she would be out on the street, an outcast. Perhaps we've got something to learn from those days. I'll tell you this: if young girls knew that there was no housing for them, no dole money, then there'd be a darn sight fewer single mothers.'

'Wanker,' I said and threw my cigarette packet at the screen, missing wildly.

The applause from the audience was even more fervent than before and the chairman struggled to make himself heard.

'We also have with us Dr Caspar Holt, who apart from being a philosopher also happens to be a single father with custody of a young daughter. Dr Holt, what's your response to Sir Giles?'

The camera cut to the nervous-looking face of a middle-aged man who seemed familiar from somewhere or other.

'I'm not sure I've got one, really,' he said. 'I distrust easy answers to complicated social problems. But I can't help thinking that if Sir Giles Whittell really believes that young girls are getting pregnant as a matter of financial calculation, he should ask himself who created this individualist culture in which anything except the selfish struggle for maximum financial gain is literally unintelligible. I'm also, well, *amused* by the belief that the very rich can only be encouraged by giving them even more money while the very poor should be encouraged by taking their money away.'

I started clapping.

'Hear hear.'

There was no other applause at all and the speaker was immediately subject to barracking from all sides. Then I remembered who he was. He was the man I had sat next to during Alan's débâcle at the ICA. I had the impression that I had been rude to him. I felt a stab of remorse. I went to the desk in the corner and searched through a pile of postcards. A grotesque nude by George Grosz. Too explicit. *The Annunciation* by Fra Angelico. Too austere. Watercolours of British mice. Too twee. *The Flaying of Marsyas* by Titian. Too much like the way I felt. *The Reverend Robert Walker Skating on Duddingston Loch.* That was about right. I turned it over and removed some dried Blu Tack, a reminder that it had once been attached to the wall above my desk. 'Dear Caspar Holt,' – I was stuck and looked back at the screen where he was now murmuring something about nursery education and being shouted down – 'I was the woman who was rude to you at the ICA. I'm writing this while watching you being sensible and brave on TV. I'm sorry that the one time I met you I behaved not very well. This isn't very coherent but you're saying the sorts of things I want to say but never think of at the time. Yours, Jane Martello.' I found a stamp in my purse and went straight out and posted the card. I needed some fresh air. The cold of the evening felt good, insofar as I could feel it.

Seventeen

'Do you remember how you used to come here to play?'

Although it was bitterly cold, Martha had insisted that we walk round the garden together. We stood by the giant oak tree, inside whose vast, hollow trunk we had hidden as children. I rubbed my hand over the mossy bark.

'Here's where Claud and Theo and Paul carved their initials. We thought they'd last for as long as the tree. They've nearly disappeared.'

We walked on in silence. I felt that I was treading in the footsteps of my childhood. The barns, the fallen trees, the stone walls, the herb garden, the flat patch where there used to be a swing, the skeletal branches, emaciated shrubs. When the wind blew Martha's jacket flat against her body, I realised how thin she'd become.

'Are you all right, Martha?'

She stooped gracefully to pluck up a weed.

'I have cancer, Jane.' She held up her hand to stop me from saying anything. 'I've known for a long time. It started as breast cancer, but it's spread.'

I took her chilly hand in my own and stroked it. The wind rushed at us from over the brow of the hill.

'What do the doctors say? What are they doing?'

'Not much. I mean, they don't say much, let me draw my own conclusions. And I'm not going to have chemo-therapy or radiotherapy or anything, except pain relief of course. I'm sixty-seven, Jane, that's a good time to get cancer: it advances more slowly.' She laughed. 'I'll probably die of a stroke at ninety-three.' Then, more soberly: 'I hope so. I can't imagine Alan managing very well on his own.'

'I'm sorry. I'm really so sorry, Martha. I wish that there was something that I could do.'

We walked back towards the house hand in hand.

'Martha,' I said abruptly, 'do you wish that the body had never been found?'

She looked at me strangely.

'That's not a question that makes any sense,' she replied at last. 'We found Natalie, and that's that. If you mean, was I *happier* before that, then the answer is yes, of course I was. I was even happy, sometimes. When Natalie was found, I had to start the mourning all over again. That old raw grief.'

She pushed open the back door.

'Let me make you some tea.'

'I'll make it,' I said.

'I'm not dying yet, Jane; sit down.'

I sat at the kitchen table, and noticed that Martha had made piles of all the children's books she had illustrated over the years. There were dozens. I started leafing through them. The pictures were familiar, of course, my own children had grown up on them, but still as wonderful as ever: funny, crowded and very colourful. She loved drawing large families: energetic grannies and harassed-looking parents and hordes of minute children with scabby knees and messy hair. There was lots of food in her illustrations – the kind of food that children love, like sticky chocolate cake, and wobbly purple jellies with bright yellow custard on top; mountains of spaghetti quivering on plates. And she loved drawing children running wild: over one double page spread a line of tiny, paunchy toddlers marched in red wellingtons; on another, children's faces peered joyously through the branches of trees. I paused at a drawing of a small girl holding a daisy chain, while a stupendous orange sun set behind her. It was unusual for Martha to draw children on their own – usually they were outnumbering and overpowering the adults.

'Before we found Natalie, Martha, were there ever times when you'd go a whole day without remembering her?'

It was the wrong question, I knew that, I knew the answer, yet I also knew that we had to talk about Natalie. Martha poured boiling water over the tea leaves, and lifted a large cake tin down from the cupboard.

'What do you think?' She put a ginger cake and knife on the table. 'For a long time I felt guilty. Not just about her going, or dying, or whatever, though that too, of course. About our relationship.'

I waited.

Martha poured two cups of tea and sat down at the table. 'My last memory of Natalie is of her shouting at me.' She looked into her tea, then said, 'No, that's not what I mean really. My last memory is of me shouting at her. Of course we used to have lots of trivial rows, cigarettes on her breath, that sort of thing. And she would give me this slightly distant smile that she always had when she was being told off and it would make me angry. It's the sort of row that is a part of being a parent, but this one we never made up. Sometimes I wonder if she died hating me.' She gave a sad smile. 'When Alan and I came back from that awful anniversary cruise and arrived at the big party, I wanted to talk to Natalie but there were so many people I had to see and I didn't and then it was too late.'

'Of course you blame yourself and feel guilty, Martha,' I said, 'and of course you shouldn't.'

I remembered experiencing a shadow version of the same feeling when my mother died. In the weeks after her burial I'd been in an agony of loss, remembering all the times I'd criticised her, been contemptuous of her, not appreciated her, not thanked her enough, not had that final settling of accounts, when we'd somehow have reconciled ourselves to all the raggedness and imperfections in our relationship.

'You have to remember the whole life, Martha, and not just the last weeks or days,' I said, lamely.

'I do. But the last quarrel somehow summed up all that was wrong with us.' Martha looked at me steadily. 'I've never said this to anyone, Jane.'

'Said what?'

'I've never told anyone about my quarrel with Natalie.'

'What was the quarrel about?'

Martha picked up the knife and cut two slices of cake. She must have baked it for me when she heard I was coming. 'Drink up your tea; it'll get cold.'

I sipped obediently.

'It was about your father and me, Jane. Our affair.'

I went on sipping my tea, but my hands felt very large and clumsy around the tea cup. Carefully, I put the cup back on the table, with an effort so that it wouldn't spill.

'Go on.'

'I had had a brief affair with your father in the summer of the previous year. He and your mother were not getting on very well, and you know what Alan was like. He was away in America for much of the summer. I was lonely; all the children were growing up and I felt my life was slipping by.' She stopped and made a sharp gesture with her hand. 'Enough, I don't want to make excuses for myself. I'm not proud of it, and it didn't last long. We never told anyone. Christopher didn't tell your mother; I never told Alan. And we were very secretive about it. We never wanted to hurt anyone.'

She took a very small, neat bite of cake.

'Natalie found a letter Christopher had written to me. She must have gone through all my drawers. She confronted me with it: she wasn't angry exactly, that was the funny thing, more triumphant. She said that I pretended to be so much better than Alan, and really I was just the same. She said she was going to tell your mother and Alan. She said' – Martha's voice was dry – 'that it was her duty.'

Martha stopped, and the kitchen felt very still as she waited for me to speak.

'Did she tell anybody?'

'I don't think so. Not that I ever knew.'

'But she might have told Alan.'

'I don't know.'

'Why are you telling me now, after all these years?'

Martha gave a weary shrug. 'Perhaps because it's a good time to uncover family secrets. Perhaps because I will die sometime soon, and I needed to confess, and I thought you might understand. Perhaps because you're the one who's rooting around for the truth.'

I didn't say anything. I didn't know what to say, and I didn't know what I was thinking. I tried to imagine my father with Martha, but I could only picture them as they were now: old, with papery skin and liver spots and stubborn habits. Martha turned back the pages to the drawing of the little girl and the setting sun.

'That's Natalie,' she said. 'I know it doesn't look like Natalie, except the mouth maybe. But it's how I always think of Natalie. She was a loner, you know. She snooped round other people's lives and she had boyfriends and went to parties, but she was always alone. I was her mother, but sometimes I felt she was a stranger. All the boys, oh they pretended to be grown up and independent, and they shrugged me away or were rude to me when their friends came round, but they *needed* me and they were always so transparent. Natalie, though, I often felt rejected by Natalie. I'd always thought we would have an intimate relationship, two women in a house of men.'

She stood up and cleared away our plates.

'You make those phone calls you were talking about; I'm going to get those cuttings for your garden.' Pulling on her jacket, she picked up a pair of secateurs and disappeared into the garden.

Mechanically, I did as Martha suggested, and hunted through my address book until I came across the name of Judith Parsons (*née* Gill, one of my best friends from school). She was surprised and thrilled to hear from me: how was I in London, how were my sons, isn't it awful how time flies, yes it would be wonderful to meet up – sometimes she and Brendon came to London and then she'd be sure to give me a ring. As we were about to say goodbye to each other I asked, casually, guiltily, oh, by the way, did she happen to have Chrissie Pilkington's phone number. I was going to be working near where she lived for a few days and thought it would be jolly to catch up with her. Judith's enthusiasm dampened slightly. Yes, she had the number, but she was Christina Colvin now: I jotted the details down in my address book, dialled again.

Christina Pilkington-now-Colvin was not so happy to hear from me. I could understand that. It had been twenty-five years since we'd last seen each other. I brought back memories she must have wanted suppressed. But she reluctantly agreed to have me round for tea later that afternoon. I wrote down directions, and just before I put the phone down she said, suddenly, 'My husband will be there, Jane.'

Martha loaded the cuttings into the back of my car, then gestured towards the pile of children's books on the table.

'They're for your grandchildren, Jane. One day.' And then, at last, we hugged each other.

The Colvins lived just outside Oxford in a large neo-Tudor house, all timber and diamond windows, with a swimming pool in the garden, and an avenue of rhododendrons. I've always hated rhododendrons. Bright flowers and shiny leaves and nothing lives under them.

I would not have recognised Chrissie. When I knew her she was thin and tall, with startling blonde hair always piled on top of her head. Now she seemed shorter – or perhaps she seemed shorter because she was so much wider. Her substantial body was packed tightly into smart white trousers and a green shirt, and placed on high heels. Her wild skinny beauty was quite gone. I could see she was anxious beneath her make-up. We shook hands; neither of us could decide whether to kiss each other on the cheek, and as we were havering, a stout man in a grey suit came out of the house, hugged me warmly and said over the top of Chrissie's half-hearted introduction:

'How lovely for Chrissie to see an old schoolfriend. I've heard so much about you, Jane.' I doubted that. 'Tea? Or would you like something stronger?'

'Tea would be fine, thank you.'

'Right. Then I'll leave you two lovely ladies to talk. You must have so much to catch up on.'

'Ian's a company director,' said Chrissie, as if in explanation. We went into the house. I could hear a dutiful tinkling from a piano upstairs. 'My daughter, Chloe. Leonore's with a friend.'

We sat in the living room, among plumped up cushions and prints of flowers and landscapes. Chrissie didn't offer me tea.

'Why have you really come?' she asked.

'Have you heard about Natalie?'

She nodded.

'That's why I've come.'

Chrissie looked nervously round, as if her husband might be standing in the doorway. 'I've nothing to say, Jane. That was over twenty years ago, and I don't even want to think about it, let alone talk about it.'

'Twenty-five years.'

'Twenty-five years, then. Please, Jane.'

'When did you last see Alan?'

'I said I don't want to talk about it. I don't want to think about it.'

'Does your husband know that when you were fifteen you had a sexual relationship with Alan Martello? Is he understanding about it?'

Chrissie started and looked me in the eyes. I felt sorry for her, but triumphant also because I could see that she was going to talk to me. She shrugged.

'I haven't seen Alan since Natalie disappeared. I don't

expect you to understand, but he was so . . . glamorous, if you can believe it. I was just a kid, and he was this famous man and he gave me things and told me how beautiful I was.' She laughed bitterly. 'It seems strange now, doesn't it? When he wanted to sleep with me I didn't stand a chance.' She looked down at her perfect red nails and then said, almost smugly, 'He nearly ruined my life. Why don't you blame Alan, not me?'

'Come on, Chrissie, don't exaggerate. It was only sex. Didn't you enjoy it at all?'

'I don't know. I don't think about it.'

'So why did you tell Natalie?'

Chrissie looked surprised.

'I didn't. She followed us to the woods once. And she saw us, you know.'

Chrissie had an air of prim triumph.

'Did you see that she was there?'

'Yes.'

'So what happened?'

'What do you expect? Alan started sort of wailing. He crawled over to Natalie and he started tugging her skirt, and saying that she was his darling girl and how could she ever forgive her old dad, and you know what men are like, and how Martha would suffer. It was pretty embarrassing really.'

'What did Natalie do?'

'She just walked away.'

'What did Alan do then?'

Chrissie looked straight at me. For the first time I could see the provocative heedless look of the adolescent Chrissie.

'He pushed me back onto the ground and fucked me. I think it had excited him. That was the last time, though.'

There was a chilly silence. 'Now you can tell my husband all about it.'

'You went out with Theo after that, didn't you?'

'Ask him.'

'What about Natalie? You know she was pregnant, don't you?'

'I've seen the papers.'

'Who do you think was the father?'

'I don't know. Whatever his name was – Luke McCann, I suppose.'

As I left, Chrissie's successful husband waved cheerfully. 'Do come again soon, Jane, it's always nice to see Chrissie's old chums.'

From the car, I saw Chrissie, a middle-aged woman wearing too much lipstick, and I saw what must have been Chloe, the piano-playing daughter, standing at an upstairs window. She looked just like the Chrissie of twenty-five years ago. That must have been hard for Chrissie to bear. I drove away with an embarrassing screech of tyres, and all the way back to London I thought about sex and its strangeness and embarrassments.

Eighteen

Against all expectations, I felt that my analysis was making me less judgemental than I had been. Instead of brooding about Martha and about Chrissie, or conducting a sterile debate about it all in my mind, I could talk to Alex about it. He wasn't shocked by the things I was telling him and he wasn't pruriently interested and although he could be critical of me, scathing indeed, I never had to apologise to him. When it came down to it, I believed that he was on my side. I trusted him. Well, who else could I trust?

The day after returning to London, I arrived at Alex's house with bundles of Christmas shopping, like a traveller passing through. I leant the bags against the couch. Occasionally, as I talked, I ran my fingers along their rumpled plastic, a sensation of normality. I needed it. When I told him about Martha and my father, I almost thought he might laugh, it seemed so excessive and sleazy and pathetic. But he didn't and he didn't offer any stupid sympathy. And when I described the encounter with Chrissie, I thought he might be irritated by this new example of my amateur detective work. I was a bit apologetic and defensive as I repeated what she had said about all the awfulness with Alan and Natalie and I was surprised when Alex only nodded with interest.

'I'm not going to be able to dissuade you from this

sleuthing, am I?' There was a note of exasperation, but it was okay.

'It's not sleuthing, Alex. It's just pottering around, really. I have this feeling I'm looking for something. I just don't know exactly what it is.'

'Yes.' Alex sounded pensive. 'I just wonder if you might be looking in the wrong place.'

'What do you mean by that?'

'You intrigue me, Jane. You have the technique of a magician. When you point me in one direction, I feel it's a sleight-of-hand and the important thing is happening somewhere else.'

'That all sounds too clever for me.'

'You're deceiving yourself as well, of course. Something is looming ahead and you both want and don't want to find it.'

'What do you mean, Alex? Do you think I'm on the right track?'

There was another of Alex's long pauses. I could feel my own breathing and my heart like a ball bouncing inside my chest. Something was coming. When he spoke it was with great deliberation.

'What I feel, Jane, is that you are on the right track in the sense that I think there is something definite to be found. But you're looking for it in the wrong place. You're going to talk to people who are never going to be able to solve your problem. Where you should really be looking is in there.'

I felt Alex's cool hand on my brow and I almost jumped away from the couch. It wasn't the first time he had ever touched me, but it felt startlingly intimate. Surely he had missed my point.

'Alex, I'm not denying that your therapy is important

177

and helpful. But when I'm talking to people, then, in my confused and pathetic way, I'm looking for something specific. I'm trying to find something that's out there, the truth about something that actually happened.'

'Do you think I'm saying any different, Jane?'

'What are you talking about? Are you saying that I already know the answer? That I know who killed Natalie?'

'*Know* is a complicated word.'

I felt a sudden crawling sensation on my skin. 'Are you accusing me of something?'

Alex laughed soothingly. 'No, Jane, of course not.'

'But if I knew, well, then I'd . . . er, know, wouldn't I? I would remember.'

'Would you? Wait a second.'

Alex got up and left the room and then returned with a battered yellow folder and a ring-bound notebook. 'Let me take the initiative for a moment,' he said as he sat down again. 'I want to ask you a series of questions about yourself.'

'Am I being tested for something?'

'Don't think about that. Just answer. Only if you want to, but I think it will be a help.'

'All right.'

'I'm going to ask quite a few questions. You can be as brief as you like with your answers. Just yes or no, if you want. Okay?' Alex clicked his pen and began. After each answer he scribbled a brief note.

'Are you scared of the dark, Jane?'

'Yes.'

'Have you been having bad dreams?'

'I think so. I'm not very good at remembering them.'

'Do you ever worry about your body? Are there bits about it that you don't like?'

'Yes, of course, but only in the way everybody does.'

This was fun. It reminded me of the personality tests I find irresistible in magazines.

'Have you ever suffered from gynaecological problems?'

'I used to get cystitis a lot. I don't know if that counts.'

'Headaches? Arthritis?'

'Not arthritis, but I get headaches quite a lot. I used to suffer from migraines. I got one every Friday after dinner for years. Unless we were going out somewhere. Then it would come on Saturday night instead.'

'Have you ever avoided looking in mirrors?'

'Yes, well see answer given above on subject of body.'

'Have you ever wanted to change your name?'

'Are you serious? I *did* change it. I've recently toyed with the idea of changing it back, but it's a bit late now. All those labels and standing orders that would need alteration.'

'Do you ever wear what might seem like an inappropriate amount of clothing?'

'I suffer from quite bad circulation so I do sometimes feel cold even when it's sunny. So, yes, I suppose I do. Is that a crime?'

'Do you have any phobias?'

'No. I don't mind heights, I rather like spiders. Confined spaces are cosy. Now you mention it, I do have an irrational hatred of breakfast cereal and spent much of my boys' childhood trying to keep it out of the house. And I don't like Mother's Day or ploughman's lunches or anything else that was invented by advertising people.'

'Any eating disorders?'

'No.'

'Ever had a problem with drink or drugs?'

'No problem at all.'

'Have you ever obsessively stayed away from them?'

'Not really. I cut down a bit on drinking in the days before I took finals and that sort of thing. I could never really be bothered with drugs. It was the paraphernalia and the culture that went with them. And I was a bit scared of being arrested. I don't think I was puritanical about it.'

'Any examples of compulsive behaviour?'

'Oh, loads.'

'Have you ever had a wish to be invisible?'

'If I did, it was granted for large parts of my marriage. Sorry. The honest answer is that the temptation has never presented itself even as a fantasy.'

'Have you ever suffered from depression?'

'Yes.'

'Low self-esteem?'

'Oh yes.'

'Do you ever cry for no reason at all?'

'That's almost a philosophical question, but roughly speaking I would say yes to that.'

'Any suicidal impulses or thoughts?'

'Not seriously.'

'Did you ever feel a need to be spotlessly good, or to be the opposite, terribly bad?'

'I know what you mean. I recognise the feeling.'

'Have you ever felt that you're a victim?'

'Only in my weaker moments. I hope that I've never seriously thought of myself as a victim.'

'Have you ever had a feeling of having possession of a secret? Perhaps with an urge to tell it and a feeling that nobody would believe it if you did?'

'I'm not sure I understand the question. I don't think
so.'

'Have you ever taken dangerous risks?'

'No. I sometimes wish I had.'

'Have you ever felt an incapacity for taking risks?'

'Yes.'

'Do you ever daydream?'

'What did you say? I was miles away. Sorry. Joking.
Sometimes, maybe.'

'Do you feel you've ever blocked out a period of your
life, especially when you were young?'

'I don't know. It's hard to say. Obviously there are lots
of things I don't remember.'

'Do you ever worry about being noisy? I mean in
experiences such as sex or in social situations or even
in the lavatory.'

'This *is* getting personal, isn't it? All right, I'm not
embarrassed, I'll answer. To take them in order. I think
I'm quite sexually uninhibited, so I suppose I groan and
scream. I'm irritated by people who bray and guffaw
at dinner parties and I probably come across as quite
restrained in public. I probably attempt to be fairly quiet
on the lavatory when there are other people in the vicinity.
Don't most people?'

'Have you ever felt that sex is dirty?'

'No, not intrinsically.'

'Have you ever disliked being touched?'

'Do you mean sexually?'

'Not necessarily.'

'I sometimes dislike it when men paw me but in an
unfair sort of way it all depends on the man. There have
been occasions when I haven't wanted sex, and then I've
said so.'

'What about by a gynaecologist?'

'I used to dislike being examined by a male gynaecologist. When I was, oh, in my latish twenties, Claud found me a wonderful woman and I've been with her ever since. I've no problem at all with Sylvia.'

'Are you repelled by particular sex acts?'

'I suppose there are one or two that I don't especially like.'

'Are there any you are strongly attracted to?'

'Oh yes.'

'Have you ever been compulsively promiscuous?'

'No. That might have been fun for a bit and I imagine that college would have been the opportunity to experiment a bit with that but I was involved with Claud quite quickly.'

'Have you ever been compulsively asexual?'

'No.'

'Are you ever preoccupied with thoughts about sex?'

'I don't know what you mean by preoccupied. I think about it now and then.'

'Do you have an impulse to be highly in control of your emotions?'

'I don't like to be emotionally *un*controlled.'

'Do you feel a need to control situations?'

'Sometimes I try to.'

'Do you obsessively try to control things that aren't important?'

'I can be madly neat or organised sometimes. Compared with Claud I was a real slut.'

'Do you find it difficult to be happy?'

'I have felt that about myself.'

'Do you find it difficult to relax?'

'Yes.'

'Do you find it difficult to work?'

'Lately it's been a bit of a problem.'

'Do you ever feel you're crazy?'

'Yes.'

'Have you ever invented fantasy worlds? Or fantasy relationships?'

'Not since I was a girl.'

'Have you ever felt that you were real and everything else was a sham?'

'I know what you mean but I can't honestly say that I have. I've always been a bit too boringly rational. I probably felt it when I was little, the way everybody does.'

'Or vice versa?'

'You mean that *I* was a sham? That's more likely. I still sometimes have the sense that everybody else is a real grown-up and I'm just pretending to be one and that I'm still really a child.'

'Are you afraid to succeed?'

'Sometimes.'

'Do any kinds of food or tastes frighten or disgust you?'

'No, but I will make the secret confession that deep down I've never really cared for sprouts or cauliflower.'

'Do you ever feel a sense of doom?'

'Yes.'

Now Alex didn't speak for a long time but wrote furiously on his notepad, occasionally flicking the pages back. After a painful few minutes he closed it.

'How did I do? Did I pass?'

When Alex replied, he was more serious than I'd ever heard him before.

'It has been said that if you answer positively to more than half a dozen or so of the questions I put to you, then this may be evidence of a submerged trauma.'

'What do you mean "submerged"?'

'An event, or a series of events, that you have made yourself forget.'

'Come on, Alex, the things in that list of questions could apply to anybody. Who on earth *wouldn't* say yes to some of them?'

'Don't try to brush this off, Jane. You've gone along with this very conscientiously until now. The questions are carefully constructed to uncover symptoms of anxiety which may be evidence of something deeper. I'm not making a diagnosis but it's something we ought to think about. Tell me, Jane, you've been putting yourself back into the landscape from where Natalie disappeared. You've been doing it with great commitment. I'm very impressed. But tell me, what does that landscape make you feel? Does it give you any feeling of dread? Do you feel that there is something there? Something hidden?'

I suddenly felt cold, lying there on the couch, as I always do when I lie still for an extended period of time, even in a well heated house such as Alex's. It was my bad circulation again.

'Yes, it scares me. What is it that interests you about it, Alex?'

'I've always tried to follow your lead, Jane. I asked you about Natalie's disappearance and you gave me a landscape. I want to send you into that landscape and see what you find. Does that seem worth trying?'

'Yes, all right.'

So we went through our familiar ritual. I felt pleased with Alex's approval, as if I was becoming his star pupil. He talked softly to me. My body relaxed, I closed my eyes and placed myself back there beside the Col. Session by

184

session, this was becoming easier and the world in which I found myself was each time more vivid.

I was sitting down, my back resting on the dry mossy stone at the foot of Cree's Top, the river on my left flowing away, the last screwed up pieces of paper floating round the curve, the elms on the edge of the woods to my right.

Without any prompting I was able to stand up and turn round. The river was now on my right flowing towards me and away behind me, the elms and the woods were on my left. Now I was looking at the path winding up the slope of Cree's Top. There were thick bushes by its side, and it occasionally disappeared from view as it snaked its way up the slope, but I could see almost all of it. It was all more vivid than before. The leaves were greener and more defined against the sunlight from above. As I moved my head round I could focus on any part of my surroundings and move in on them, on to the small stones on the path that had been pushed to the sides by the passage of feet that had also worn the ground down, exposing larger stones and the roots of trees. Almost without an impulse on my part I started to step forward along the path. Looking down, I saw my feet wearing black gym shoes of a kind I hadn't owned since I was at school. I was now well along the path and moving up the hill and away from where I had been sitting. When I turned to my right, I was looking down the slope at the river. When I turned to my left, I was looking into the woods towards the Stead. Suddenly all became dark. I looked up and a heavy black cloud was passing overhead. The air turned cold, a shiver passed through me and I turned and ran down the hill. I carefully sat myself in my original position, the stone crusty against my spine.

I described to Alex what had happened.

'Why didn't you go on?'

'I was afraid.'

'Big girls don't need to be afraid.'

Nineteen

'Yes.'

'May I speak to Jane Martello, please.'

'Yes, what is it?'

I wasn't in a good mood. This would be the fourth time in one morning that someone from the council had rung me about changes to the hostel. The next day, the committee was going to meet to give the go-ahead – or not – to the revised budget for a building that had already been so cut back, compromised and revised that I hardly wanted my name attached to it any more.

'Jane, this is Caspar, Caspar Holt.'

'What?'

'It wasn't necessary, but thank you for your postcard.'

It was the philosopher. I sat down, and breathed deeply.

'Oh, yes, well, I wanted to apologise for my behaviour that evening.'

'In the circumstances, I think that you behaved with aplomb. I wondered if you'd like to meet?'

Oh God, a date.

'Um, fine, I mean, when did you have in mind?'

'How about now?'

'Now?'

'Well, in half an hour, then.'

I needed to sort out the final details for the next day's committee meeting, I needed to go to the office, I desperately needed to wash my hair. It wasn't a good day; it was my day for a rush and a sour bad mood.

'Give me an hour. Where shall we meet?'

'Number thirteen, Lincoln's Inn Fields. I'll meet you outside.'

I didn't manage to sort out the committee details or phone the office. But I did wash my hair.

He was standing outside wearing the same bulky tweed coat he had worn at the ICA. He was engrossed in a paperback book so I was able to observe him before he saw me. His hair was ash-blond, long, curly and swept back off his forehead. He had round wire-framed glasses.

'Sir John Soane's Museum,' I said to him. 'Is this where you usually take girls on their first date?'

He looked up in surprise.

'Yes, it probably explains my luck with women. But it's free and it's like walking around inside a man's brain.'

'Is that good?'

He put his hand lightly on my shoulder as we went through the front door, and into the strange interior, the space extending into the upper floors and down into the basement. He steered me into a room that was painted a dark rusty red. There were strange objects, architectural fragments, archaic instruments, eccentric works of art on every surface.

'Look at that,' said Caspar, pointing out something shapeless. 'That's a fungus from Sumatra.'

'A what?'

'Actually, it's a sponge.'

We walked on through improbably tiny corridors giving on to sudden even more improbable vistas, up and down, everything lined with a baffling array of objects.

'Each room is like a separate part of the mind that planned it,' he said. I noticed his hands were splashed with red paint at the knuckles, and his shirt collar was frayed.

'Like a man's brain, perhaps,' I said.

He smiled. 'You mean compartmentalised. Full of objects. Maybe. Maybe you're right. It's not a woman's house, is it? I come here sometimes at lunchtime. I marvel at how a lifetime can be packed into a house. It's such an introverted place, don't you think? And extroverted as well, of course.'

'Is this your standard lecture?' I asked.

'Sorry, am I irritating you?'

'I was only joking.'

We went upstairs, into the high picture room painted green and deep saffron yellow. The winter sun flooding in through the arched windows illuminated the dull, rich colours; the room felt cool and grave as a church. We walked together along Hogarth's *The Rake's Progress*, all that savagery and anger. Caspar paused in front of 'The rake in Bedlam'.

'Look,' he said. 'By cell fifty-five, that man with a sceptre and a pot on his head, he's urinating. Can you see the look on the faces of those two fashionable ladies?'

I peered at the grotesque scene, making out dim and writhing figures, and shivered.

'It's Bethlehem Hospital, Bedlam. It was in Moorfields, just outside the city wall. Hogarth's father was in prison for debt, it made a great impression on him. Look at the face of that old woman on her knees, Jane, she seems only half-human.'

I watched his face, his steady grey eyes. I noticed how he used my name. It suddenly occurred to me that it had been a very long time since I had last felt happy. Standing with Caspar, in a house like a man's brain, it was as if I was looking out from the gloom I had inhabited for so long, through a window, into a different kind of future: brighter. I could see views, sky. For a minute, I stood quite still, while hope clutched me. I caught his eye for a moment.

'Hang on,' he said. 'I want to show you something.'

We descended the stairs again and crossed two rooms.

'Look through there.'

I saw what looked like a totem pole made up of fragments from different columns. On it was carved the name 'Fanny'. I turned to Caspar with raised eyebrows.

'Yes?' I asked.

'That's the tomb of the dog that belonged to John Soane's wife. But it's also the name of my little daughter.'

'I thought Fanny was one of those names we can't use any more.'

'I've tried to revive it.'

'Are you married?'

'No. I live on my own.'

'I'm sorry.'

'Don't be.'

Outside, blinking in the chilly light, we grinned stupidly at each other. Then Caspar glanced at his watch.

'Lunch?'

'I shouldn't.'

'Please.'

'All right.'

We walked to Soho, past the delicatessens and the porn shops, and stopped at an Italian café-cum-restaurant. We had goat's cheese half-melted on crisp toast, and green salad, and a glass of white wine each. He looked at my ringless hands and asked if I was married, and I told him I was separated. And I asked him how old his daughter was. She was five. Lots of people, he said, thought he was some kind of superman just because he did what hundreds of thousands of women did without anyone noticing them at all.

'I didn't know about love before Fanny, silly thing that she is,' he said.

I told him about Robert and Jerome, how grown-up and tall they were, how they protected me, were always on my side, and he said he'd love to meet them one day. And then the possibility of there being a future to this, a 'one day', opened up before me and I felt dizzy and scared, and I lit a cigarette. I said I had to go. He didn't try to stop me, just saw me to my bike and watched as I got tangled up with the lock and the helmet and wobbled off.

I felt like an adolescent, dizzy with excitement, and I felt like a terrified old woman being dragged back into a prison by hundreds of thin, sharp ties. I could have an affair with Caspar – no, I knew when I thought of his hand lightly on my shoulder, or his straight grey gaze, that I could have a *relationship* with Caspar. We wouldn't just climb into bed with each other one night after a bottle of wine, we'd dig back into each other's past, uncover old wounds, give ourselves up to the addictive grief of love. And it wasn't that I wasn't ready – that's what counsellors always say, that you have to wait, to grow strong again, to learn to live with loneliness. I was ready, all right. It had been a long time since I'd lost myself to love. I was ready, but I was scared. I felt tired. A mild headache thrummed in my temples. Wine at lunchtime.

I rode my bike along Oxford Street, which, in the winter

afternoon, was already lit up by its Christmas lights. God, I hate the way we now have massive Disney characters hanging across the roads. I hadn't finished Christmas shopping yet, though I'd bought a pair of binoculars for Dad, and lots of ridiculous stocking presents from Father Christmas, who had always come to the house, long after the children had discovered he was me. It had always been my favourite bit of Christmas Day – the early morning, when everyone would crowd into my bedroom, sit on the bed, pull knickers and soap and corkscrews from their pillow cases. It suddenly occurred to me that I might be alone this Christmas morning: the boys would come for dinner, of course, and so would Dad, and maybe I should invite Claud because I couldn't bear to think of him eating a neat meal for one, though probably he'd go to Alan's and Martha's. But maybe I'd wake up on Christmas morning in an empty house.

For a moment I contemplated going into the hot jaws of one of the department stores, thick with perfume, to grasp wildly at shirts and ties and jerseys for the boys. But they hated shirts and ties from department stores, and it had been a long time since I'd stopped choosing their clothes for them. On an impulse, I rode to one of my favourite shops in London, the hat shop in Jermyn Street, and I bought three fabulous and expensive trilbys: a brown one for Jerome, a black one for Robert, and a bottle-green one for Kim. I hung the bag on my handlebars, and pedalled towards Camden, where I bought lots of tiny paper cases for the chocolate truffles I was going to make for everyone, and some handsome green jars. In one shop, I saw a pair of earrings in the shape of tiny silver boxes. Far too expensive. I bought them for Hana and carried them away in a pretty, ribboned box.

That evening, I played my three Neil Young albums while I made tomato chutney and ladled it into the green jars, which I labelled, and I made chocolate truffles with bitter dark chocolate. I rolled them in cocoa, and laid them in their little cases. Tomorrow I would make boxes for them. The kitchen smelt of vinegar and bitter chocolate. I still felt excitedly energetic, so I poured myself a glass of red wine, lit a cigarette, and with a satisfyingly sharp pencil and my favourite ruler (long, with one flat edge), I made an architect's drawing of my house. I doodled a fat kitsch cherub against the clean lines of the roof. When I went to the office, I would photocopy the drawing onto white card, and send off the copies as Christmas cards.

I poured another glass of wine – the headache was gone – and smoked a cigarette. Perhaps I would give up smoking for New Year. Through the window, I saw that the moon was quite full, and on an impulse I put on a thick overcoat, belonging to Robert, and went into the garden. It was a beautiful night, clear and bitingly cold. The stars looked close, and the branches of the pear and cherry trees were stark.

At one end, under the overgrown bay tree, was the unmarked graveyard of the boys' numerous pets: hamsters, guinea pigs, two rabbits, a budgie. The boys used to play football on the lawn, churning it into mud. In spring and autumn, we would have binge gardening weekends, planting seeds that the neighbourhood cats would dig up. In April, the trees would blossom, the froth of pear and cherry and the waxy candles of the magnolia tree, and for a few weeks the garden would become a place of astonishing loveliness and grace. Claud and I used to sit out here with our drinks when the weather was fine. We'd had summer parties, with Pimm's and strawberries, and the boys had handed out crisps. We'd had loads of barbecues, some of the hot dogs and fizzy drink kind, some with prawns on kebabs, and cajun mackerel, and flat mushrooms marinaded in a spicy sauce. My recall snagged again: there was something I wasn't remembering. What had Alex told me to do – *let* myself remember.

Clutching my wine and cigarette, I made my private New Year's resolution early: that I would not rest until I had walked through the landscape of my memory and reached its heart, and that I would give myself permission to be happy.

It never occurred to me that I could make the second resolution without the first.

Twenty

'He what?'

'He wants to come for Christmas dinner with a television crew.'

'But that's ridiculous. For a start, what television crew would agree to work on Christmas Day?'

'I think his would. It'll be like the Queen's message to the Commonwealth.'

'Jane, you haven't agreed?' Kim never squeaked; now she was squeaking.

'Well, it was so difficult. I mean, this clearly means so much to Paul, and he's already done so much work on it, and I suppose I feel that if I've gone this far down the road with it, I might as well go all the way.'

'Are you seriously suggesting that Paul and Erica should arrive on Christmas Day, plus Rosie, of course, with cameras rolling, and film you cooking turkey? Christ, Jane, your *father's* going to be there. And Robert and Jerome. And *I'm* going to be there with Andreas.'

'They're not going to be there all day. They'll just get an impression of a bit of the family at Christmas. They'll go away long before we eat.'

There was a gurgle from the other end of the phone, and I realised with relief and something approaching delight that Kim was giggling.

'Will you help me, Kim? Get through it, I mean?'

'Never mind that, what shall I wear? I've never been on telly before. Is it stripes or hoops that are verboten?'

'Here you are. One dry sherry, one mince pie.'

The sherry was pale yellow, the mince pie hot and spicy. I sat carefully on the sofa that looked as if it had just arrived, cushions plumped up, from the department store. I felt like a stranger, a polite guest.

'It's very nice here.'

The room was immaculate, like a space that was about to be photographed for a colour supplement. On the ivory walls hung six small prints. A square rug lay exactly in the middle of the wooden floor. On either side of the new sofa sat two new armchairs. A book about Norman churches and the *Guardian*, folded, lay on the small table. A cactus flowered prettily on top of the old piano, newly polished. In the corner, on a clever elevated stand, was a small Christmas tree with white lights. From where I sat, delicately holding my sherry and mince pie, I could see a kitchen that was so immaculate that I wondered if Claud had ever cooked himself a meal in it.

'Yes, I'm pleased with it. I did it just as I wanted.'

We smiled nervously at each other across the ordered space. I thought of the clutter in my kitchen: great bowls of squashy winter tangerines, piles of bills and unanswered letters, lists I'd made out to myself and then never looked at again, broken plates I'd been meaning to mend for days, Christmas cards I was going to hang on string along the eaves but hadn't yet got round to, a regretted but not discarded bunch of mistletoe tucked among the cups on the dresser, daffodils thrust into vases and dotted around the room in untidy bursts of yellow, bits of architectural drawings I'd started then abandoned, photographs I had not got round to putting in the album, dozens of books, several recipes cut out from magazines and not filed, a half-finished bottle of wine. And, of course, a moulting spruce whose decorations, courtesy of the boys, looked as if they'd been thrown on in drunken handfuls. Indeed, they had been thrown on in drunken handfuls: Jerome and Robert had been horrified by the coordinated aestheticism I'd achieved this year. Christmas trees, they said, should be gaudy and brash. They'd dug out the great pink and turquoise globes and glittery stars, all the baubles we'd accumulated over the years, and hurled them at the tree.

I brightly suggested we have some music.

'There is no music,' Claud said.

'Where are all your CDs?'

'They belonged to a previous existence.'

'If you didn't want them, why did you take them?'

'They weren't yours.'

'Are you seriously telling me' – I was appalled – 'that all the music you've collected over your whole life, you've just, just, *binned*.'

'Yes.'

I looked around the room. I realised that, with surgical ruthlessness, Claud had sliced away any evidence of our life together, of our family. This wasn't order. This was emptiness.

'Claud,' I blurted out, 'how do you remember Natalie?' Even as I asked, I knew my question was odd, oblique.

'*How* do I remember her?'

'I mean, I've been talking to people about her and it struck me as odd that we've never really talked to each other about our versions of her.'

Claud sat down in a chair and scrutinised me with the professional air that had always infuriated me.

'Don't you think that your preoccupation is going a bit far now, Jane. I mean, all of us – her *real* family, to put it frankly – we're trying to pick up our lives. I'm not sure it's entirely helpful to have you poking about in our past for your own private psychological reasons. Is this what your analyst has been encouraging you to do?'

His manner was mild and correct, and I felt like a schoolchild, unkempt and fidgety on his neat sofa.

'Okay, Claud, lecture over – so how do you remember her?'

'She was sweet and bright and loving.'

I stared at him.

'Don't look at me like that, Jane. Just because you're in therapy, you suspect anything that's straightforward. She was my little sister, and she was a dear child, on the brink of womanhood when she tragically died. That's that. That's how I remember her and that's how I want to remember her. I don't want you sullying her, even if she has been dead for twenty-five years. Okay?'

I poured another slug of sherry into my miniature glass, and took a sip.

'All right, what are your last memories of her, then?'

This time Claud did seem to think a bit before answering – or perhaps he was just thinking about whether to answer at all. Then he nodded with an expression almost of pity.

'I don't know what you're doing, but if you insist. We were all at the Stead arranging the anniversary party for when they arrived back from their cruise. I was to fly off to Bombay the following morning. Like most of us, Natalie was helping. On the day of the party and in the morning, you and Natalie and I were rushing about doing errands. Remember?'

'It's a long time ago,' I said.

'I remember taking her in the car to collect Alan and Martha's present, and we talked about what she was going to wear, I think. All I remember after that is that I took charge of the barbecue, and I didn't move from it until the early hours of the morning.' He looked at me. 'But you wouldn't know about that, would you? You were too tied up with Theo. Then I left before dawn the next morning with Alec. The first I heard of Natalie's disappearance was two months later when I came back home.'

I carefully picked up the crumbs on my plate with my forefinger.

'Did you see Natalie in the morning?'

'Of course not. I saw nobody, except mother, who drove Alec and me to the station at about three thirty in the morning. As you know. Come on, Jane, you're just going over and over old ground. And I can't help you much: I wasn't there the day she disappeared.'

He passed his hand over his forehead, and I realised how tired he was. Then he smiled at me, a goofy little intimate half-smile; the hostility went from the atmosphere and was replaced by something else, just as disturbing.

'Don't you know,' he said almost dreamily, 'how much I regret not being there? For a long time, I thought that if I hadn't gone off, then it wouldn't have happened. That I could have prevented it or something ridiculous. And I feel still as if I were separated from the rest of the family because they were all together in it, and I was apart.' He grinned mirthlessly at me. 'You always called me the bureaucrat of the family, didn't you, Jane? Perhaps it's because that's how I can feel properly a part of it.'

'Claud, I'm sorry if I've been blundering around.'

Without thinking, I took his hand, and he didn't take it away, but looked down at our fingers interlocking. We sat in thick silence for a few seconds, and then I drew back, embarrassed.

'What are you doing for Christmas?' My voice was too bright.

It was his turn to look embarrassed. 'Didn't you know? I was going to Martha's and Alan's, but Paul invited me to spend it with him and Peggy.'

'But they're coming to me.' A nasty thought struck me.

'Paul didn't think you'd mind.'

'It's impossible, Claud. It's impossible. Dad will be there, and Kim and her new lover, and the boys and Hana. Oh, shit, there'll be a TV crew there as well, filming us all. What do you want us all to do? Play happy families for the cameras?'

'It was you who said we could still be friends.'

I had said that. It was a stupid cliché, a fake consolation, and a lie, but I had said it.

'And I want to be with my sons at Christmas.'

I knew it was a terrible mistake. What was Kim going to say to me?

'All right.'

Twenty-One

I was sitting down, the dry moss of the stone scraping the curved ridge of my spine. I knew that Cree's Top was behind me. The River Col was on my left, its surface slate grey, reflecting the cloud cover which had obscured the sun. It was suddenly cold in my sleeveless dress and I hugged myself with my prickly, goosepimpled arms. The screwed-up pieces of paper were almost lost in the murky surface and, flowing away from me, they disappeared into the shades and reflections long before they were carried round the bend. The branches in the elms on my right rustled and swayed with a sudden breath of wind that threatened rain.

I stood and turned round until I was facing Cree's Top and looking along the path that wound up its slope. Sometimes bushes hid its progress until it disappeared into twilight. I walked determinedly up it. Each time I returned to this river and this hill which separated me from Natalie, the objects seemed more vividly present. The grass was a richer green, the river more detailed in all its ripples and flurries. On this occasion, the detail was not just more precise but somehow harder as well. The water looked heavier and more solid, the path was more rigid under my feet, even the leaves looked like blades that would cut the fingers that brushed against them.

This was a hostile, unyielding landscape that seemed reluctant to give up its secrets. I was nearing the brow of Cree's Top and I had a palpable sense that there was something bad on the other side. That was why the landscape had darkened. My body, my whole spirit, sagged in despair. Did I really want this? One moment of weakness was enough. I turned and ran down the hill, away from whatever was awaiting me. Were there not other places to go in this beloved landscape of my memory? I reached the foot of Cree's Top and ran along the Col. I knew instinctively that the path would wind away from the river and take me back towards the Stead and there I would find my family as they once were: Theo, tall and saturnine; Martha, dark-haired and beautiful, laughing and strong; my father, handsome and still hopeful for a life that could be fulfilling. There would be the remnants of that golden summer party.

But the path quickly became unrecognisable, as if I had wandered beyond the bounds of permitted territory. The woods thickened, the sky was closed away and I came to myself there on Alex's couch with tears running hot down my face, across my cheeks. I had to sit up and, with a sense of absurdity, wipe my neck and ears. Alex was standing over me with a look of concern. I explained to him what I had tried to do and he nodded his head reprovingly.

'Jane, you're not in Narnia or Oz or some theme park where you can wander off in whatever direction you like. This is your own memory you're exploring. You have to give yourself up to where it's leading you. Don't you feel that you're almost there?'

Alex Dermot-Brown was not the sort of person whom I would normally have considered to be my type. He was a scruffy man who lived in a scruffy house. His jeans were worn in the knees, his navy blue sweater was stained and dotted with fluff, it was obvious that the only styling his long curly hair received was when he frequently ran his fingers through it while in animated conversational flight. Yet I had become attracted to him, of course, because he was the person to whom I had opened up, the man whose approval I was seeking. I recognised all that. But now I realised with some excitement that he was as avid about my quest as I was, and as hopeful about its prospects. I felt a lurch deep in my belly at the same time. It reminded me of the early contractions I had had with Jerome, those little pre-shocks warning me that I was really going to have to give birth. Soon I was going to have to face up to something.

A balding man in a grey suit stood up. He looked as if he had come to the hall straight from work.

'Well *I've* got something to say.'

Do you know those public meetings or discussions when the chair calls for questions and there is a long silence and nobody dares to say anything and it's all rather embarrassing? This wasn't like that at all. Everybody had something to say and most of them were trying to say it at the same time.

We had realised from the start that the local residents would have to be involved, at least on an informal basis, in the setting up of the hostel. There'd been a meeting of the Grandison Road residents' association to discuss the issue and they had demanded a public meeting with the authorities responsible for the hostel. It wasn't clear quite what this demand meant, or whether it even needed to be acknowledged, but it was decided as a matter of tact to respond. Chris Miller of the council planning department was notionally in charge of the project and was going to chair it and Dr Chohan, a psychiatrist from the out-patients department of St Christopher's hospital, was going to be there, and Pauline Tindall from social services and then at a very late stage Chris had rung me and asked if I could come along as well.

I reluctantly agreed, if only to keep an eye on any rash spending commitments that Chris might make which would then duly come off my budget. This was an evening on which I had arranged to meet Caspar for a drink. I rang to cancel and apologise but when I mentioned to him what I was doing, he became interested and asked if he could pop along and sit in the audience. He said he wanted to see me at work. I told him not to bother and that it would be only a formality.

'It won't be a formality,' he said. 'These are people's homes you're dealing with. You're going to be bringing mad people into their area. The only worse thing you could be proposing would be a veal factory or a vivisection laboratory. I don't want to miss this, Jane. Public meetings like this are what the British do now instead of watching a bear being baited or a public hanging.'

'Come off it, Caspar, this is a totally uncontroversial project.'

'We'll see. Meanwhile, you must remind me to show you an interesting study that was done a few years ago at Yale. It suggested that when people have made a public commitment to a position, then contrary evidence, however strong, only reinforces their commitment.'

'So what are you saying?'

'Don't expect to convince anybody by rational argument.'

'I don't need a study from Yale University to tell me that. Maybe I'll see you there.'

'I might be lost in the mob but I'll see *you*.'

I locked my bicycle to a parking meter outside the community hall just five minutes before the meeting was due to start. When I entered I thought at first I must have come to the wrong occasion. I had expected a few old ladies who had come to get out of the rain. This looked more like a warehouse party or a poll tax demonstration. But there on the distant platform were Chris and the gang. Not only was every seat taken but the aisles were crammed and I had to squeeze my way through in a flurry of apologies in order to reach the platform where Chris was looking red-faced and nervous. He kept coughing and filling his glass with water from a jug. As I sat down on the municipal plastic chair reserved for me, he leant across and whispered hoarsely:

'Big turn-out.'

'Why?' I whispered back.

'There's the Grandison Road lot,' he said. 'But there's a whole lot from Clarissa Road and Pamela Road and Lovelace Avenue as well.'

'Why are they all interested in a little hostel?'

Chris shrugged. He looked at his watch and then, after a nod at Chohan and Tindall, he stood up and called for silence. The boiling hubbub settled down to a light simmer. Chris introduced us all and then said a few words about how this policy reflected the local council's ommitment to make care in the community effective. It was to be hoped that this hostel would be the first of several in the borough, and that it would be a model of humane, practical and cost-effective treatment for recovering mental patients. Did anybody have any questions? There was a forest of hands but the balding man in the suit was the most assertive.

'Before I ask a question,' he said, 'I would first like to express what I think is the mood of the meeting which is that we local residents are appalled that we were not consulted about this institution being placed in our area and that we consider it to have been done in a disgracefully underhand way.'

Chris tried to protest but the man brushed him aside.

'Please let me continue, Mr Miller. You have had your say. Now it is time for us to have ours.'

It was a speech rather than a question but the thrust seemed to be that it was quite unsuitable for a mental institution to be installed in a residential street. When he had finished, Chris took me completely aback by turning to me and asking for my comments. I said something about the hostel not being an institution. My entire brief had been to design a building for people who had no need of residential care. The only supervision that would be necessary would be, in certain cases, to ensure that pre-scribed medication was taken. That the hostel was another house in a residential area was the whole point.

A woman stood up and said that she had four children, aged seven, six, four and almost two, and that it was all very well to talk about care in the community but she had her children to worry about. And for that matter there was the Richardson Road primary school which was only two streets away. Could the doctors absolutely guarantee that the patients in the hostel would be no danger whatso-ever to local children?

Dr Chohan tried to explain that these were not patients. They were people who had been discharged, just like a person who has left hospital after suffering a broken leg.

And just as such a person might require a crutch for a few weeks, so some mental patients require some lightly supervised accommodation. Patients, *people* he corrected himself, who were a potential danger in any way at all would not be in this hostel.

But what about this medication? How could the doctors guarantee that these mental patients would take their medication? Pauline said that this was at the heart of the way the hostel system functioned. She said that she understood local concerns and that they had all been addressed at the earliest stage of planning. Potentially dangerous people (of whom there were extremely few) and people who refused to take their medication would not be considered for a hostel of this type. Then Pauline made what seemed to me afterwards to be the fatal mistake. She concluded by saying that we mustn't allow uninformed prejudices about the mentally ill to influence policy. If this was a tactic to shame the audience into accepting our position, it backfired disastrously.

A man stood up and said that all the arguments about medical matters were one thing but this was also an issue of property values. There were people in this meeting, he said, living in houses for which they had saved their entire lives. There were people sitting on negative equity who had just seen the first signs of growth in the housing market. Why should these people sacrifice their homes to a trendy new dogma invented by sociologists who probably lived safely away in Hampstead?

Chris, who sounded as if he were trying to speak while simultaneously swallowing his tongue, replied that he had hoped that the medical explanations would allay all fears of this kind. But the man stood up again. All the medical explanations were a bloody waste of time, he proclaimed.

It was all very well for outsiders to talk about so-called prejudices. Whether they were true or not, house-buyers would be put off.

Chris foolishly asked how he could possibly dispel concerns of that kind and the man shouted back that the local residents were not interested in concerns being dispelled. They wanted the hostel project to be abandoned, that was all. Then a good-looking man in a tweed jacket and an open-necked shirt stood up. Oh, God. It was Caspar.

'I'd like to make a comment rather than ask a question,' he said, blinking through his wire-rimmed spectacles. 'I wonder whether it might be best for people here to imagine, as a sort of thought-experiment, that we are discussing a hostel that is going to be constructed in another British city altogether. Would we approve the project if we had no personal stake in it?'

'You fuck off,' said the property man to a startled Caspar. 'Why do you think we're here at all? If they want to build somewhere for these people that nobody wants, why don't they do it on an industrial estate somewhere or in an old factory?'

'Or perhaps in one of those closed-down Victorian lunatic asylums,' suggested Caspar.

'Aren't you supposed to put raw meat on things like this?' asked Caspar. 'Ow!'

Caspar flinched as I dabbed his eye with cotton wool.

'I've got to clean out the wound first. Anyway, I haven't got any raw meat. All I've got are some sausages in the freezer.'

'We could eat them,' Caspar suggested hopefully, and then flinched once more. 'Do you think there are any bits of glass in the wound?'

'I don't think so. The lens just broke into a few big pieces. The cut was caused by the frame. And that man's fist, of course. And can I just say for one last time that I'm really, really sorry about what happened. I regard it as completely my fault.'

'Not completely.'

We were back in my house. Paul Stephen Avery of Grandison Road had been taken away between two large policemen. The meeting had broken up in disarray. Caspar had refused all medical treatment but had been unable to drive himself home because his spectacles had been damaged. So I'd pushed my bike into the back of his car and driven him to my house where I'd insisted on getting something to put on his eye.

'I thought you didn't believe in intellectual debate,' I said, as he flinched once more. 'Sorry, I'm being as careful as I can.'

'In theory, I don't. I intended just to look at you in action but when that man was talking I suddenly thought of the model that Rawls's *Theory of Justice* was based on and felt I had to intervene. It may have been salutary in a way. You know, one has this fantasy that if at various crucial points of world history a linguistic philosopher had been on hand to make sure that everyone's terminology had been consistent then the world would be a better place. It's probably good to be punched in the face occasionally. Do you think I'll get a black eye?'

'You certainly will.'

'Have you got a mirror?'

I passed Caspar a mirror from my medicine box. He scrutinised himself with awe.

'Amazing. It's a pity I'm not going into college until Tuesday. They would be very impressed.'

'Don't worry. That black eye is going to mature like a fine wine. It'll be even more spectacular by next week.'

'So long as it doesn't scare Fanny. Speaking of whom . . .'

'I'll give you a lift. In your car. Don't worry. My bike is still in the back.'

Twenty-Two

'What do you want, Jane?' Alan asked, staring at me over his half-moon spectacles.

Characteristic blankness. 'I haven't made up my mind. Paul can go first.'

'Paul?'

'You know, I always have this existential problem with menus. I can never decide why I should order one dish rather than another.'

'Oh, for God's sake,' Alan exploded. 'We'll all start with the smoked salmon. Anybody object? Good. Then I'll have steak and kidney pudding. I recommend it if you want some decent old-fashioned food.'

'All right,' said Paul, rather shiftily.

'Jane?'

'I'm not really hungry. I'll just have a salad.'

Alan turned to the waiter. 'Did you get that? And some rabbit food for the lady here. And just tell Grimley we'll have a bottle of my white and a bottle of my red and I'll start with a large Bloody Mary. The others will probably want some overpriced mineral water with a foreign name.'

'I'll have a Bloody Mary as well,' I said impulsively.

'Well done, Jane.'

Alan handed the menu to the waiter, removed his spectacles and sat back.

'Salad,' he said in horror. 'That's the sort of thing that kept women out of this bloody place for so long.'

This seedy ornate dining room south of Piccadilly Circus, with its third-rate old masters, its tired club architecture, the faded hangings, the smoke, the male chatter, this was Alan's habitat: Blades, the club he had belonged to for over thirty years. Today he seemed ill at ease, prickly and depressed, and I didn't feel that Paul and I were the people to snap him out of it. Paul was preoccupied with his programme. He had told me as we were walking down Lower Regent Street that Alan was the key to the structure, the bit that he had to get right and he wasn't sure how to use him. As I sat at the table lighting one cigarette after another I felt I was looking at a callow fisherman dangling a fly in front of the nose of an ancient salmon. And me? Was I any good to Alan at that moment? The Bloody Marys and the mineral water arrived. Alan took a large gulp.

'How did the lunch with your publisher go?' I asked.

'Waste of time,' Alan said. 'Can you believe that lunch used to be my favourite part of the day? When Frank Mason was my editor, we used to spend three or four hours over it. We once took so long that we went straight on to dinner in the same restaurant Yesterday I met this new editor called Amy. Wore some sort of suit. Drank water. Ate a first course and nothing else. I was going to really show her: gin and tonic to start, three courses, couple of bottles of wine, brandy, cigar, everything.'

'So what happened?' Paul asked.

'I didn't,' Alan said with a shrug. 'And do you know why? She thought I was a bore. Alan Martello, the reactionary old drunk who hasn't produced a book since the seventies. Twenty-five years ago girls like her wanted to sleep with me. Queued up to get into my bed. Now they try to keep their lunches with me as short as possible. She was back in the office by two fifteen.'

I took a sip of my drink, the vodka astringent under the tomato's sweetness.

'What did Martha think of those queues of eager girls?' I asked.

'Good old Jane, always talking about how people feel. Wanting to make everything smooth and perfect. The answer is that we muddled along like most people.'

'She didn't mind?'

Alan shrugged. 'She understood.'

'How *is* Martha, Alan?'

'Oh, she's all right,' Alan said distractedly. 'Her treatment's getting her down a bit, that's all. She'll be better when it's over. It's just those bloody doctors worrying her.'

I felt a rush of emotion for this blustering, self-deceiving, famous man with his stained beard and his florid face and his novel he'd been working on since we were all children. A man who didn't want to think about his dying wife, who didn't want to be with her. But what emotion?

'I've been thinking a lot about Natalie lately,' I said.

Alan waved the waiter over and ordered two more Bloody Marys. I didn't bother to protest.

'I know,' Alan said, after the waiter had gone. 'And I hear you've been seeing one of these head people. All been a bit much for you, has it?'

'Yes, I think it has been, in a way.'

'And then snooping around. What are you doing? Trying to find out who killed my daughter?'

'I don't know. Trying to get things sorted out in my mind.'

'Then you, Paul, and your programme. Haven't either of you got a family of your own to mess around with?'

The vodka was taking effect on Alan. I knew this mood. He would taunt us, probe for weak spots, try to goad us into losing our tempers. I sneaked a look over at Paul who smiled back at me. We were a match for him and, anyway, this wasn't the old Alan, dominating, seductive. He only picked at the smoked salmon but he cheered up when the steak and kidney pudding arrived in its bowl, and the heavy opaque claret was poured into his large glass.

'Salad, indeed,' he said, tying his napkin around his neck like a bib.

I've seen the old pictures of Alan, the angry young man, and in the early fifties he had a slim, austere look. Now he was overweight, florid. His dimpled, veined nose was a testimony to decades of over-consumption. But there were still those lively blue eyes, flirtatious and imperious. They held people, especially women, and even now I could imagine the fascination they would arouse and the impulse to sleep with him.

'How many women have you slept with, Alan?'

I couldn't believe I'd said it, and I waited almost in horror to see what he would say. To my surprise, he laughed.

'How many men have you slept with, Jane?'

'I'll say if you say.'

'All right. Go on then.'

Christ, it was my own fault.

'Not very many, I'm afraid. About seven, eight maybe.'

'And a quarter of them are sons of mine.'

I flushed red in embarrassment. Even my toes, under their layers of leather and cotton, must have been blushing.

'What about *you* then?'

'Isn't Paul going to tell us?'

Paul looked genuinely alarmed.

'I didn't promise anything,' he said, gulping.

'Come on, don't be shy. You're expecting everybody else to bleat about their private lives in your ridiculous telly programme.'

'God, Alan, this is pretty juvenile, isn't it? If you must know, I have probably had sex with about thirteen women, maybe fifteen. Are you satisfied?'

'I win then,' said Alan. 'I would estimate that I have slept with something over a hundred women, probably over a hundred and twenty-five.'

'Oh, well done, Alan,' I said in my driest of tones. 'Especially as you had the handicap of being married with children.'

Alan was well into the claret now. 'Ah, the true, the blushful Hippocrene,' he said as he drank deep and then wiped his mouth with his napkin. 'It wasn't a handicap. Do you know one of the good things about literary success?'

Paul and I looked quizzical. We knew that no actual answer was required.

'The women,' said Alan. 'When you write a successful novel and become a representative, however misleadingly, of a younger generation, you get rewarded by money and fame, of course, but also you get a lot of women whom you would not otherwise have got. It's like this,' he said, pushing his spoon into his bowl and lifting out some gobbets of flesh. 'We're meant to pretend not to like this sort of thing, aren't we? The blood of the meat and the kidneys with their fine tang of faintly scented urine. And we're supposed to whine and winge about the sufferings of animals. I *like* meat. I like veal. I love foie gras. Who cares about the calf growing up in the dark or how the goose was fed?'

'I'm sorry, Alan,' I interrupted, 'but is this all because I ordered a salad for lunch? I wasn't making a political gesture. I'm having a big meal tonight.'

He continued as if I hadn't spoken.

'When I meet a woman, any woman, I imagine what she'd be like in bed. All men do, but most of them never dare to act on it. I did. If I met a woman and I was attracted to her, I'd invite her to bed. A lot of the time they'd accept.' He pushed a large spoonful of steak and kidney pudding into his mouth and chewed it vigorously. 'People aren't supposed to say things like that, are they?'

'Any woman at all?' I asked.

'That's right.'

'Like Chrissie Pilkington?'

'Who?'

The steaming spoon halted half-way between bowl and mouth. Dead flesh in grease. Alan's brow was furrowed with the effort of memory.

'You don't remember them all by name?'

'Of course not.'

'She was a schoolfriend of Natalie's. Long curly silver hair, like a model for a pre-Raphaelite painting. Freckles. Small breasts. Tall. Fifteen years old.'

'Yes, I remember,' Alan said wistfully. 'She was probably sixteen, wasn't she?' he added with a note of prudence.

'Girls are beautiful at that age, don't you think?' I said.

'Yes, I do,' Alan replied. He looked wary. He liked to be in control of the conversation. He didn't know where this was going.

'Their skin is unblemished. Their bodies are firm, especially their breasts.'

'That's right.'

'And they've got a particular sexual attraction. I could even see it in the girls that Jerome and Robert used to bring home. They're still a bit like children but they've got adult bodies. And I bet they're sexually submissive, and eager as well. I bet they'll do almost anything you want and be grateful for it. Isn't that right?'

'Sometimes,' Alan said, laughing uneasily. 'That was all a long time ago.'

Paul looked uneasy as well. He was wondering what sort of private fight he had wandered into and what he should do about it.

'It was all so perfect, wasn't it? It was 1969 and the little girls were on the Pill and suddenly it wasn't adultery or seduction any more. It was sexual liberation. Unfortunately it didn't always work out. Like with Chrissie. Natalie found out. And she told Martha. And for once Martha didn't get cross with you, or do nothing. She had an affair with my father. What did you think of that?'

'What?' said Paul, deeply shocked.

Alan's steak and kidney pudding was finished. He noisily scraped the last streak of gravy from around the inside of the pie dish and licked it off his spoon. He used to say that this insistence on finishing every last particle of his food was a legacy from wartime. He couldn't sustain his tirades the way he once had and he looked tired.

'I thought it was a pathetic gesture,' he said. 'If Martha wanted to fuck someone . . .' He wasn't shouting but this was loud enough to make one or two of the pin-striped lunchers on adjacent tables turn their heads. Oh, it was that writer fellow being outrageous again. 'If she wanted to fuck someone she should have gone and done it and had a really good fuck. Instead, she wanted to make a gesture, so she seduced your poor father. I don't think your mother ever got over it. I think that Martha behaved contemptibly.' Paul's head was in his hands now.

'Not only that,' I added. 'Natalie was threatening the family, that beautiful protected world that you had built up between the Martellos and the Cranes, just to make a stupid little point. I would have been angry if it had been me.'

Alan drained his glass. He no longer looked like a man who could manage a four-hour lunch.

'I *was* angry,' he said, but he was speaking in a muted tone now.

'What did you do about it, Alan?'

He laid his spoon gently down into his bowl. 'I think we've talked enough about sex for one lunch,' he muttered.

'You started it,' I said, but he was too preoccupied to listen.

'Our family – and I mean you as well – was a wonderful thing,' Alan said. 'It was terrible to put all that at risk just to hit out at me. Unforgivable. And in the end, the only person who was hurt was Felicity. Do you ever think about that, Jane? Darling, gentle Martha and your spiritual sister, Natalie, did that terrible thing to your mother.'

'Natalie was hurt as well.'

Alan's reactions had slowed down now. He had the befuddled look of an old man roused from sleep.

'Natalie? It was Martha, really, not Natalie.'

'It all came to a climax in the same summer, didn't it? Chrissie and you, the revelation about Martha and my father, then Natalie. That's going to be a lot to get into a sixty-minute film, Paul. Won't you need a series?'

Paul pushed his pie dish aside. It was still half full.

'What is it you want, Jane?' he said quietly.

'And what is it that *you* want, Paul,' interjected Alan, always eager to toss petrol on the flames.

'Alan, I love you, I love you all, that's what I want to capture on film.'

'We shall see,' said Alan wearily. 'Hurry up, Jane, we want our pudding.'

I prodded a tired quarter of tomato with my fork. The thought of food in my mouth made me want to gag.

Twenty-Three

The water in the sink was scummy with dark brown goose fat ('Why are we having goose?' Robert had complained, sounding about eleven. 'We *always* have turkey!'). I pulled the plug, lifted out the greasy plates and stacked them neatly on the side. Bits of red cabbage and a couple of cigarette butts – mine, I supposed – lay at the bottom of the sink, along with a whole arsenal of cutlery. I swilled down the dirt, put the plug back in, and filled the sink with hot and very soapy water. Then I went back to the dining room to assess the damage.

A chair still lay on its side where Jerome had thrown it before storming out ('You've gone too far this time, *Mother*!'), dragging Hana with him, listing gracefully on her thin black heels. I picked it up and sat down heavily on it. Candles guttered in the centre of the table, casting flickery light over the debris. A capsized half-demolished Christmas pudding lay, as unappetising as a ruptured football, among a smeary array of wine glasses, tumblers, port glasses, empty bottles. How much had we drunk? Not enough – not enough to blank out the memory, which anyway had been relentlessly filmed by the TV crew.

I picked up a green paper crown and stuck it on my head, then lit a cigarette. This was nice, being alone again. As I smoked, slowly, I shovelled the empty crackers together, and threw them on the glowing fire, which briefly flared, then returned to gold-speckled ash. A cracker joke caught my eye. 'How many ears does Davy Crockett have? – Three: a left ear, a right ear, and a wild front ear.' Oh, how Kim – in a stinging yellow gown – and Erica (roaring purple) had giggled. They'd giggled most of the evening, unexpected allies, mad molls in their absurd finery. They'd laughed at all the usual cracker jokes ('What did the policeman say to his tummy? – You're under a vest'; 'Knock, knock. – Who's there? – Boo. – Boo who? – Ah don't cry.'); at Andreas, who clearly disapproved of Erica and this new-model Kim; at Paul's directorial solemnity; at the cameras themselves. They'd sat on either side of Dad (who had gone into slow motion as everyone else had speeded up) and flirted with him outrageously, until he'd given grudging half-smiles, charmed by their loony girlishness.

I stubbed out my cigarette and carried the glasses to the kitchen. I washed the crockery and cutlery, rinsed it. Lovely silence. What a lot of shouting there had been: Paul at Erica ('Are you trying to ruin my film?'), Andreas at Kim ('You've had quite enough to drink'), Kim to Andreas ('Piss off, you old fart, it's Christmas and I'm not on call'), Jerome at Robert ('If you can't be polite to Hana, get out'), Robert at me ('Still trying to make everyone one happy family?'). Dad hadn't shouted, but then he'd hardly spoken. Claud hadn't shouted, but he had followed me into the kitchen and hissed: 'Who's Caspar, Jane?' I hadn't shouted until the cameraman, backing away from a long take of Erica and Kim singing 'Oh Little Town of Bethlehem', had bumped into my precious green-glass decanter, knocking it to the floor.

The plates were done, lined up in a gleaming row of white. Glasses done. I lifted a tray of disparate objects (matches, a set of keys, paper clip, pen, thimble, paper-knife, ear-ring, Remembrance Day poppy, screwdriver, black pawn from a chess set) and winced at the memory. Oh God, we'd played the Memory Game. Claud had organised it, of course, explaining the rules to a half-sozzled company ('Memorise what's on the tray, then I'll cover it up, and you must write down everything you can, then we'll uncover the tray and see who's remembered the most objects'). It was a game we'd played a lot as children. One of the objects on the tray, staring up at a suddenly sober company, had been a photograph of Claud and me and the boys, taken years ago (By whom? I could no longer remember). Smiling, touching each other. That's when Jerome had thrown over his chair.

I poured out a glass of port in a thick purple glug and lit a final cigarette. The rest of the mess could wait till morning. I took off my shoes, my ear-rings. Yawned. Giggled suddenly at the memory of Kim and Erica. The phone rang.

'Hello.' Who would ring at this time of night?

'Mum.' It was Jerome and he still sounded angry. 'Never do that again.'

'You mean you didn't have a good time? What a pity – I was thinking of reconvening at New Year's Eve.'

'This is exactly what I needed.'

I was lying by green water, palm trees and thick plants all around, in a thick white towelling robe. We were drinking mango juice, and I was feeling more relaxed than I had done in a very long time. My muscles had unstrung, my bones felt supple, my skin soft, green light danced against my eyeballs. The winter sun, slanting in through the tall windows, stroked my bare legs. The echoey room was filled with low murmurs of women, like a harem without a master. I could feel my heart-beat smooth and comforting. Soon I would have a swim, then a massage. Then I would lie down again, and flick through women's magazines, reading advertisements for sun lotion and lip gloss.

Kim had called me the evening before, when I'd been feeling wearily sad. She'd bought two day passes for The Nunnery, a women-only health centre, and wasn't asking but insisting that I came along. I'd protested, but feebly, and at the sound of her voice, so matter-of-fact and familiar, my eyes had filled with tears. I'd felt as if, at last, I were coming unravelled; all my seams undoing at once.

When I'd put the phone down, it had rung again almost immediately. It was Catherine, from a payphone. Paul had come round, she said, and he and Peggy were quarrelling; they weren't even bothering to keep their voices low. It was awful, awful, like the days before Paul had left the family for good. They were shouting at each other and it all had something to do with Natalie, and please please could I tell her what was going on. I couldn't tell her because I didn't know. I said something banal about Paul and Peggy loving her a lot, and she must never forget that, then realised that I was talking to her as if she were six, so stopped. But instead of being surly down the phone, Catherine started sobbing noisily. I imagined her leaning her beautiful skinny body against the grubby kiosk, and wiping her tears with her black T-shirt, her sharp knobbly elbows icy in the winter air. I muttered something, and she sobbed on. The money ran out on a gasping sniff.

When Robert and Jerome had been little, it had been so easy to comfort them. Even now, I could vividly recall how their bunchy bodies could be gathered up, heads tucked into my neck, my chin on their smooth crowns, their determined legs wrapped fiercely round my waist; how I'd croon nonsense as I wiped away tears that smarted on their flushed cheeks . . . My little darling . . . it'll all be okay . . . Mummy'll protect you . . . there, pigeon, there, humdinger . . . don't you fret, don't fret a bit . . . Mummy's here, my sweet love . . . my darling one.

Then, slowly, they had stopped wanting me to touch them. One day, I'd realised they no longer got into bed with me in the mornings, that they closed the bathroom door. When something was wrong, they'd go to their rooms, and I'd have to fight against the urge to follow them, pretend that Mummy could still make it better. When Robert was bullied at school, and went around in a fog of mute shame, and it was only when I heard one little boy calling him sissy that with a punch in the gut I knew what was going on; when Jerome had his first sweetheart and sewed absurd felt hearts (so uncool) onto his jeans, and then she chucked him after one date, so we had to spend an evening unpicking them and he pretended to be indifferent, not to care, he winced at my sympathy; when Robert quarrelled with Claud about smoking, and neither of them could talk to the other for days, pompous gits, and I longed to shake them both, but instead I busied myself around them, and I thought, even then, what a waste of *time* this is. There were days when all I wanted to do was to hug them, touch them, my boys, my lovely sons – but they'd twitch embarrassedly, good humour-edly: don't be soppy.

Ever since they'd been born, they'd been leaving me. I remembered Mum, just before she died, saying: 'The best gift I could give you was your independence. But you were always in such a *hurry* to go from me.' Children are always in such a hurry to go. I remembered Robert, aged five or so, at the beach. His shoe lace was undone and he was crying because we'd left him behind. He stood, a little blocky shape on a great expanse of sand. I ran back, stooped down to help, and he pushed me away: '*I can do it.*' They practise being grown-up for such a long time, and then one day you notice that they really are grown-up. Where had all that time gone? How had it happened that I was middle-aged and on my own, and never again would I know the swamping joy of holding a child under my chin and saying: Don't fret, it'll be all right, I promise you it'll be all right.

I wept myself to sleep, great raw spasms of weeping, and felt as if something was breaking up inside me. In the morning – a great ice-blue sky and skeletal frost-covered branches – I pulled on a track suit, packed shampoo and *Jane Eyre* into a shoulder bag, and went to meet Kim. Now, lying side by side, eyes shut in the white and green space, I spoke dreamily. Today, to Kim, I could say anything at all. Words floated in the air between us, clouds of explanation. Water lapped, and green ripples danced across my closed eyes. My body was water; my heart had dissolved; emotion was running softly through me, like a dreamy river.

'I feel I'm in trouble, Kim.'

'This is Natalie?'

Kim held my hand, our fingers locked, our arms hanging between the sun-beds. Was this despair that I was feeling? Despair didn't have to be vicious and hard; it could be like warm liquid filling up every crevice in my body.

'It might have been a stranger, some random tragedy.'

'Yes.' My voice came out in a whisper.

'Luke is probably the most likely suspect, even though he wasn't the father of the baby. Maybe he killed her because he knew he *wasn't* the father.'

'Maybe.'

'Whatever it is, it certainly isn't your responsibility to find out.'

'No, of course not.'

'You couldn't possibly have anyone else in mind? Darling Jane, you're not going to make a fool of yourself.'

We lay a little longer in silence. I still had my eyes shut; the only part of me that felt solid were my fingers, where they clasped Kim's.

I had a massage. A woman smelling of lemons, her dark blonde hair tied back in a smooth pony-tail, her feet bare, stood over me and dug her strong fingers into all my aches and pains. My last resistance was pushed up the channels of my body, out. My tears ran onto the couch, puddled against my cheek. I felt empty.

I collected my car from the car-park on St Martin's Lane – God, what an indulgence – and headed over to Charing Cross Road and north. I turned on the radio. I didn't want music. I didn't want to be trapped with my own thoughts, so I pushed the button until I found someone speaking.

'What has not been taken on board by the sleepy Establishment that still rules this country is that the most valuable commodity in the world will soon be something that you can't hold in your hands; it's not oil or even gold, but information.'

'Oh, shit,' I yelled in the safe confines of my car.

'Now, the implications of this are almost infinite, but let me just make two points. One, it's irreversible, entirely beyond the control of any national legislation or administration. Two, any organisation that is left outside that information world will wither and be left behind.'

'Oh, fuck,' I shouted.

A jaunty DJ's voice wondered if 'Theo' could give an example.

'All right, take one of our most respected institutions, the police force. Let's just say that if you were creating an organisation to do the job of the police force you wouldn't create anything like what we now have. It is a typical, unmanaged, manpower-heavy structure, which takes more money every year only to produce worse results, and one of the main reasons for this is that its role is based on a myth. An efficient police force is about rational management of staff and the ordering of information.'

'What about the bobby on the beat?'

'The idea is a joke. If we want people to walk up and down streets doing nothing, let's get retired people to do it at a pound an hour. It has nothing to do with policework.'

'We'll take a break there. We're talking to Dr Theo Martello about his new book, *The Communication Cord*. This is Capital Radio.'

I was in Tottenham Court Road and realised with amusement that I was about to drive past the Capital Tower. I crossed Euston Road and, on an impulse, turned right off Hampstead Road and parked next to the army surplus store. I sat with the radio on listening to Theo rhapsodising about the breaking down of frontiers, the collapse of institutions, the end of the state, of welfare, of income tax, of almost everything. Finally, he drew to a close with yet another plug for the book from the DJ. I got out of the car, crossed the road to the Capital Tower and waited a few yards away from the revolving door.

Theo didn't notice me at first. He was in his business

227

uniform, a suit whose lapels were so high and ugly that it must have been fashionable and expensive. He carried a briefcase about the size and slimness of a magazine. His head gleamed through his close-cropped hair in the cold winter sunshine.

'Carry your case for you, guv?' I asked brightly.

He started.

'What's this?' he said. 'Am I on *This is Your Life* or something?'

'No, I heard you on the radio and realised I was just passing.'

He laughed.

'Good. It's good to see you, Jane.'

'Can I give you a lift somewhere?'

'Is Bush House on your way?'

'No, but I'll take you.'

Theo told a waiting taxi to go away and we set off in my car.

'How can you manage with a briefcase that small? I go around with shopping bags full of papers crammed into my saddlebag.'

Theo shook his head.

'It's a waste of space as it is. In five years I'll have something the size and weight of a credit card.'

'I keep losing my credit card.'

'I'm afraid that the information revolution hasn't got anything yet to deal with your brain, my dear. You want to go left ahead and then right.'

'I know the way,' I said irritably. 'You weren't very nice about our constabulary were you?'

'It's the sort of thing that makes people sit up, isn't it?'

There was a short silence and I waited, hoping that

Theo wouldn't change the subject but not daring to take the plunge. I had to.

'Theo, what are you up to with Helen Auster?'

There was no reaction but the pause was a few beats too long.

'What do you mean?'

'Oh, come on, Theo, I'm not blind.'

I saw his grip on his case tighten.

'Oh, you know, it's something about women in uniform, isn't it?'

'Helen Auster doesn't wear a uniform.'

'Not literally, but she wears a metaphorical uniform. There's something erotic about symbols of authority yielding and being conquered.'

I didn't know where to begin.

'Theo, this is a woman involved in the investigation of your sister's murder.'

'Come off it, Jane. Nobody's going to solve Natalie's murder. The investigation is a farce. There is no evidence. Nothing's going to happen.'

'Am I missing something, Theo? I thought you were married. Where does Frances fit into all this?'

Theo turned to me with a secure smile.

'What do you want me to say, Jane? That my wife doesn't understand me? This isn't a debating society.'

'And isn't Helen Auster married?'

'To the supermarket manager, yes. I haven't noticed any signs of reluctance on her part.' I glanced at his face. He had a faint smile that seemed to challenge, even taunt me. 'Helen is a passionate woman, Jane. Very uninhibited, with a bit of encouragement.'

'Are you going to leave Frances?'

'No, it's just a bit of fun.'

It had been horribly easy. I felt nauseous, but I couldn't stop myself from continuing.

'I saw Chrissie Pilkington the other day. Well, she's not called Pilkington any more.'

'Yes?'

'She mentioned your name.'

'What's all this about?'

'She was an old flame of yours. After your father had finished with her.'

'Briefly.' There was a pause. 'Are you all right, Jane?'

'What do you mean?'

'Do you want to know what I mean?' Theo said, angry now for the first time. 'I'm trying to remember who was my flame – as you put it – after Chrissie? I wonder who that was?' He looked around agitatedly. We were totally stuck in Gower Street. 'I'll walk from here or get a taxi. Thanks for the lift.'

He opened the car, got out and walked quickly away. I sat, stuck in traffic, furious and shamed.

Twenty-Four

I was in the bath when the phone rang. I turned the hot tap off with my toe, sank back into the foam, and listened. I'd forgotten to switch the answering machine on. Should I bother to answer it? If I got out of the bath now, it would stop before I reached it. But it went on ringing stubbornly. I pulled myself out of the water, which suddenly seemed irresistible, wrapped a towel around my boiled body, and ran to the bedroom.

'Hello.'

'Jane, it's Fred.'

'Fred? I haven't heard from you for . . .'

'It's Martha. She's going.'

'Going?'

'She's dying Jane, she's dying fast. She wants to see you. She asked me to bring you with me. I'm going tomorrow, crack of dawn.'

'Shouldn't we go straight away?'

'Not quite up to it, I'm afraid.' I heard that his voice was slurred. 'Anyway, she's asleep.'

'All right, Fred, what time?'

'I'll pick you up at five-ish, that way we'll beat all the traffic and be there by eight. She's best in the mornings. She sleeps most of the afternoon.'

I had made this journey too often, recently: for the family

mushroom hunt, for the funeral, for my bungled confrontation with Martha and then Chrissie. Fred had been drinking – but had that been last night or this morning? I offered to drive but he waved me away. We drove through the dark morning in silence in his smooth, purring company car. Lynn had packed him a Thermos flask of good black coffee, and some sandwiches, cut into neat triangles and thinly spread with damson jam. I refused the sandwiches but accepted the coffee. Alfred opened the window when I smoked. I inserted one of the tapes I had brought up for Martha into his machine: songs by Grieg, pure and clear, filled the car.

At Birmingham, I said: 'Do you remember how she used to sing to all of us. At supper, or on walks, suddenly she'd start singing; not just humming, or singing so that we'd all join in, but belting it out loud, really loud.'

Alfred just grunted. Well, of course he remembered. But I couldn't stop.

'Or how she rode that old bicycle of hers, sitting up so straight in the saddle with her hair flowing back. We all used to laugh at her but she always got to the top of the hills first. Or how she used to sketch us. We'd be playing together, and not even know she was there, and suddenly she'd show us her drawing. Some of them were lovely. I wonder where they all went to. I'd love to have one.'

'I have this vivid image of her sitting in the greenhouse.' Alfred's voice was gruff and he kept his eyes fixed on the road. 'Every morning, she would go to the greenhouse and just sit on that tall stool. When we got up in the mornings, we'd often see her, absolutely still, gazing out at the garden, like a sentinel. I always found it oddly reassuring. Whatever else happened, Mum was there keeping watch on our bit of the world. Have some more coffee.'

'Thanks. Do you mind if I smoke another cigarette?'

'Go ahead.'

We left the motorway and followed signs for Bromsgrove.

'Alfred, about Natalie . . .'

'No.' His voice was sharp, like the screech of a brake.

'I just wanted to ask . . .'

'No, I said, Jane. Later. After Martha. Wait.'

Martha's room was full of flowers and chocolates, like a hospital ward.

'It's extraordinary how people think that when you grow old, or ill, you like sweet things,' she laughed. She thanked me for my tapes; and Alfred gave her the cards his children had made for her. She looked at them all attentively, and put them carefully on the table beside her bed. We sat there, appalled at the thinness of her face. Her body barely disturbed the drape of the sheet, and her fingers lay like five whitening bones on the covers. There was an awkward pause as we tried to think of a suitable topic of conversation for a death bed.

'It's also funny,' she continued, 'how when it's most important to talk – like now, when I'm dying – it also seems most impossible. Or embarrassing. Look at you, Alfred, you were about to ask me about the garden, or the weather or something, weren't you? And yet you might never see me again.'

'Mummy,' said Fred. It seemed shocking that a grown-up man should call anyone by such a childish, trusting name. I looked down at my hands, clutched in my lap.

'Fred, my love, why don't you go and see Alan. He's

stalking round the garden somewhere. I want to talk to Jane, alone. And then to you alone. All right?'

When it was just the two of us, Martha said, 'I've had a long time to get used to dying, but it doesn't seem to make it any easier.'

'Are you scared?' I asked.

'Terrified is more like it. I think about this great black hole waiting for me, and it doesn't seem as if my life has really happened yet. It's gone too fast, I feel cheated somehow. I can't talk to Alan about that, though. He keeps talking about when I'm better, and where we should go on holiday this year. Half the time he's fussing over me so that I can't even drink a glass of water without him rushing to steady my glass,' she lifted a trembling hand up, 'then other times he's saying I should get out of bed today, perhaps go for a walk in the garden. He cuts recipes out of magazines, and encourages me to try to cook them. Or he tries to cook meals for me, dumplings and things, and he puts about five times as much as I can possibly eat on my plate and watches me. He won't talk about arrangements. Real arrangements for after I've died.'

'Can I do anything?'

She looked at me steadily, as if she knew everything. 'Yes. Alan's always trusted you. Keep an eye on him. Make sure he's all right, Jane.'

'I don't know if I can, Martha,' I said.

'Yes,' she said.

How do you say goodbye to someone whom you love, and whom you know you will never see again I leant over Martha, and she gazed up at me with milky, tired eyes.

'You're beautiful,' I said ridiculously, and brushed a

white strand of hair from her forehead. I kissed her on both cheeks, and then I kissed her on the lips.

To me she said: 'I'm sorry.'

Fred drove much too fast going home. The roads were crowded, and it was foggy, but we kept in the fast lane, braking as shapes loomed up, hooting at cars that were prudently keeping their speed down. He didn't speak at first, and I was happier that way. He listened to the news on the radio, and a play I couldn't follow. About forty miles from London, he said, 'Jane, it's got to stop.'

I didn't pretend not to understand what he meant. 'Why do you say that, Fred?'

He thumped a fist on the steering wheel, swerved to avoid something dead on the road, and replied, 'Can't you see we've had enough of all this, this nonsense. I've spoken to Claud – who I must say is being unbelievably understanding and protective of you in the circumstances – and he said it was something to do with some therapy or other. And I spoke to Theo as well. What are you playing at?'

I opened my mouth to speak but he hadn't finished.

'I don't know why you should feel the need to take revenge, since it was you who left Claud, but never mind that. The point is, we can't take you poking into all of our lives any longer. And now that Mum's dying too – can't you just lay off?'

'It's nothing really.'

'Oh, don't give me that crap. What are you trying to do to us? Leave us all alone. Get on with your nice, cosy life and your navel-gazing therapy and just *leave us all alone.*'

Fred had been drinking, of course. But was this what

235

they all felt about me? There was a part of me that just wanted to be forgiven and be welcomed back into the fold. Something stopped me. We drove the rest of the way in grim silence.

I must buy a cat, I thought, as I unlocked my front door into my cold and silent house. Without even taking off my coat, I went to the phone in the living room, and punched in Theo's number. He answered on the first ring.

'Theo, it's Jane.'

'Hello, Jane.'

He didn't sound too welcoming.

'I had to speak to you. I've just been with Fred.'

'Yes, I know, he's just called me on his mobile.'

'Do you feel the same way, Theo, that I'm just poking around in something that's not my business?'

'If you can even ask that, Jane, then you're considerably less intelligent than I've given you credit for. I think you're making a bloody fool of yourself.'

The line went dead. The doors of the Martello family were swinging closed against me.

I peered into my wardrobe. My grey gabardine suit, with a long tight skirt slit up to the knees? Too business-like. My red dress, low neck, long sleeves and tight down to my knees? Too sexy. My black dress? Too clichéd. Leggings, with a silk, Chinese-style tunic in autumn colours? Too safe. I tried them on, one after the other, turning round in front of the long mirror, and chose the Chinese tunic. Then I ran myself a bath, washed my hair, and dressed very slowly. I lined my eyes in dark green, brushed my lashes with mascara, glossed my lips in mul-berry. I smiled and an anxious face smiled back at me.

Too bright. I soaked cotton wool in make-up remover and scrubbed off the eye-liner.

It was only a dinner party, for God's sake, not an exam. I brushed my hair back and pinned it up. I chose some delicate ear-rings, amber drops, and dabbed rose water on my wrists. Just a dinner party with seven other people and Caspar's daughter in the background, and what if she took a dislike to me?

Fanny made her entrance backwards, pulling a heavy case into the room. She turned round and looked seriously at us all.

'I'm a traveller,' she said. She came to a halt at my knees, and considered me for a moment with Caspar's grey eyes. 'Who are you?'

Caspar made no move to intervene, just waited for me to reply.

'Jane.'

'Tell me all the words you can think of that rhyme with Jane. Ready-steady-go.'

'Lane, mane, deign, feign, cane, pain, rain, same, vain, grain, chain, arcane . . .'

'Now with Fanny. Go!'

'Danny, Annie, Mannie . . .'

'Those are all other names. I want real words.'

'Canny, granny . . .'

'What does canny mean?'

'Knowing, I suppose. Like you.'

'At school, people say that Fanny means vagina. They chant, "Fanny has a fanny". Do you think that's what it means?'

'Lots of words have different meanings. For some people fanny does mean vagina; for me, Fanny now means a five-year-old girl who's a traveller. When I was at school, people used to chant "Plain Jane Crane".'

Caspar stood up and said to Fanny, 'Come on, then. Bedtime for you. We'll read a chapter of *Pippi* and leave our guests on their own for a few minutes, shall we? You know where the wine.'

She held up her arms, starkly vertical, and he hoisted her onto his shoulders.

'More wine, Jane?'

'Half a glass.'

I put up a hand to signal it was enough and our fingers met. I could not breathe. My stomach turned to water and my heart flipped like a fish.

'So how did you meet Caspar?' the man next to me asked: Leonard, who worked in the Hospital for Tropical Diseases and had just come back from Angola.

'I sat next to her at a public meeting and she shouted at me,' interrupted Caspar.

'And then he came to a residents' association meeting I was involved in, and he got punched in the eye.'

'For such a pacifist,' said Carrie from across the table, 'you get in an awful lot of fights. Weren't you hit by a down-and-out for trying to give him money?'

'It was a misunderstanding.'

'Obviously,' said Eric with the red hair and bitten nails, 'and that old lady in the supermarket when you walked off with her shopping trolley. You can still see the scar in the right light.'

It had been a lovely evening, full of frivolous talk. Caspar's friends had smiled at me as if they'd heard about me in advance. Occasionally, when I looked at him, I caught him watching me. With everything I said or did,

I was aware of him across the room. Happiness rose up, whoomph, in my throat, taking all my breath away. I jumped up.

'I'm sorry, I didn't realise the time. I've got to get home.' I aimed a smile around the room. 'It was a lovely evening, thanks.'

Caspar held out my coat and I shrugged my arms into it, careful not to touch him. He opened the door, and I stepped out into air that held the promise of snow.

'Thank you, Caspar, I had a lovely time.'

'Good-night, Jane.'

We stood quite still. For a moment I thought that he would kiss me. If he kissed me I would kiss him back, wrap myself up in his long body. But then a laugh wafted out through the front door, upstairs a child coughed. I went home.

'Sorry, Jane Martello isn't here, but please leave a message after the bleep.'

'Hello, this is Paul, on Thursday evening at, ur, 10.30. I'm calling to say that my programme is being broadcast on the twenty-first of February. I'd be really pleased if you could come round to our house to celebrate it. And watch it, of course. Let me know as soon as possible.'

How could the programme possibly be ready? I mean, I'd seen Paul wandering around taking notes and things, and there was that disastrous Christmas, of course, but I'd thought it was all still in embryo. In fact, I'd secretly assumed it would never actually be broadcast at all.

'Hi, Jane, it's Kim, just wanted to know that you're all right.'

'It's me, Alan.' He sounded pissed. 'Please ring.'

I was right: Alan was drunk. When he talked about

239

Martha he cried down the phone. 'Oh Jane, Jane,' he wailed and I shuddered at his clumsy, childish need and my sophisticated and furtive betrayal.

'She thinks of you as her daughter.' Not quite, but I knew what he meant. I, too, thought of her as my not-quite mother.

'Is there no hope for you and Claud? It would make her so happy.' No, no hope, no hope at all. Martha knew it was over and done.

'I'll never write again, never. I'm an old man and done for, Jane.'

I pulled out my packet of cigarettes.

'Don't desert us, Jane.'

He was gabbling about Natalie – such a gorgeous child – so loving – why did she get so hostile in the last years? – they'd tried to be good parents, hadn't they? – what had they done so wrong? – he knew he'd been weak with women, but surely that couldn't explain – once she'd spat at him – memories are a terrible thing, a terrible thing, a terrible thing.

Twenty-Five

I rang Caspar. I thought about him all day and then in the evening I rang him.

'It's Jane. Will you meet me at Highgate Cemetery on Sunday?'

'Yes. What time?'

'Three o'clock, by George Eliot's grave.'

'How will I find it?'

'It'll be the one with me standing next to it at three o'clock.'

'All right. I'll be the one carrying a copy of *Daniel Deronda* with half of the pages unread. Un*cut*, in fact.'

That was it, two dozen words, and the most erotic phone conversation I'd ever had. I baked two Madeira cakes, three loaves of brown bread, and a plain sponge cake for the freezer. I drank four glasses of red wine, smoked eight cigarettes, listened to unromantic Bach. On Saturday I cleaned the house from top to bottom. Really cleaned it, taking books off shelves and washing them down. I put up some pictures that had been standing in my study for months, I tore down posters of old churches that Claud had left curling on the walls. I stuck photographs from the last year into the photo album. They were all of buildings, except for one of Hana with a cloche hat obscuring her face. In the afternoon, I went to Hampstead and bought a coat. It didn't cost anything. I just paid for it with a credit card. I pushed all thought of Natalie out of my mind. This was my weekend.

In the evening I made a rice salad, and ate it with half a bottle of red wine left over from not that long ago. I pulled a box down from the attic, lit a candle, and browsed through Claud's love letters to me. Almost all of them dated from the year before and the year after our marriage. After that, nothing except the odd postcard from a conference: 'Missing you.' He probably was.

The letters were in meticulous script. On some, the ink had faded. 'My sweetest Jane,' he wrote, 'you were lovely in your blue dress.' 'My darling, I wish I were with you tonight.' The earliest letter was dated October 1970 – a few months after Natalie had disappeared. Odd that I'd forgotten it: it was a kind, grown-up letter saying how the family was holding together. 'She'll come home,' he had written, 'but of course nothing will ever be the same again. The first part of our life is over.' He was right. I thought of him in his tidy flat, with his books about churches and his correspondence arranged alphabetically. I wondered if he still hoped that I would change my mind and if he'd walked through the door at that moment, the evening before my date with Caspar, I believe that I would have let him stay. I've never been good at partings.

He was there on time, but so was Fanny, hair in wild curls around her face and wearing jeans about two sizes too big for her wiry little frame. She uncurled her gloved fist to show me the stones she'd collected while they'd waited. Her face was blotchy with cold and smudged with dirt.

'The friend she was going to spend the day with is ill,' explained Caspar.

'I'm glad to see her again,' I lied. 'Come this way,

Fanny, and I'll show you an obelisk with a dog's snout set in it. The dog was called Emperor.'

'What's an obelisk?'

'A pointy thing.'

We wandered off the main gravelled path. Brambles caught at our legs.

'Have you noticed,' said Caspar, 'how many children are buried here. Look, little Samuel aged five here, that's the same age as Fanny, and there's a baby of eleven months.' We stopped at a family gravestone: five names, all under ten. On some neat gravestones there were flowers. Most were overgrown with nettles and ivy; moss sank into the lettering, obscuring it.

'Look at that,' I said. A few yards away, through a thicket of trees, a headless angel stood guard over a buried slab. 'We've forgotten how to mourn, haven't we? How to remember. I'd like a monument like that. But people would say it was kitsch, or morbid.'

Caspar smiled. 'Morbid? To be planning your funerary sculpture at the age of forty? The thought never entered my head.'

'I'm forty-one. Look.'

Four dreamy pre-Raphaelite heads clustered mournfully in a circle of stone.

'Where are the pets buried, Jane?' Fanny ran back from her detour through a line of toppled graves.

I pointed up the path. 'There. A bit further on.'

She rushed off, her scarf trailing its fringes behind her.

'Come here, Jane.'

I made my way through the thickets to where Caspar stood. I walked very slowly. Nothing would ever again be as good as this moment. I stopped a foot away from him and we looked at each other.

'Plain Jane Crane,' he said. With one forefinger he traced my lips. Carefully, as if I were precious, he cupped the back of my skull. I took off my gloves, dropped them among the nettles, and slid my hands under his coat, jersey, shirt. He smelt of wood smoke. I could see my face in his eyes, and then he closed his eyes and kissed me. So many layers of clothing; we leant into each other. My body ached.

'Caspar! Caspar, where are you? Come and see what I've found. There you are. Why are you hiding? Jane, Jane you've dropped your gloves. Come on. Hurry.'

When I found myself in my remembered world again, the first stones of Cree's Top hard against the curve of my spine, I felt cold and afraid. As soon as I had mounted my bike and free-wheeled down Swain's Lane leaving Caspar and Fanny holding hands on the pavement, the kiss in the cemetery had seemed like a dream and I was returning to what was real. The holiday was over and I was going back to school.

Alex and I hardly spoke. We made no eye contact. I lay on the couch and as he spoke the ritualistic few words, I felt the room slip away from me and I was back where I had to be. The surface of the River Col on my left rippled sickeningly, as if it were thick oil rather than flowing water. It moved heavily away round the bend. I stood and turned, shivering a little in my gym shoes and thin cotton dress, black like the one that Natalie had worn so often that summer. The breeze blew it back and it outlined my firm young body, the body I had given to Theo just the day before, caressed and peeled and finally penetrated out in the shadowed woods with the laughing and the music of the party humming in our ears. I had taken my notebook, with my silly girlish fancies and fantasies, and ripped them from the book one by one. Their childish illusions repelled me now and it was with a sense of burnt bridges that I'd screwed them up and tossed them one by one into the water where they'd lost themselves in the broken surface of light and ripples which disguised where air ended and water began. I was a woman now, wasn't I?

I turned round to face Cree's Top. A wave of dread flowed through me and I felt giddy, so that my legs would scarcely bear me. The elms on my left swayed and tipped, or it might have been that they were still and I that was swaying. I began to make my way up the narrow and steep path that was familiar and so long lost. I could see the sludgy water of the stream down through the bushes to my right but this time I made an effort not to look anywhere but up the path, this path of my own shuttered mind. Branches brushed against me, snagging my dress, thorns against the flesh of my bare arms and calves, as if I was being held back. I strode through them unheeding. I was now directly on the summit of Cree's Top, though the visibility was obscured in all directions by the thick gorse bushes that covered it. The peak was very small and after just a few steps I began to descend.

I stopped and listened. Now I knew. Movement was visible through the bushes ahead, glimpses of something. Sounds also, muffled and indistinct. It was there. It was there. Things I had buried in my own mind for a quarter of a century and all I had to do was step forward, through the barriers I had erected for myself. When I opened my eyes and blinked, unseeing at first, at Alex, it was not with the fear of before but with an icy resolve. It was there. But I wasn't quite ready. Not quite.

Twenty-Six

I woke on the morning of Wednesday 15 February with a sense of imminence. There had been rain for days – the lawn was bloated with it – but the weather was suddenly cold and bright. From my back window the spire and the television mast on Highgate Hill looked unnaturally clear. The everyday objects in my kitchen were different, charged with meaning. My skin prickled. It was as if every object that I looked at was illuminated from behind, its outline accentuated and made harder, more vivid. Myself, too. I felt capable, precise. I needed to do things.

I had shopped the day before and was partly prepared. On the table I placed my heavy scales and weights, a bag of wholemeal flour and a bag of strong white flour, small polythene bags of pumpkin seeds, sunflower seeds and sesame seeds, yeast like soft modelling clay, sea salt, vitamin C powder in an orange medicinal pot, a plastic bottle of grapeseed oil, a bag of hard, thick muscovado sugar. This was a process I could go through in subconscious bliss. The yeast awoke with jewelled bubbles. I forked the salt into the sandy wholemeal flour, then added everything else with the beery puddle of yeast. I smoked cigarettes in the garden for half an hour, not thinking of anything, then returned and mashed and kneaded the two large patties of dough, leaning on the heels of my hands, folding and folding. Cut, rolled, pushed into four tins.

Another pause. I deliriously circulated round the house, folding shirts, arranging the books back on the shelves. I painted the top of the ballooning loaves with briny water, sprinkled them with sesame seeds and then slid them into the searing oven. The smell of controlled burning, of yeasty rebirth, filled the house so that I was almost drunk with it. After what seemed like no time at all I rapped the bottom of the tins, they resounded hollow, and I tipped them out onto wire trays. Tiny toasted seeds pattered across the worktop and I wetted my fingers and dabbed them and crunched them between my teeth.

Three loaves were put aside, ready to be wrapped and stored in the freezer. From the fourth, I cut a warm slice, spread it with salted butter and cold, sour goat's cheese and gobbled it greedily with nothing to drink but tap water. No wine, no coffee: I didn't need them; I wouldn't have been able to bear them. Buzzing, trembling, I got on my bike and cycled through the cold clear air to my office, where Duncan and I had arranged what we over-ambitiously called a meeting. I arrived in the office just after two and opened the last few days' mail, which consisted largely of circulars from mailing lists from which I hadn't yet been dropped. I threw almost everything away. If I hadn't had other things to worry about, I would have been worrying about my job.

I was no more purposeless than anybody else. For want of anything more constructive with which to occupy her time, Gina was re-ordering our filing system. A week earlier, the result had looked apocalyptic with the entire past of CFM regurgitated in paper form and arranged around the office. Now the papers were disappearing into their newly designated places, accompanied by the snap of ring binders and the clatter of filing cabinets. We were now only a day or two from achieving perfect order, like Pompeii. It would be almost a pity to disturb the taxonomic perfection with any new work.

Duncan was engrossed with the technicalities of the espresso machine, one of our major capital expenditures in the boom days of the late eighties. He brought me over a thimbleful of coffee which gave me an almost instantaneous jolt of caffeine as I despatched it in a single, tiny gulp. He told me of his new scheme which he was discussing with the council for putting homeless families ('homilies' he camply called them) into derelict houses and enabling them to restore the buildings themselves. I nodded with enthusiasm. It was extremely cost-effective (except for us), practical, socially beneficial, had little to do with architecture in any traditional sense, and was almost certain to be rejected out of hand by the housing department. An ideal CFM project. Then we moved on to my hostel.

'I read about the torchlight procession of local residents in the local paper,' Duncan said. 'Your allaying of the anxieties of the community obviously wasn't a total success. Does that mean that the hostel scheme has been abandoned?'

'Not necessarily,' I said. 'A council lawyer has come up with a slightly underhand way of pushing it through. Because of the fight at the meeting and the arrest that followed it, there's a court hearing coming up. The ruse is, as far as I can understand it, that the matter is all *sub judice*, which means that we can't respond to questions on the issue. Or at least that's what we'll say. Meanwhile, the plans are moving towards completion. The objectors will end up having to deal with a hostel that is up and running and that will bring its own problems. Local residents attacking arrogant council officials and a modernist architect is one thing. That would go down well in the local press. Nimbys assaulting the mentally ill who have been returned to the community is another. Anyway, that's the grand strategy.'

'Did you explain to them that if these people weren't in their back yards, they would be on their pavements and in their shop doorways and public benches?'

'No. Events intruded.'

The meeting was adjourned in fairly good spirits and I returned to my desk where I smoked cigarettes and tapped my phone with my pencil and realised I wasn't doing anything and that maybe I had better leave. I had the conviction that I was seeing everything with extreme clarity and that I had other places to be and other things to do. Gina asked after my health but I was unable to pay proper attention to what she was saying and I left, without even saying goodbye to Duncan. I would explain everything later.

Back at home, I opened a bottle of red wine and I stood on a chair and looked through a cupboard and found some salted cashew nuts and a rolled-up quarter of a bag of pistachio nuts and a little packet of scampi-flavoured somethings that were a bit like crisps. That would do for my supper. I drank the wine and ate these bits of crisps and watched TV and flicked between channels. There was a quiz show with questions I found elusive, a local news broadcast, an American science fiction show that I assumed must be *Star Trek* but turned out not to be, not even the new *Star Trek*. There was a programme about albatrosses, the long journeys they take navigating on the trade winds and the lifelong devotion the albatross shows to its mate, and a comedy show set in an American high school, and then another news programme.

After I had watched too many of these programmes, I switched the sound off and rang up the Stead because I wanted to talk to Martha but somebody else answered and took me by surprise. It was Jonah and he spoke in a very calm official sort of voice and told me that Martha had sunk into a coma in the morning and then had died very quietly that afternoon. I tried to ask some questions, not wanting to break the connection, but Jonah said he was sorry but he had to go. On the television I saw a man in a grey suit silently opening and closing his mouth like a fish in a bowl. I had to phone somebody. I rang Claud and got an answering machine. I rang Caspar and a woman answered and I hung up. And I rang Alex Dermot-Brown and Alex answered. He was surprised and said at first that we had a session the next day and asked if it couldn't wait but after I had talked a bit he told me to come straight over and asked if I was all right about getting over on my own or should he come and get me. I insisted and cycled over without a hat or gloves, though there was already rime on the car windows.

Alex looked very slightly different when he opened the door. Although this was where I had always seen him and he never dressed up, I felt like a schoolgirl calling on her teacher at home, illicitly, after hours. He greeted me with obvious concern. He spoke quietly and I could hear voices from the kitchen downstairs. I dimly realised that I might have interrupted something but I wasn't in a position to care. He led me up to his room. I asked something about the children. He said that they were asleep, way up at the top of the house and I didn't need to think about them. He put the light on and it dazzled me. With the darkness outside and the brown cosy illumination in the hall and on the stairs, it seemed clinical and interrogative. I lay on the couch and he sat behind me.

'Martha's dead,' I said.

I was breathing deeply and deliberately as I had in earlier times on board ship while struggling not to vomit. Alex waited a long time before speaking and when he did he was gentle but determined.

'I want you to think again of the day when Natalie disappeared,' he said.

It was more than I could bear.

'I can't, Alex, I can't.'

Suddenly, he was kneeling beside me. I could feel his sweet warm breath against my cheek, his hand was on my hair.

'Jane, this woman you dearly loved has died. I know what you are suffering. But you haven't come to see me in order to be comforted. You want to use this emotion. Am I right?'

'I don't know what I want to do,' I said, and I knew that all resistance was gone.

'Let's do it then,' he said.

Alex spoke the soft, soothing words that were now a familiar incantation, like half-heard music from a distant room. I experienced a profound relief in letting my body relax and my will slacken and I was there. This time I really was there. The charred moss against my back, my thighs resting on tiny twigs and stones. As I stood up and brushed my dress down I could feel the marks they had left in my flesh, like a raffia mat on the back of my thighs. The sun was lost behind a cloud and it left the River Col in heavy shadow. The stained, shadowy surface rippled lethargically and drifted away. The twisted torn paper fragments were gone, along with the childish fantasies they had represented. That was all over.

I turned, shivering in the flurries of wind, drops of moisture threatening rain, that now blew against me. The black dress was pressed against my body, my sexually awakened body, the breasts and thighs now somebody else's as well as my own. I felt a cold clarity of purpose. Cree's Top was ahead of me, the river lapping down on the bank by my right foot. I began to run up the narrow, steep path and into the wood and gorse that covered this lump of nature. There were sounds, not of birds or of the wind or the stream but strange creakings and whistlings and groans. I paid them no attention. I ran and could hear myself panting and feel the pain in my constricted chest. The trees around me looked dead, the bushes bare, the river below me on my right, brown and sluggish. My duty now was not to think and reason but to proceed regardless. Branches scratched my face, thorns tore me, my clothes snagged. I had reached the summit of Cree's Top and ran across and began to make my way down the slope on the other side. On Natalie's side. Through the bushes ahead I saw movement, fragmentary glimpses between branches, I heard screams, unintelligible shouts. My decision had already been made. I ran forward and burst through the bushes into the sunlight.

For the first moment I could see nothing with the sun burning my eyes, nothing but speckled gold explosions. I narrowed my gaze and forced myself to look. It was clear. Simultaneous perceptions: A girl lying on the grass. Screaming and screaming. Natalie. Dark hair, flaming eyes. Held down. Above her was a man, his hands about her throat. Her arms and legs flapped uselessly, then slowed and stopped. I tried to shout but it was as if my mouth was stopped with ashes. I tried to run, but my feet were stone blocks. The girl was let fall and lay still. The man had his back to me. He was dark haired, not grey. He was slim not stout. He was clean-shaven, not bearded. But there was no doubt. It was Alan.

Suddenly, I was screaming and screaming and I was being gripped and it was Alex and he was holding me tight and whispering in my ear. I pulled myself up. My hair was streaked over my face. I was spent. I had been skinned and turned inside out. I said I was going to be sick, now, and Alex reached for the wastebasket and I retched and then vomited and vomited, emptying myself. I lay back on the couch, stretched out, helpless, snotty, spots of vomit on my face, tear-stained, groaning, crying, gasping. Utterly spent, disgraced, appalled.

I felt a voice, intimate in my ear:

'You got there, Jane. You're all right. You're safe.'

Twenty-Seven

I woke up in my own bed, didn't know how I'd got there. Yes, Alex had brought me in his car. Had I made a scene and scared his children? My bike must still be locked to a parking meter outside his house. I picked up the alarm clock. Almost ten o'clock. Morning or evening? Must be morning. If it was night, it would be twenty o'clock. No, twenty-two. There was something on the edge of my consciousness not wanting to be thought about. I made myself think about it. I had to be quick to get to the lavatory. I leant into the bowl and retched and retched, bringing up nothing but a few hot, stinging splashes.

I washed around my mouth with a flannel. I was still wearing my clothes. I let them fall where I stood and stepped into the shower. Very hot water followed by very cold water. I dressed myself in jeans and an old corduroy shirt. My fingers trembled so much I could hardly fasten the buttons. I decided that I should eat something and went down to the kitchen. There were two bags of coffee beans in my freezer and I chose the darker ones. I filled a large cafetière. After hunting round a bit, I found an unopened packet of cigarettes in the pocket of the coat I'd been wearing the previous night. I emptied the cafetière, cup by cup, and smoked my way through the packet.

The phone rang a few times and I heard various voices on the answering machine. Duncan, Caspar, my father. I would deal with them later, some other day. When I heard Alex Dermot-Brown's voice, I ran across the room and picked up the receiver. He was concerned about me. He asked if I was all right and then said he wanted me to come round. Straight away, if possible. I said I'd be there in an hour. It was cold outside but bright, sunny. I put on a long flapping coat, wound a scarf about my neck, put a flat cap on my head and set off for the Heath. The wind blew about me in gusts and when I reached the top of Kite Hill, London was miraculously clear at my feet. I could see right across it to the Surrey hills beyond. I walked down and left the Heath at Parliament Hill and passed the Royal Free hospital. Claud had told me about a mental patient there who had been possessed by a neurotic compulsion to count the number of windows. Since he never achieved the same figure twice, it was an eternal task.

The things we do to give order to our lives. I had once read a poem about a man arrested for filling in the 'o's in library books. Did he think of all the 'o's that he *had* filled in, or all the 'o's that he hadn't? It was a long, hard trek and I was out of breath by the time I knocked at Alex's door. All the cigarettes. I almost laughed as I caught myself resolving to give up. Not yet. Not yet.

When the door opened, Alex surprised me, almost overwhelmed me, by taking me in his arms and holding me tight to him, murmuring comforting words in my ear as if I was one of his little children, scared of the dark. It was what I wanted more than anything else in the world. After the reassurance, his look turned serious as he asked me once more if I was all right.

'I don't know. I've been vomiting and I still feel sick. My head feels like somebody's trying to inflate it with a bicycle pump.'

Alex smiled. 'Don't worry,' he said. 'It's just what I would expect. It's like a fever breaking. Think of it as your body trying to expel a quarter of a century of poisons and impurities that have been trapped inside you. You're purifying yourself.'

'Am I going mad, Alex?'

'You're becoming sane. You're discovering the agony of a life without illusions.'

'But Alex, can it be true? Can it really be true? Could a man like Alan have got his own daughter pregnant? Could he have killed her?'

Very gently, Alex held my face in his hands and looked closely in my eyes.

'You're the one, Jane, who has broken through all the barriers and lies to uncover this. You've made the journey, Jane. You tell me, do you think it's impossible that he could have done this?'

It seemed an immense effort to reply. I stepped back and his hands dropped away from me. I slowly shook my head.

'No,' I said in little more than a whisper. 'I don't think it's impossible.'

A couple of minutes later I was back on the couch and Alex was in his chair. I started trying to reconstruct the details of what had happened all those years before but Alex was firm. All that could wait, he said. Instead he talked to me softly, as he had so often before, and he took me back into my memory, back to the scene of the murder. During that session and again during another on the following day, and again on the day after that, he took me over and over the events and they became clearer and more precise. It was like a photographic image that already seemed satisfactory coming more and more into focus, bringing with it new details and nuances. I saw Natalie struggling, I could see what she was wearing, from that familiar braided hair-band to the black plimsolls that I always associate with her. I could see Alan, strong and heavy, holding her down, grasping her throat, tightening his grip until all movement ceased.

'Couldn't I have done something?'

'What could you have done? Your mind saved you by shielding you from the horror of what happened. Now we've broken through that shield.'

I found the process of reliving the event unspeakably harsh. The crime was so vivid and violent, and I was so close – just metres away in the bushes – that I felt I could intervene, do something, maybe just shout. But I knew that I had not intervened and that it was now beyond my power and that there was nothing to be done. The shock and pain remained constant. There was no coming to terms, no catharsis, no getting beyond the pain or working my way through it. I achieved no distance from the events, I was not able to think about them in a balanced way. These were days of sobbing, retching grief, of smoking instead of eating, of drinking on my own at home.

Sprinkle some celery salt into the jug, followed by a few twists of black pepper, three splashes of Tabasco, an improbable amount of Lea & Perrins, the juice of half a lemon and a shake of tomato ketchup. Always begin with the cheapest ingredients. If you are using a whole litre carton of tomato juice, as I was, you will need a good tumbler of iced Russian vodka. Finally, the secret ingredient: half a wineglass of dry sherry. A handful of ice in your chunky tumbler and you have a drink substantial enough to replace dinner. A middle-period Bartok string quartet would have suited my mood but I listened to

Rigoletto. Woman is mobile. This one wasn't. I had gone inside myself and been horrified by what I had found. Outside was cold and dark. I would have to go out there soon and deal with things in the world. That was next.

When I had drained the last watery little puddle from my glass, I decided to go outside. Everything had to be done with utmost care. It was cold. I put on a sweater. I put on a coat and a hat. I found my keys and my purse and put them in the pocket of the coat. Outside, the icy air cleared my head a little. I had destroyed my marriage. I had done God-knows-what to my children. I had damaged my own mental health. I had uncovered horrors. People I loved were already appalled by my actions. What catastrophe was I now going to inflict on the family that meant more to me than anything in the world? The wind was blowing stingingly cold drops of rain into my face. Life had become horrible for me.

I was walking past shops now. A man, his hair in long matted ringlets, sat outside the supermarket with a mangy pathetic-looking dog of indeterminate breed. His hand was extended towards me. This was what happened to people who removed themselves from the world of family and society and work. I opened my purse and found a coin which I gave him, holding it precisely between two fingers so that I wouldn't fumble it.

I knew that I was projecting my misery out onto the world – however miserable some of its individual components might have been in their own right – so that I wasn't all that surprised when I stood in front of the TV rental shop and saw images of Alan mouthing silently on a dozen screens. There was the patriarch, justifying himself in words that I couldn't understand. For a moment, I thought that I had gone entirely mad, that the real world and the worlds of my memories and my nightmares had become one and that Alan had defeated me, utterly and finally. Then I remembered.

'Oh, fuck.'

I looked around, dazed but shocked into action. I saw a yellow 'For Hire' sign and flagged the taxi down. I gave a Westbourne Grove address. As we drove towards Swiss Cottage, Paddington and beyond, I held my face against the ferocious blast at the open window.

'All right, love?' the driver asked.

I nodded, not trusting myself to speak coherently. When I knocked at the door, Erica let me in.

'It's almost over,' she said. 'Drink?'

'Water,' I replied as I followed her up the stairs.

'Off the drink?'

'On it.'

She ushered me into a dark room, lit only by a vast television screen. The chairs were all occupied by indistinguishable silhouettes and I found myself a spot on the floor. Erica handed me something that rattled. My water. I held the damp glass against my forehead. I had thought of Paul's documentary about our family as a series of interviews. I hadn't prepared myself for what it would actually look like. When I started to pay attention to what was happening there was a photograph of Natalie on the screen, a hazy blow-up of a class picture that didn't do her justice. Someone was saying something about the lost spirit of the sixties, Jonah, I think, but it may have been Fred. From Natalie, the image changed to a picture of the Stead, seen, I guessed, from Chantry's Hill. At first, I thought it too was a photograph, but there were tiny things, a tremble of the camera, barely distinguishable flutters of leaves, shimmers of light, that showed this was being filmed. The camera began to move until it settled on Paul. He was looking down on the house, his face hidden from us. Then he turned and began to walk, accompanied by the camera. He addressed it as if it was a friend. What a pro.

Paul talked about the family as home and home as the place where, when you go there, they have to let you in; the family as the symbol of our affections; and the family as the symbol of society with its ties and obligations. I found it a bit difficult to concentrate, befuddled as I was, but I understood that he was telling some story from his golden childhood. At the moment he finished the story he came to a halt. The camera pulled back from his face and we could see that he had reached the spot where Natalie's body had been discovered. The hole was still there and he stood looking soulful. The camera pulled back and back until it could take in the whole scene: pensive Paul peering into the hole, the Stead, early morning sunlight, a tweeting bird. Some Delius-style music struck up and the credits began to roll. Someone switched the light on.

'Where were you?' Paul nudged me from behind.

'Sorry.'

'I'm glad you saw the final sequence though,' he said. 'That was a real *tour de force*. Four and a half minutes without a cut. I walked all the way down the hill, and hit the mark at the moment I finished the reminiscence. It's the most technically demanding thing I've ever tried. When I said cut, even the technicians applauded. But I want you to see the whole thing. I'll get a tape sent round.'

'Thanks,' I said. 'I've got to go now.'

'You've only just arrived, Jane. There are people I want you to meet.'

'I've got to go now.'

I hadn't even taken my hat or coat off, so I walked straight down the stairs and out. I thought I might have spent the last of my money on the taxi but I didn't check. I walked all the way home. I went through Regent's Park on the way. It took me an hour and a half and I was bleakly sober by the time I unlocked my front door.

Twenty-Eight

When I got up the next morning, after a night of lurching dreams, I felt so dizzy and sick that I had to hold onto the edge of the bed and breathe deeply for several seconds. In the long mirror facing me I saw an ageing and distraught figure with a chalky face and unwashed hair. I hadn't eaten properly for days, and my mouth tasted of decay. A week before, I had kissed Caspar and felt my body come alive. This scrawny woman staring at me was a different person altogether, shuffling and sickly, belonging to dark corners.

The image of Alan's stooped figure wouldn't go away. I saw him; I saw him as clear as ever. I didn't need Alex's help any longer. The monster had come out of its hiding place, into the glare of day. I wouldn't be able to push him back again. I remembered everything. I had witnessed a murder, a double murder, and now I witnessed it once again. I could watch myself watching. I took shallow, queasy breaths, and saw Alan standing over Natalie, triumphant and appalled.

I put on my dressing-gown, and went to the kitchen, where I ground coffee beans and made myself two pieces of toast. I smeared them with butter and marmalade, sat at the table and stared at them. After five minutes, I took a bite. Then another. It felt like grit. I chewed and swallowed, chewed and swallowed. Nausea hit me again, and beads of sweat broke out on my cold forehead. I rushed to the bathroom, where I was sick until my throat hurt and eyes stung.

I ran a bath and scrubbed myself. I brushed my teeth, but could still taste the vomit and the panic in my mouth. I lit a cigarette and filled my lungs with ash. Ashes to ashes.

I dressed in black jeans and a black polo-neck sweater. I brushed my hair back from my face. I sat on a chair in the kitchen and drank cooling brackish coffee, smoked another cigarette and stared out of the window at the rain which made the untended garden look grainy. It was nine o'clock and I had no idea how to get through the rest of the day. The rest of my life.

I rang Kim at work. She was busy with a patient, so I left a message to call. 'As soon as possible. Please,' I said. My voice was a croaky whisper. The receptionist probably thought that I was dying. Another cigarette. I heard the mail plop through the letter box onto the hall floor, but I didn't move. My body was heavy and hollow. The phone rang.

'Jane.'

I opened my mouth but I couldn't speak.

'Jane. It's Kim, Jane, tell me what's happening.'

'Oh Go-o-o-od!' Was that thin wail coming from me?

'Jane, listen, I'm coming over. Don't move. I'll be there in fifteen minutes. All right? Fifteen minutes. It's going to be all right.'

'I can't tell you. I can't tell you. Oh God. I can't.'

'Drink your tea, Jane.'

I sipped obediently and grimaced: it was milky and sweet, food for a baby.

'Now, I'm going to ask you some questions, okay?'

I nodded.

'Is it to do with Natalie?'

I nodded.

'Do you think you know something about Natalie's death?'

I nodded again.

'Do you think you know who the murderer is?'

Nod.

'Have you arrived at this through your therapy?'

'Yes.'

'Listen, Jane, will you tell me who you think murdered Natalie, but remember, telling doesn't make it any truer.'

'I – I – oh Christ, oh Jesus Christ, Kim, I can't.'

'You can. Is it one of your family?'

'Of my extended family, yes.'

'Tell me the name, Jane.'

I couldn't say his name. I used a word that didn't seem to fit him: 'My father-in-law.'

My father-in-law. My father's best friend. My sons' grandfather. The man I had known all my life, and who, until a few weeks ago, I casually would have said that I loved. As I gasped it out to Kim, I could see his leering face.

'He must have killed her because she was pregnant. Maybe he got her pregnant. He could have done. I can imagine it. Another thrill, and an act of revenge against Martha. Or somebody else made her pregnant and he found out about it. All the time I've been asking questions about Natalie, people kept talking about how, how *peculiar* she was: manipulative, calculating, private, charming, sexy, sexually hung-up. It all makes sense now.'

Bile rose from my stomach again and I rushed from the

room, but I only had milky tea to bring up. When I came back, Kim was staring out of the window. She was frowning.

'Jane,' she said. 'This is a huge thing you're saying.'

'I know,' I gulped.

'This is your family, Jane. Are you sure?'

'I saw it as clearly as I'm seeing you now.'

'So you're saying that Alan Martello murdered his own daughter, perhaps having made her pregnant as well, and buried her outside his front door?'

'Yes.'

'Have you told the police?'

'No.'

'What will you do?'

I stared at a magpie – one for sorrow – hopping across the soggy lawn.

'Talk to somebody. Claud, probably. Whatever else, I owe him that.'

'I think you do. And Jane, think this through. Don't do anything yet, just think about it. Okay?'

'Jane, it's Caspar, when can we see each other? What are you doing tonight?'

'Oh, I can't, I mean it's not convenient.'

'All right, tomorrow maybe?'

'No, I can't.'

'Are you okay?'

'Yes, fine.'

'All right.' His voice shaded from warmth to polite hurt. 'If you want to see me, call.'

'I will. Caspar.'

'Yes?'

'Nothing. Goodbye.'

★

265

'You look dreadful, are you ill?'

Claud, back from work in a pale grey suit, stood at the door, his face stretched in concern. I knew I looked awful, I'd seen myself in the mirror before setting out and had been shocked by the pinched face that stared back at me. At the sight of Claud, a pain screwed between my eyes. I thought my knees would buckle.

'Come in, come and sit down.'

He led me to the sofa – he wouldn't be so friendly and tender after I'd told him. Oh no. I was the wrecker.

'Tell me what's the trouble.'

His doctor's voice. At another time I would have been irritated by his professional calm. Now I admired it, and welcomed the distance it put between us. I took a deep breath.

'Alan murdered Natalie.'

Horribly, the expression on Claud's face would have been comical under almost any other circumstances. There was complete silence.

'I saw him doing it. I tried to forget, and now I've remembered.'

'What are you talking about? What do you mean you *saw* him?'

I gave him a summary of my therapy with Alex Dermot-Brown. I thought I would be sick again. Claud's face swam in and out of focus. His fingers gripped my shoulder like a desperate claw.

'You're talking about my *father*. You're saying my father murdered my sister. Who was the father of the baby, then?'

I shrugged.

'Excuse me a minute.'

Claud got up and left the room. I heard the sound of

266

running water, then he returned, drying his face on a small towel. He replaced his glasses and looked at me.

'Is there any reason that I shouldn't throw you out?'

'I don't know what to do, Claud.'

He stood there, gazing down at me. I didn't want him to throw me out.

'Can I get you a drink?'

'Yes,' I said in relief.

Claud poured us a tumbler of whisky each and he stood over me while I drank a good half of it. It scalded my throat, and burnt a passage through to my hollow stomach, where it took fire.

'Are you all right?'

I nodded, gulped more whisky. Claud took my hand and I let him straighten my fingers and stroke them. He rubbed my bare ring finger.

'Jane, I'm not happy with this therapy revelation. You've ended your marriage, your sons have left home, you discovered Natalie's body – are you sure you're not just in a turbulent state?'

'You think I'm making it up?'

'You're talking about my *father*, Jane.'

'Sorry. Oh God, I'm sorry sorry sorry. What can I do?'

'Suddenly you're running to me, Jane, and asking for advice?'

I stayed silent. He walked over to the window and stared out into the opaque darkness for fully five minutes, occasionally sipping his whisky. I remained entirely immobile. Trying not to make a sound. Finally he returned to his chair and sat himself opposite me.

'You've got no evidence,' he said.

'I know what I saw, Claud.'

'Yes,' he said doubtfully. 'I'm going to be candid with

you, Jane. I don't believe that my father killed Natalie. But I'll try to help you sort out this muddle that you've got yourself into. I have two reasons. I have my feelings for you, which you know about. And I want to stop a further disaster happening to the family. Which is what will happen, one way or another, if you go around making accusations like this. If we can demonstrate Alan's innocence, so much the better.'

'So what can I do, Claud?'

'That's a good question. No physical evidence. No possible witness, apart from you.' Claud raised his eyebrow as he said this. Now there was another long pause. 'I've got one thought, Jane, for what it's worth. Have you ever been in father's study?'

'Not since I was a girl.'

'Do you know what's up there?'

'His manuscripts, I suppose, and working papers and copies of his books and reference books.'

'And his diaries.'

'Oh, for God's sake, Claud, he's not likely to have murdered his daughter and then written about it.'

'But I'm the one who thinks he's innocent, remember? If you could get hold of the journals for that year, they might give him an alibi for the time when you say you saw him and there might be witnesses who could be checked. If not, there might at least be some suggestions of his feelings in earlier entries.'

'It doesn't seem much of an idea to me.'

'Doesn't it?' he said with bitter sarcasm. 'Well then, I apologise for forcing my help on you. Perhaps you should try someone else, like Theo or Jonah.'

'I'm sorry, Claud, I didn't mean that. I'm grateful I really am. It's a very good idea, how can we do it?'

'When are you going up for the funeral?'

'What? Oh, I don't know, Saturday, I suppose. What about you?'

'I'm going tomorrow. Look, if I have the opportunity, I'll try to get in there. If I can't manage it, you'll have to do it. I'll do anything I can. Anything.'

Claud stood up, and looked down at me. I looked back, unsmiling; our gazes locked, and I couldn't look away. Then his face crumpled, and he sat heavily on the sofa beside me. This time it was me who picked up his hand. His ring was still on his fourth finger, and I turned it slowly. Tears were running in a smooth sheet down his face; carefully I wiped them away, cupped his face in my hands.

'I'm sorry, Claud.'

He groaned and moved towards me and I didn't stop him. How could I? He nuzzled into my neck and I let him. He slipped down and put his streaming face on my lap.

'Jane, Jane, please don't leave me. I can't, I can't, without you. Nothing's the same without you. I can't go through this on my own. You've always been with me. You've always helped me. Always. When I've most needed you, you've been there. You've saved me. Don't go now. Not now.'

'Ssssh.' I stroked his hair, and felt his breath hot against my thigh. This felt like incest. 'Ssssh. There, Claud, don't cry. I can't bear it if you cry.' He lay there like a heavy child, and I raised him up and cradled him against my breast.

Twenty-Nine

I was back where I'd started, in Alex Dermot-Brown's kitchen drinking coffee out of a thick mug. Alex was on the phone to someone, making non-committal noises, um-ing and ah-ing, obviously trying to get the caller off the line. Every so often, he looked across at me and smiled encouragingly. I gazed around the room. It was the kind of kitchen I felt at home in: cluttered, recipes tacked to notice-boards, bills in a pile on the table, newspapers scattered, photographs propped up against candle-sticks, breakfast dishes stacked in the sink, garlic cloves in a bowl and flowers in a vase. I noticed a photograph on the window ledge of a woman with dark hair and a self-conscious smile: his wife, I supposed. I wondered how important Alex's kitchen had been to the whole process of my therapy. Would I have trusted myself to a man whose kitchen was neat and cold?

He put the phone down, and sat down across the table from me.

'More coffee?'

'Please.'

It felt odd to be on an equal level to him, meeting his direct gaze.

'You're looking a bit better.'

This morning I had put on a low-waisted woollen dress and a funny little hat, and I'd applied lipstick and mascara.

'I'm feeling a bit better. I think.'

I'd wept so many tears I felt drained of them.

Alex leant across the table. 'Jane,' he said in his low, pleasant voice, 'you have shown enormous courage, and I'm very proud of you. I know it's been hard.'

'Why don't I feel any better?' I burst out. 'You said it was like bursting an abscess. So why do I feel so terrible? Not just about all of them, but about me. I feel terrible about *me*.'

Alex passed me a tissue.

'Bursting an abscess is painful and brings problems of its own. At a very vulnerable stage in your life, just when you were crossing over from childhood to adulthood, you witnessed something so atrocious that your mind censored it. You can't expect everything to be all right immediately. Knowledge is painful; to take control over your own life is hard; and healing takes time. But you have to realise, Jane, that you can't go back to your previous state. You'll never forget again.'

I shivered.

'What shall I do?'

'You agree that you can't run away from this new knowledge?'

'Yes.'

'Do you think you could live with it and do nothing?'

'No, I suppose not.'

'You do realise, of course, that if you did decide to do nothing, just to live with this terrible memory, that you'd still be exercising your power, making a choice.'

'Yes, I know that.'

'Who matters to you?'

The question took me aback.

'What?'

'I said, "Who matters to you?"'

'Robert and Jerome.' Their names came out of my mouth so quickly I realised that my sons, the horror they would experience from all of this, had been near the front of my mind all the time, suppressed. 'Dad. Kim. And Hana now.'

'Who else?'

'Well, Claud in a way. Still.'

'Who else?'

'After that, lots of people. But not so much.'

'Alan?'

'No, of course not,' I said almost in weariness. I could hardly bear the mention of his name now.

'No one else in particular?'

'Not especially.'

'Nobody?'

'Alex, what is this?'

'What about you?'

'Me?'

I didn't understand.

'Don't you matter to yourself, Jane?'

'Yeah, right, I know what you mean but . . .'

'Don't you think, Jane, that you owe it to yourself to acknowledge this openly. You're thinking of your sons, your father, your ex-husband. You are so busy thinking of the world beyond you that you haven't thought of the most important thing of all.'

'But I have to think of everyone else. I'm wrecking their world.'

Alex leant further forward, stared at me intently. 'I have dealt with cases similar to yours before,' he said. 'In all of them, women have had to be brave and determined. They have not just had to deal with their own considerable pain but with the simple disbelief of the people they know, of the authorities. You don't just owe it to yourself to go through with this, you owe it to them, Jane, all those women who know the pain of repressing their memories, and all those who have found the courage to speak out. Don't cry.'

His voice became gentle again. He handed me another tissue and I blew noisily into it.

'I don't suppose you'd let me have a cigarette?'

He smiled. 'We could go into the garden.'

Outside it was damp and cold. Mud seeped up through the balding lawn. Snowdrops wilted in pots by the door. I put a cigarette in my mouth and struck a match; it flared and blew out. I struck again, shielding the flame with my hand. Inhaled gratefully.

'Those other women,' I said at last, 'what did they do?'

'Most of them,' Alex replied, 'remembered being abused themselves, not witnessing an atrocity like you. We're starting to discover that the mind is capable of a self-protective amnesia. But the hidden memories are not lost. They are like files in a computer which can be recovered with the right triggers. Some kinds of therapy can retrieve this information.'

'Yes, but what did they *do*? After they knew.'

'Some did nothing, of course, except cut themselves off from their abusers.'

'And the others?'

'They brought their injuries into the open. They confronted their abusers; they even went to the police. They refused to remain victims.'

I lit another cigarette and walked to the end of the garden. Alex made no attempt to follow me. He watched as I paced. Eventually I said:

'So you think I should confront Alan?'

He said nothing, just looked at me.

'Or go to the police?'

Still Alex said nothing. All at once I felt massively angry. Rage danced across my eyeballs. I felt itchily hot in the cold air.

'You have no idea,' I shouted into his face, 'what you are asking me to do, no idea. This is my family we're talking about here. My whole life. I won't have anywhere I belong any more. I'll be an outcast.' My face stung with tears. 'How can I just go to the police and tell them about Alan. He was like my father. I *loved* him.'

I stopped on a wail, and there was silence. A few gardens away I heard the thin gulpy scream of a baby who's been crying a long time, and isn't going to stop. I fumbled in my pocket for my cigarettes, lit one, and incompetently dabbed at my messed-up face with a soggy tissue.

'Here.' Alex gave me another one.

'Sorry. I'm ravaging your tissue store.'

'It's all right. I have a tissue mountain. I get an EC grant for maintaining it.'

We turned back to the house. At the door, Alex stopped and put his hand on my shoulder.

'I'm not *asking* you to do anything, you know. Of course you have to decide that for yourself. I'm just asking you if you can do nothing.'

Inside, Alex made us some more coffee, while I went to the bathroom to wash my face. I looked terrible. Mascara ran in rivulets down my face, my hair straggled out from under my hat and stuck to my snotty cheeks in strands, my eyes were puffy and my nose was red from the cold. 'Pull yourself together,' I muttered to the woman in the mirror, and watched a mirthless rictus spread over

274

her grubby face. I whistled a tune: 'You'll never get to heaven.' A song all of us used to sing at the Stead. Never mind, it had been a long time since I'd believed in heaven.

Alex had put a tin of biscuits on the table. I dunked a shortbread into my coffee and ate it ravenously. When I had finished, he picked up the cups and took them to the sink. The conversation was over.

'Thanks Alex,' I said as I got on my bike.

As I reached Camden Lock, I knew there was something I had to tell him, so I cycled back and knocked on the door. He opened it almost at once, with the smallest flicker of surprise.

'I'll go forward,' I said.

He didn't move, just gazed at me steadily. Then he nodded.

'So be it,' he said.

It sounded alarmingly biblical. I cycled away without another word.

Thirty

I had been ready for half an hour when the car horn sounded outside the house. It was snowing, beautiful snow that wafted down in large flakes, settled like feathers on trees and houses and parked cars. In the half-light, London looked pure and serene, and I sat by the window smoking and thinking. Rusting vans, dustbins, empty milk bottles had become clean white shapes. All sounds were softened. Even the security screens on the house across the road were a sparkling grid. Tonight it would be muddy slush. Tonight, Martha would be lying beside her only daughter. I was glad she was dead.

I put on the coat I had bought before going to kiss Caspar in Highgate Cemetery. I pulled on a brown felt hat and brown leather gloves, and went out to meet Claud. He had insisted on driving all the way down to fetch me. In this weather. He said he wanted to make sure I came.

We were silent at first. I smoked and watched London turn to countryside. He fiddled with tapes and drove at a steady seventy up the M1. The windscreen wipers methodically pushed snow into compacted lines of grime.

'Well?' I said, finally.

'Well, what?'

'You know.'

Claud frowned.

'Alan has been ensconced up in his study the whole

time I've been at the Stead. And when he's not there, the door is firmly locked.'

'Jesus,' I said.

'Don't worry, Jane, together we can sort out something.'

I just grunted in assent, watched Birmingham with its sprawled blocks of flats pass by. Tried not to think about cigarettes. I hadn't thought what I was going to say to Alan. I hadn't even prepared myself for the sight of him. I fumbled in my bag and found a comb which I dragged through my hair before rearranging the felt hat. Claud glanced sideways at me.

'Nervous?'

It occurred to me that Claud was the only member of the Martello family with whom I could now sit like this.

'You've been good over all this,' I said.

He stared ahead.

'I hope so,' he replied.

Under the thin spread of snow, Natalie's grave still looked neat and new. There were spring flowers – snowdrops, aconites – pushed into the holes of a stone vase. I wondered if anyone would come to tend it now. Beside it was an ugly clay hole, agape. The last bitter snow fell into it like spittle.

A small crowd of mourners in dark clothes stood and watched as Martha's four sons carried her coffin towards us. They looked sombrely handsome under their burden, generic grieving sons carrying the remains of their beloved mother. A man in front of me took off his hat, and I recognised him suddenly as Jim Weston, an improbability in a long dark coat. I'd last seen him at the side of another grave. Sort of grave. I took off my hat, too. Snow drizzled onto my hair. I placed myself right at the edge of the crowd of mourners to avoid any chance of encountering Alan. Later, he'd want to give me a long hard hug and mutter intimately into my ear about his loss. All that could wait. I felt a nudge beside me and turned. It was Helen Auster.

'I just wanted to show my face,' she said with a little smile.

I gave her a quick hug while the familiar words were being intoned once more.

I heard Alan before I saw him. As Martha's coffin was lowered into the waiting pit, a howl ripped the air. All heads moved forward. Suddenly, through a gap, the scene became clear. Alan was leant over the coffin, roaring into it or at it. His greasy grey hair was whipped back in the wind; in spite of the chill, he was wearing no coat, and his black suit was grubby and unbuttoned. Tears cascaded down his blotchy face unchecked and he lifted up his cane and shook it in the air like an unrehearsed King Lear.

'Martha!' he yelled. 'Martha!'

The four sons closed in on him; they stood tall and straight around their fat, wild father, who was addled with grief and drink. Alan put his hands over his face; tears streamed through them as he groaned and wept. The rest of us remained silent. This was a one-man show.

'Forgive me,' he yelled. 'I'm sorry.'

Claud put his arm around Alan, who leant against him and mumbled and wept. A woman next to me whom I'd never seen before started crying quietly into her demure hanky. Erica, standing back from the scene with Paul and Dad beside her, blew her nose noisily and gave a single hiccuping wail. For my part, I felt clear-headed and as cold as the day. I had already said my last goodbye to

Martha. Now I was about to defy her last request to me. *Look after Alan.*

Cold pebbles of soil splattered onto the coffin. Martha and Natalie lay side by side, and Alan wept noisily on.

Helen put her arm through mine and we peeled away from the group, stepping off the path and among the gravestones.

'You don't look well,' she said.

'I haven't been well. I think I'm better now, though. How are *you* doing?'

She smiled.

'I wanted to tell you. We've found a use for one of our lists. We're going to make an announcement on Monday. We're asking every male person who was present in the environs of the Stead on the twenty-seventh of July, the day after the party, the day when Natalie was last seen, to give a blood sample for DNA fingerprinting.'

'To find the father?'

'Maybe.'

'And the murderer?'

'It wouldn't be proof in itself.'

'Still, it sounds a positive step.'

'We think so.'

We walked along for a few more moments in silence. The graveyard was empty now except for us. I forced myself to speak:

'But how are *you*, Helen?'

'Me?'

She was obviously thrown.

'You know, of course?' she said.

'Yes.'

Helen stopped and sat on the edge of a plinth bearing

279

a stone urn half covered with a stone cloth. She looked up at me, almost a supplicant.

'What do you want me to say?'

'Helen, I'm not looking for some sort of justification from you. My only concern is how you are.'

'Me? I'm totally confused. My life has been turned upside-down.' She took a tissue from her pocket, clumsily unfolding it in the cold, and blew her nose. 'I'm behaving unprofessionally. I'm breaking my marriage up. I promise you I've never done anything like this before and I feel I'll have to tell Barry – that's my husband – about this soon. And it sounds awful, but I feel happy and excited as well. Of course, I needn't tell you. You of all people know what Theo is like.'

'Yes.'

'I'm suddenly thinking about things differently, seeing new possibilities. I feel a bit drunk with it all.'

'What are you going to do?'

'I keep planning different things. What will probably happen is that we'll wait until this inquiry is over and then I'll tell my husband and move out and then we'll move in together.'

'Is that what Theo has said?'

'Yes.' She glanced up at me again. 'You don't look as if you approve.'

'It's not a matter of approval.' I sat down, very uncomfortably, on the edge of the plinth, next to Helen. 'Look, I don't want to give advice and you may be completely right in what you say will happen. I just think you ought to be wary of the Martello family. They're fascinating and seductive and they draw people in and I think they can be deceptive.'

'But *you're* a member of the Martello family.'

'Yes, I know, and all Cretans are liars.'

'What?'

'Never mind. I don't know what I'm saying. Don't go up without a parachute, something like that.'

'But you loved Theo, didn't you?'

'How do you know?'

She was silent.

'Just be careful about smashing up your life and career,' I said.

She turned to me with an expression that reminded me unbearably of a sad small child.

'I thought you would just say congratulations or good luck.'

Then she broke down and cried as I held her.

'It's so stupid and embarrassing I can hardly admit it,' she said. 'I had this fantasy of us being friends and being brought closer by this.'

'But look, look,' I said, holding her damp face, 'it has brought us closer.'

'No, I meant more than that. Almost like sisters.'

I hugged her.

'I need a friend more than I need a sister,' I whispered to the back of her head.

I need not have worried about how to meet Alan; he didn't want to meet me, or anyone else. By the time I arrived back at the house, he had scuttled, like a giant crab with its old shell cracked, up to his study. 'To write,' he had said.

The kitchen and the living room were crowded with mourners; some I recognised and others I had never seen before. I thought I glimpsed the beaky nose and high cheekbones of Luke, but what would he be doing here?

Jim Weston shuffled up, looking ill at ease in his tight wide-lapelled brown suit. It could almost have been his demob suit. He clutched my sleeve and murmured something, but I didn't catch it. Conversations hummed around me, meaningless sounds. I saw mouths open and close. People were wiping their eyes. Laughing. Pushing sandwiches down their throats. Lifting delicate cups of tea between forefinger and thumb. Bodies jostled against me.

I was hot; my legs itched in their tights; my hands were sweaty; there was a nervous tic pulsing invisibly under my left eye. Pain flowered in my head. Theo was standing in front of me, frowning. Paul was holding me by the shoulder, saying something in my ear about Dad, and needing to leave soon. The vicar – a young man with an Adam's apple jiggling nervously above his dog collar – shook my sweaty hand with his sweaty hand and spoke vaguely about peace at last. Luke – it *was* Luke – asked if I was all right and someone passed me a glass of water. Peggy was in grey and Erica was in navy blue. Dad sat in a chair near the patio door and occasionally a hat would bob down to his level and then come back to its own. He looked old and miserable and aggrieved.

I put my coat back on and walked briskly around the garden. I smoked the rest of my packet of cigarettes and returned to the house only when I saw people starting their cars and driving away.

We were a strange, temporary household, lacking our usual sense of common purpose. Paul and Erica drove back to London almost straight away. The next morning Jonah and his family left, and Theo drove Frances to the station. Fred and a worried-looking Lynn stayed on. And Claud, of course. What were we all doing there? The material remnants of Martha's life didn't need ordering. On the morning of the funeral we looked through her drawers and wardrobes. Every item of clothing had been cleaned, folded and stowed. Some were in cardboard boxes with destinations marked in her clear, assertive handwriting. Her workroom seemed empty but that was because it had been given a terminal organisation. I knew that she had completed her last book a couple of months before she'd died and she had used her last months systematically. Notes and many of her old papers had been thrown away. A couple of drawers opened at random showed that every file, every stapler was in its place. This was Martha's last great gesture. There was not a corner of the house where we could catch her ghost unawares, in dishabille. Before she had departed, she had left everything signed, sealed and as she wanted it. The realisation of it was the only thing that made me smile that day.

The brothers had nothing to do there. They didn't talk much – Fred was scarcely more sober than his father – but I believed that the three of them could not imagine the idea of leaving Alan alone in that house. As it turned out, they never would.

Lunch was a dismal affair. Bread, cheese, wine and some weirdly bright conversation, with even Alan joining in occasionally. This wasn't the real world. We were teetering along a ledge between existences. The acknowledged old life organised by Martha had not been relinquished, and what the new life might be, nobody spoke of or imagined. Did they think we could all just go and leave Alan to run this house alone?

When we were finished, Claud almost physically prevailed on Alan to stay downstairs.

'You and me and Jane are going for a quick walk,' he said.

Alan looked at the two of us with a start, and I was scarcely less surprised.

'Are we?' I asked.

'Yes, it's a bracing day,' Claud said cheerily.

I looked out of the window and saw lowering clouds.

'Let's all get our coats on,' he continued.

He helped Alan on with his waterproof, his hat, scarf and boots, and put his old stick in his fist. We pulled on old coats that we found hanging there (with a shiver I realised that I was wearing one of Martha's) and Alan was firmly led out between us. As we made our way across the lawn, Claud talked about the walk he had taken the day before, how he thought he had seen an owl's nest in an ash by the drive and he thought we might take a look at it. Suddenly, he slapped his forehead.

'Bloody hell, I forgot the binoculars. Nip back and get them will you, Janey?'

We were married again, it seemed.

'Where are they?'

'In the boot room. Which I locked, of course.'

'What on earth for?' asked Alan.

'Hang on, I'll give you my keys,' Claud said, pushing into his various pockets. 'No, sorry, I must have put them somewhere. Dad, could you give Janey your keys?'

Alan took a large bunch of keys from his pocket and gave them to Claud, who passed them over to me without any traceable expression except for a possible flicker of irritation at his own forgetfulness. They say doctors have to be actors as well.

'See you in a minute,' I said and turned and ran back up the lawn.

★

Hall, first floor, up the steep stairs that led to the large attic. My legs were trembling so much I thought I might fall and I gripped the handrail tightly. I tried several keys until one fitted and I pushed the door open and stepped into Alan's space. It was sacrosanct and indeed it oddly resembled a church nave, lodged as it was under the roof. There were skylights on each incline and they diffused a grey light through the space that gently illuminated it, even before I switched the light on. I had been in here only a few times in my life. This was where Alan wrote and pretended to write. If it had been empty it would have seemed large. As it was, it was cramped and almost impassable. The daily bills, receipts, letters from publishers and universities, junk mail, pamphlets, requests from students who were studying him, old newspapers, postcards from his sons, invitations, many letters that had not even been opened. I checked a postmark at random: 1993. I stared around at the piles of books higgledy-piggledy on the floor, the scrunched-up tissues in the corner, the line of coffee cups growing mould, the nearly empty whisky bottle on the window ledge.

Alan's desk was the one clear space in the room. His ancient heavy German typewriter squatted like a tank at its centre. Next to it was a beaker full of pens and pencils and a blank memo pad. On the shelf above were dozens of copies of *The Town Drain* in a Babel of languages. It had always been a difficult title to translate. I pulled open some drawers. Notebooks with fragmented jottings, unused postcards, typewriter ribbons, drawing pins, a stapler, old batteries and a few entirely incomprehensible objects. I looked around the room. There was a grey metal filing cabinet against one wall, and right along another wall was a row of low cupboards. You don't keep diaries in a filing cabinet. I opened cupboard doors. The first contained large cardboard boxes piled on top of each other. I could return to them later, if necessary. The next contained piles of old files arranged on shelves. The next had only a large box file on which was written: *Arthur's Bosom (provisional title)*. I peeped inside and found just a few pieces of paper, covered in Alan's thick scrawl. Snatches of dialogue, unconnected sentences, descriptions trailing away. This was the great novel, Alan's long-awaited comeback, the master-work he climbed the stairs so regularly to attend to. In spite of myself, I felt a spasm of pity for him. What a life.

The next cupboard was crammed with magazines and newspapers, probably old reviews and interviews. The next was what I was looking for. Piled along the shelves were dozens of hard-backed notebooks. I pulled one out at random. On its cover was written *1970*. I was close. I thumbed through the pages, all of which were densely filled in with the events of a day. I picked another volume and then another. They were all the same. At least he had kept up one form of writing. From far down in the house I could hear voices, the chink of china. Nobody was coming up here.

I quickly found the volume I was looking for. I opened it and a piece of paper fluttered out and landed at my feet. I hurriedly flicked through the volume but when I reached July I found something I hadn't expected, the stubs of pages which had been ripped from the book. From the beginning of July until September there was nothing. Then the entries resumed as before. I felt stymied. Almost as a reflex, I bent down to pick up the slip of paper that had fallen from the book. It was a yellowing piece of lined paper, full size, folded in half. I opened it out. It looked as if it had been hastily torn from a notebook because it was ripped jaggedly across the top. I instantly recognised the blue-biro handwriting as Natalie's. I still knew her handwriting as well as I knew my own. It read:

I don't know what the point is of avoiding me. We're in the same house! You know what you've done to me. You know what's happening. Do you think you can do nothing? Do you think you can get away with this? Okay, don't talk to me. So long as you know that I'm going to do what I have to even if it brings the whole family down. I'll tell everything and I don't care then if I have to kill myself. I still can't believe it. I thought families were about protection.

Natalie

I felt entirely calm now. I refolded Natalie's note, and slipped it back inside the diary volume. I turned and saw Alan standing in the doorway. He was still wearing his large coat and the rubber boots which had masked his footsteps on the stair carpet. He was breathing heavily from his climb.

'I think you'd be more likely to find the binoculars downstairs.'

'I wasn't looking for the binoculars. Where's Claud?'

'Downstairs. If you're going to break into my study, Jane, you ought to be more careful about switching the light on. From the wood opposite it was not unlike the Blackpool Illuminations. What are you doing here, Jane? I see you've been reading my great works.'

'I saw you, Alan.'

'Indeed?'

'I saw you kill Natalie. I saw you strangle her. I forgot and I've remembered again. And now I've got proof.'

'What do you mean "saw me"? What proof?'

He approached me. I tried to move past him but he caught me by the wrist, and the book fell to the floor. I cried out in pain as he pushed me down into a chair. I struggled to get up and he pushed me back down with his other hand on my neck, then both hands.

'Is this what you saw? Was it like this?'

I couldn't speak. I couldn't breathe. I was rocked by spasms as I fought for breath. Then he let go. As I coughed and gasped, he slowly bent down and picked up the diary. He quickly found Natalie's note and opened it up and read it. He replaced it in the book and closed it. He handed it to me.

'You raped your daughter and killed her,' I said. 'But I saw it.'

Alan started to blubber messily. Then he struck himself on the head repeatedly, while snotty liquid poured down his cheeks.

'You did, didn't you Alan?' I shouted. 'You fucked your daughter and murdered her?'

A thin trickle of blood made its way down his face. He touched the blood with a finger and held it up.

'Guilty. Guilty guilty guilty!'

Then he subsided. He slumped down on the floor and sat there in silence, apparently unaware even of my presence. I got up from the chair, clutching the book, and tiptoed past him.

Thirty-One

I didn't want to meet anybody. I crept down the stairs and out of the back door. I slipped the notebook safely into the inside pocket of my thick coat and strode away from the house. I chose one of the walks I knew best, one of the longest, most exposed and one of the most familiar, which I knew I could manage without any thought. I walked through woods and then up hills with winds so strong they almost blew me over and, on this cold, blustery day, such a view that I could have sworn that I could see all the way to the Beacons in Wales.

I went on and on, never turning for home. When it was getting dark I reached a pub and I phoned the Stead and told Claud not to expect me back for supper and I'd explain everything later. I ate a lasagne with some warm frothy beer, followed by an astringent rhubarb crumble with custard and black coffee. The woman behind the bar showed me a map and I was able to walk back to the Stead along the road under the illumination of the fullest of moons. By the time I heard my boots crunching on the drive, all the lights were out. I went straight to my room and fell heavily asleep, the diary under my pillow.

By the time I came down in the morning it was after nine. I could see Fred and Lynn outside, loading the car. Claud was fixing a shelf in the kitchen. I asked him where Alan was and he told me that Alan and Theo had driven into town. Shopping, he supposed. He gestured to the oven. Inside was a pan with eggs, tomatoes, bacon. I devoured them with tea and orange juice. Would it be all right if I borrowed Claud's car for the morning? Yes. He asked if I had anything to tell him. Not yet, I said. I swallowed the last of the tea, took his keys and went to the car, hugging Fred and Lynn on the way.

At the front desk of Kirklow police station, I asked for Helen Auster. She was away.

'Can I see whoever's standing in for her, then?'

I looked at the posters until a thickset young man appeared and introduced himself as Detective Sergeant Braswell. I showed him the diary and Natalie's note and in a few sentences explained where I had found it. He looked startled and led me through the station to the office of Kirklow CID, pleasingly modern and industrial in design. A hum of conversation stopped as I entered and several people looked at me in curiosity. Braswell led me through them and out to an interview room. He asked if he could take the diary for a moment. Within a very short time he returned with two more men, the younger of them carrying a blue plastic moulded chair which he placed in a corner. The other, obviously the senior officer, was a slight man, with a florid face and dull brown hair, combed flat with obvious effort. He stepped forward and shook my hand.

'I'm Detective Superintendent Wilks. I'm in charge of this inquiry,' he said. 'And I think you've met Detective Constable Turnbull before.'

I nodded at the young man hovering in the corner. We all sat as Wilks continued.

'DS Braswell, assisted by DC Turnbull, will do any

interviewing that is necessary. I just wanted to sit in for a preliminary chat, if that's agreeable to you. First, is there anything we can get you? Tea? Coffee?'

Turnbull was dispatched to get four teas.

'Where's Detective Sergeant Auster?' I asked.

'On leave,' Wilks said.

'In the middle of the case?'

'DS Auster is no longer on the case,' said Wilks. 'At her own request.'

'Oh.'

'Now, Mrs Martello, can you tell us about this diary?'

I described in detail how I had searched Alan's study and found it and the note inside.

'Yes,' said Wilks, lifting up the note which was now encased in a plastic folder. 'There is no doubt that that is the handwriting of Natalie Martello?'

'None at all. There is still lots of her writing in trunks at home if you want to check it.'

'Good. You say that Alan Martello found you there. What happened?'

I described the squalid scene as calmly as I could, the hands on my neck, the collapse, the guilty guilty guilty.

'Why did you search Alan Martello's study, Mrs Martello?'

'I'm sorry?'

'On the face of it, it seems odd to suspect one's father-in-law of murdering his daughter. Why did you suspect him?'

I took a deep breath. This was the bit I had been dreading. Now I told the full story of the therapy with Alex, my cheeks burning hot. I had expected the officers to smile and exchange glances but Wilks's frown of concentration never faltered and he remained silent except when he asked two or three questions about the circumstances of the therapy – how often it was conducted, where, in what way. When I had finished, there was a silence. Wilks broke it.

'So, Mrs Martello, let us get this straight. You are claiming to have witnessed the murder?'

'Yes.'

'Are you willing to make an official statement to that effect?'

'Yes.'

'With the possibility of appearing in court as a prosecution witness.'

'Yes.'

'Good.'

Wilks stood up and put his hands in his pockets. I looked around at the three officers.

'I was afraid you might laugh at me,' I said.

'Why should we do that?' asked Wilks.

'I thought you might not believe that I had regained the memory of seeing Alan.'

'You obviously had some doubts about it yourself.'

'What do you mean?'

Wilks shrugged. 'You didn't come and see us with your suspicions. Instead, you undertook a personal investigation, in the course of which material evidence seems to have been handled both by you and Alan Martello.'

'That's not very grateful.'

'I don't want to seem ungracious but it might have been better if you'd come straight to us. You might have been hurt as well.'

'So what happens now?'

'If you're willing, and I hope you are, DS Braswell and DC Turnbull here will take a detailed statement from you, which will probably take a couple of hours. I should add that you are fully entitled to have the advice of a lawyer before making any statement. We can supply a name or two if you want.'

'That's all right. And what will you do then? Will you bring Alan in for questioning?'

'No.'

'Why on earth not?'

Wilks gave a smile, beneath which was just the smallest trace of puzzlement.

'Because he's already here.'

'How on earth did you get him so quickly?'

'He came by himself. He said he wanted to make a statement. He was clocked into the station at 09.12 and twenty-five minutes later, Alan Edward Dugdale Martello confessed, unprompted, to the murder of his daughter, Natalie.'

'What?'

'He's currently in a cell in the basement pending the preparation of charges.'

I was stunned.

'Has he . . .? Did he say, well, why and how he did it?'

'No. He said nothing else.'

'Are you going to charge him?'

'False confessions are always a possibility. Some wicked cynics have even accused the police of encouraging them. However, off the record,' Wilks raised an eyebrow at me, 'having heard what you have to say and seen the diary and the letter, I now feel disposed to prefer charges. But let's wait until we have your statement, shall we? Guy and Stuart will sort out any problems you may have. See you later.'

DC Turnbull rummaged in a cardboard box at his feet

and produced a bulky cassette recorder with two sets of spools. While Turnbull noisily searched through some cassette cases, DS Braswell was slipping a carbon between a thick pad of forms. He caught my eye and smiled.

'You thought you'd done the hard bit. You haven't seen the forms you've got to go through.'

Thirty-Two

At nine o'clock in the evening of the day after Alan's confession, I was phoned at home by a reporter from the *Daily Mail*. What he described as 'a source' had told the newspaper that Alan Martello was about to be charged with the murder of his pregnant daughter, twenty-five years after the event, because I had suddenly remembered having witnessed it. Would I be prepared to give the newspaper an interview? I was so shocked that I had to sit down before I could speak, but I managed to control my voice. I said that, as far as I understood, if Alan was charged, it would be because of his own confession. The man seemed sure of his ground. He asked me if it was true that I had witnessed the murder.

For a moment my mind was blank. Should I lie? Would it be best to co-operate? I thought of my last venture into the public realm, with my doomed attempt to defend my hostel to the local community that it was designed to benefit. That settled it. I told the reporter that it would be best to deal directly with the police. Then an idea occurred to me. I said that, since a charge was probably imminent, the matter was now *sub judice*. The man seemed dissatisfied but he let me get off the line.

I phoned Alex Dermot-Brown immediately and told him what had happened. I expected him to be sympathetic and shocked but he laughed.

'Really?' was his only reaction.

'It's terrible, isn't it?' I said.

Alex didn't seem to think it was all that terrible. He said it was only to be expected and it was what I had taken on when I decided to do something about Alan. I felt dissatisfied, somehow. He resumed in a cheerful tone.

'I'm glad you rang, because I was going to get in touch with you. Are you doing anything tomorrow afternoon?'

'Nothing especially urgent. What is it? Do you want me to come for an extra session?'

'No, I want to take you somewhere. I'll pick you up at about eleven thirty.'

'What's all this about?'

'I'll tell you on the way. Bye.'

I was tempted to ring Alex back and tell him I was busy, but I couldn't be bothered and, anyway, I was curious.

It took a couple of pills to get me to sleep, which meant that I awoke with a headache. I had a few aspirin with my black coffee and grapefruit. I showered and, since I didn't know where I was going, dressed in clothes selected for neutrality. Dark, longish skirt, grey sweater, discreet necklace, a touch of lipstick and eye-liner, flat shoes. If I looked like a mental patient, then at least it was one who could safely be released back into the community. When I was ready, it was only ten thirty, so I fidgeted for an hour, smoking, listening to music, inattentively reading a novel. I should have gone out and worked in the garden, planted some bulbs, but I thought I might not hear the front door. The electric bell wasn't working.

Finally, there was a knock at the door. Alex was wearing a most improbable suit. He had shaved. His hair was neatly brushed.

'You look smart,' I said. 'This isn't a date, is it?'

'At eleven thirty in the morning? You look smart too. Come on.'

Alex drove a Volvo. There was a baby seat in the back and every surface was strewn with crisp packets and cassettes and empty cassette cases. He swept some of them off the passenger seat and onto the floor to make space for me. A flashing light instructed me to put my seat belt on and we were off, south, down Kentish Town Road.

'So where are we going?'

Alex switched on the cassette player. The car was filled with some Vivaldiesque music. For months I'd been curious about any stray details of Alex's private life that I could garner, and now, here I was in his car, with his tapes, Miles Davis and Albinoni, Blur and the Beach Boys, written in his own handwriting. For me it was as improbable as if I were to find myself in a car being driven by, I don't know, someone like Neil Young, with the added feeling that there was something forbidden, incestuous about it.

'I'm giving the keynote speech at a conference,' Alex said. 'I thought you might be interested.'

'Why *me*?'

'Because it's about recovered memory.'

'*What*?'

I was stunned.

'Are you serious?'

'Of course.'

'But I don't understand, is it something to do with *me*?'

Alex laughed.

'No, Jane, this is a subject I have an interest in.'

For the rest of the journey I stared out of the window. Alex drove into the basement car-park of the Clongowes

Hotel on Kingsway. We went up in the lift and walked across the lobby to a conference room with a sign outside saying 'Recovered Memory: Survivors and Accusers'. Alex signed us both in at the reception and I received a badge bearing my name, written in ballpoint pen. I was apparently not expected. In the hall were rows of desks, as if an exam were about to be taken. Most of them were occupied and Alex steered me to a seat at the back.

'Stay here,' he said. 'I'll be with you again in twenty minutes or so. There are one or two people I would like you to meet.'

He winked at me, then walked down the aisle towards the front. His progress was slow because he greeted almost everybody he passed, shaking hands, hugging, patting backs. A beautiful woman, dark, with olive skin, clattered towards him and gave him a hug, one high heel cocked up behind her thigh. I felt a twinge of jealousy and caught myself. I had had months of Alex to myself and it was something of a shock to see him in public. It was like seeing Dad at the office, and realising with a pang that he had a life outside his relationship with me. I made myself think of something else. On the desk in front of me was a white ballpoint pen and a small lined pad of paper, both bearing the inscription 'Mindset'. There was a folder bearing the title of the conference and inside was an assembly of documents. One contained a list of delegates, about a hundred of them. Against each name was the person's qualification. There were doctors, psychiatrists, social workers, representatives of voluntary organisations and a number of people, all women, labelled simply as 'survivors'. I supposed that I too was a survivor, and an accuser as well, for that matter.

At the front of the hall was a table with a jug of water

and four glasses. Beside it was a lectern. Displaying the charming diffidence with which I was already familiar, Alex shook hands with a final delegate and made his way to the lectern. He gave the microphone a little tap which echoed round the hall.

'It's twelve fifteen, so I suppose we'd better get underway. I'd like to welcome you all to the 1995 Recovered Memory conference, organised by Mindset, and I'm glad to see so many familiar faces here. This is *your* conference, and, like last year, it's been designed to maximise the delegates' participation, so I'll try to stem my natural eloquence, or at least that's what I call it. I'm aware of being in an audience with many distinguished fellow analysts.' There was a dutiful ripple of laughter. Alex coughed nervously, sipped from a glass of water (I was shocked to see his hand trembling) and continued.

'I'm just going to give a brief introductory talk, setting out some of our agenda. Then Dr Kit Hennessey will be giving an outline of some recent research. Then we break for lunch, which I'm told you'll find outside and to the right. Just hand in the token that you'll find in your folder. After lunch we split up for a series of workshops. Those are in different conference rooms all on this floor. You'll find the details also in your folder. I think that's about all.

'Now for my brief contribution.'

Alex opened the slim document folder he was carrying and removed some papers. This was a different Alex from the easygoing, enabling, ironic listener with whom I had spent so much of the last few months. He was passionate, unambiguous, polemical, from his opening statement: 'Recovered memory is one of the greatest hidden scandals of our time.' He spoke of how generations of people, especially women, had been compelled to hide traumas they had suffered in their early lives. When they had spoken of them they had been disbelieved, vilified, marginalised, diagnosed, lobotomised. He admitted with regret that the very medical authorities best qualified to expose the horror, the psychiatrists and analysts, and the criminal authorities, the police and lawyers, had become collaborators in its suppression.

'Law and science,' he said, 'have been misused against these victims just as in the past they have been misused against other groups wherever it has suited the interests of authority to deny the rights of victimised minorities. So-called scientific objectivity, so-called burdens of proof have themselves been used as instruments of oppression. We owe it to these victims of abuse, who have shown the courage to remember, to say, "We believe you, we support you".'

I knew now why Alex had brought me here. I had felt mad and strange and an outcast, trapped in my own private sufferings. This was part of what Alex meant by going public: the discovery that I was not alone, that other people had experienced what I had experienced. With a pang that almost made me cry as I sat there at the back of the hall doodling on the shiny dossier cover, I was reminded that this was what I had loved about Natalie: she had validated me by feeling the things I had felt. Had I, too, been buried when she had been buried?

Alex had finished. He asked if there were any questions and several hands went up. One man, a deputy director of social services, thanked Alex for his speech but said that the one omission from his survey was the political dimension. Legislation was needed. Why was there no MP among the delegates, or even a local councillor? Alex shrugged and smiled. He agreed with the delegate, he said. From personal connections, he knew a number of politicians who were sympathetic to their cause, but the implications of findings about repressed memory were so great, and the entrenched medical and legal authorities so powerful, that they were extremely unwilling to go public with any form of commitment.

'We have to push the issue another way,' he said. 'We need some high-profile legal cases to demonstrate that this phenomenon cannot be ignored. When that happens, and public awareness has increased, it will seem less dangerous. Perhaps when the bandwagon is rolling the politicians will jump on it.'

There was a round of applause. As it faded, a woman stood up. She was strikingly short, dowdily dressed, in her late forties. I expected a personal testimony of remembering abuse but she identified herself as Thelma Scott, a consultant psychiatrist at St Andrew's in central London. Alex gave her a wry nod of recognition.

'I think we all know who you are, Dr Scott.'

'I've been looking at your list of events, Dr Dermot-Brown,' she said, holding the conference folder. '"Believing and Enabling", "Listen to Us", "Legal Obstacles", "The Doctor's Dilemma", "Protecting the Patient".'

She paused.

'Yes?' said Alex, with just a hint of exasperation.

'Is this a forum for discussion and inquiry? I don't see any discussions planned here about the problems of diagnosis, the possible unreliability of recovered memory, the protection for families against false accusations.'

'That's not necessary, Dr Scott,' Alex said. 'The whole history of this subject is about protection for families against *true* accusations. We don't yet face the problem of having to *discourage* people from making accusations of abuse. The pressures against authentic sufferers are so great that it is almost impossible for them even to face up to their recovered memories, let alone make public assertions as to their legal rights.'

'And I notice another absence from the delegates,' Dr Scott said.

'Yes?'

'There is not a single neurologist here. Wouldn't it be interesting to have a contribution about the mechanics of memory?'

Alex gave an exasperated sigh. 'We don't know about the mechanics of tumour development. That doesn't prevent us from knowing that cigarette-smoking increases the risk of cancer. I'm fascinated by current neurological research, Thelma, and I share your concern. I wish we had a scientific model for the workings of memory and its suppression in the brain but the limitations of our knowledge are not going to prevent me doing my job as a doctor and helping patients in need. Now, are there any more questions?'

The proceedings petered out and, after introducing Dr Hennessey, a tall, slim man with an epically large file of papers under his arm, Alex slipped off the platform. Nodding at one or two people, he tiptoed along the side of the hall and sat down beside me. I smiled at him.

'So you haven't persuaded everybody?'

He grimaced. 'Don't mind her,' he murmured. 'I suppose that Galileo had people like Dr Scott pursuing him, except that they had instruments of torture at their disposal. There's a great myth that you can persuade people by reason alone. It's been said that the only way that a radical new scientific idea gets accepted is when all the old scientists who were committed to the old idea die off. Now, let's sneak out. There's somebody I want you to meet.'

As we tiptoed towards the door, Alex beckoned to a woman leaning against the wall and she followed us out. The ante-room outside was deserted.

'I wanted two of my stars to meet each other,' said Alex. 'Jane, this is Melanie Foster; Mel, this is Jane Martello. Why don't you two pop into the next room and grab some lunch before the mob arrives?'

Melanie was wearing a crisp, grey business suit that made me feel shabby. I guessed that she was five years older than me, but her face had many fine wrinkles, like a crushed newspaper that had been straightened out. Her hair was cut short, grey and coarse in texture, almost like the strands in a horse's tail. She wore granny glasses and had a slightly insecure smile. I took to her at once. We looked at each other, nodded and headed for the food.

A buffet was laid out and servants in white jackets were chatting in groups, waiting for the rush. I was going to take nothing but a piece of cheese and bread but Melanie loaded a large spoonful of spicy pasta onto my plate and I gave in with a giggle.

'You look thin,' she said. 'Here.' She heaped tomato salad beside the pasta, then a stack of beanshoots, until I cried 'When!' in mock horror. 'You've got to keep me company.'

We took our trays over to a small table in a corner where there was no chance of anybody joining us.

'I suppose I ought to ask how you know Alex,' I began.

'Yes,' said Melanie in a firm, schoolmarmish tone. 'But I must begin by saying that I know why *you* know Alex.'

'Really?' I said, shocked. 'Isn't it meant to be private?'

'Well, yes, of course,' she said quickly. 'But your case is a matter of public record now, isn't it?'

'I suppose so, but still . . .'

'My dear Jane, I'm here to help you and I can tell you that you will need support.'

'Why *you*, Melanie?'

Melanie had just taken a bite of bread and when she tried to reply she began to choke. I thumped her on the back. There was a long pause.

'Thank you, I can speak again now,' she said. 'I started to see Alex ten years ago. I was depressed, my marriage was in trouble, I wasn't coping with the stress of my job. You know, Jane, the normal state of the working woman.'

I smiled and nodded.

'I spent a couple of years talking about my early life and all that, but nothing seemed to change. One day, Alex said to me that he believed I had been abused by a close member of my family and that I was suppressing the memory. I was furious, I rejected the idea totally and considered stopping the analysis, but something made me continue. So we carried on, teasing away at certain episodes in my childhood, some blank spots, but nothing happened. It all seemed pointless, until Alex suggested that I should picture myself being abused and go from there.'

Melanie paused and took a gulp of water.

'It was like a floodgate opening. There were certain images tormenting me, sexual images. As I focused on them, developed them, I realised they were memories of sexual assault by my father. I won't tell you the things he did to me, they were terrible things, perverse things that I could scarcely imagine. And as Alex and I went on we uncovered more and more. I realised that my mother had conspired with my father, not just by allowing it to happen but actively helping. And my brother and my sister had been raped and abused as well.'

She spoke with uncanny calmness, as if she had schooled herself to tell this terrible story. I wondered what I could possibly say.

'That's awful,' I said, conscious of its inadequacy. 'Were you absolutely sure it was true, that you didn't imagine it?'

'I was tormented with worry and I needed a lot of help and reassurance, most of which was provided by Alex.'

'What did you do? Did you tell the police?'

'Yes, after a while. They questioned my father but he denied everything and there were never any charges.'

'What did your brother and sister say?'

'They took my parents' side completely.'

'So what happened with your family?'

'I never see them. How could I ever have any dealings with people who have ruined my life?'

'God, I'm so sorry. So what did you do? How did your husband react?'

I was appalled, but Melanie seemed detached, almost amused, when describing the wreckage of her life.

'He couldn't cope with it at all, but then for a year or two I collapsed utterly. I became terribly ill, I couldn't work, I couldn't function, I couldn't do anything. I moved away from home, I gave up my job. I lost almost a decade of my life. I always wanted children, you know. I began to see Alex when I was in my mid-thirties. I'm forty-six now. I'll never have children. It's still all I can do to look after *myself.*'

'God, Melanie, was it worth it?'

Her curious half-smile vanished. 'Worth it? My father

sodomised me when I was five years old. My mother knew about it but chose to ignore it. That's what they did to me, that's what I've got to deal with.'

I felt sick, the food dry and heavy in my mouth. I forced myself to swallow.

'Have they never apologised to you for what they did?'

'Apologise? They've never even admitted that they did *anything*.'

'So what are you doing now?'

It seemed a mad question. I just didn't know what to say.

'A couple of years ago I formed a self-help group for people like me who have recovered memories of abuse. In fact, that's why Alex suggested we should meet. We're doing a workshop this afternoon and we wondered if you'd like to sit in.'

'I don't know, Melanie.'

'They're a remarkable collection of women, Jane, I think you'd like them. Give us a try. I think we might be able to help you.' She looked at her watch. 'I've got to go ahead now. But we meet at two. It's along the corridor in CR3. Will you be there?'

I nodded. That gnarled, damaged woman stood and hoisted the strap of her bag over one shoulder, picked up a pile of files and picked her way through the crowd, nodding at people here and there. I felt she could have been at a fête or a WI meeting, but she was off to chair a seminar for the psychically damaged.

I needed a cigarette and I needed a coffee. I got in line but when I reached the piles of cups and began to pour, my hand was trembling so violently that the coffee went everywhere but in my cup.

'Here, let me do that for you,' said a woman beside me

and she poured a cup for me and one for herself. Then she led me to the nearest empty table and sat down with me. I recognised her. I thanked her and she held out her hand to me.

'Hello, I'm Thelma Scott.'

'Yes, I know. I heard your contribution to the debate earlier on.'

'And I know who *you* are,' she replied drily. 'You're Jane Martello, Alex Dermot-Brown's latest and best specimen.'

'Everybody I meet here seems to know me already.'

'You're a valuable property, Ms Martello.'

It was more than I could bear.

'Dr Scott, I'm grateful for your help but I don't really know what I'm doing here and I certainly don't want to get involved in any controversy.'

'It's a bit late for that, isn't it? Your father-in-law is about to go to prison for the rest of his life and you put him there.'

'He confessed to the crime, Dr Scott. He's going to plead guilty.'

'Yes, I know,' she said with an obvious lack of concern. 'What did you make of Melanie Foster?'

'I think she's an unbearably tragic case.'

'Yes, I agree.'

I drained my coffee cup. 'I've got to go,' I said, preparing to get up.

'Off to Melanie's workshop?'

'Yes.'

'For some sisterly reassurance? To be told that you've done the right thing?'

'That's not what I want.'

Thelma Scott raised an amused eyebrow. 'Really? That's good,' she said and began to open her purse.

'I'll pay,' I said.

'There's nothing to pay,' she said. 'Our coffee is courtesy of Mindset. I want to give you this.'

She extracted a card, wrote on the reverse and offered it to me. 'This is my card, Jane. On the back, I've written my home phone number and my address. If you ever feel that you'd like to talk to me, just give me a ring. Any time at all. And I can guarantee confidentiality, which is more than some other people in this field of inquiry.'

I took the card reluctantly. 'Dr Scott, I really don't feel we have anything to talk about.'

'Fine, then don't call. But put it in your purse. Go on, I want to see you do it.'

'Okay, okay.' I did as she said under her keen gaze. 'There it is, tucked under my Leisurecard.'

Before I could get up, Thelma Scott leant across the table and took my hand. 'Keep it there. This isn't over, Jane,' she said, with an urgency that surprised me. 'Look after yourself.'

'I always do,' I said and left her without looking back.

Conference Room 3 was much smaller than the hall we had sat in earlier. It contained ten chairs arranged in a circle, and when I entered most of them were occupied, all by women. They looked curiously at me as I sat down. Should I introduce myself? Would it be rude if I read a magazine before the workshop got going? I opened my file as if I had some urgent preparations to make. I was aware of other people coming in and sitting down and then Melanie greeted me and I looked up. All the seats were occupied and two people were standing, Alex Dermot-Brown among them, so more chairs were brought in and we all scraped backwards to give them room.

'Good afternoon,' Melanie said, when everybody was settled. 'Welcome to the "Listen to Us" section. I'll try to follow the spirit of the title and say as little as possible. As you all know, this isn't a normal meeting for our group. We have a couple of observers and a guest. I don't want to be formal about this, and I'm only going to chair this in the loosest sense. I propose that we begin by identifying ourselves and explaining what we're doing here. We'll go clockwise, starting with me. I'm Melanie, and I have recovered the memory of being abused by my father and mother.'

And the introductions began, a catalogue of suffering that I could hardly bear.

'I'm Christine and I'm here because I have recovered the memory of being abused by my stepfather.'

'My name is Joan and I'm here because I have recovered the memory of being sexually abused by my father and my uncles.'

'My name is Suzanne and I'm here because I have recovered the memory of being abused by my father.'

'Hello, I'm Alex Dermot-Brown and I'm a doctor who wants to listen to the victims of abuse and to help them to help themselves.'

'I'm called Christine.' A rueful smile. 'Another one. I recovered my memory of being sexually abused by my older brothers.'

'I'm called Sylvia and I recovered my memory of being raped as a child by my stepfather and by another man.'

'I'm called Lucy and I recovered my memory of abuse by my father and my mother.'

'My name is Petra Simmons and I'm a solicitor.' She gave a nervous laugh. 'I'm here to see what I can do. And to learn something, I hope.'

'My name is Carla and I remembered being abused. I don't know who they were, though. I was so young.'

My turn. My cheeks were burning.

'My name is Jane,' I said. 'Look, I'm not really prepared for this. I didn't know anything about it. I thought I was just going to be an observer, to see what it was like.'

'It's all right, Jane,' said Sylvia, a robustly handsome middle-aged woman. 'The first thing we have to learn is to find words for what happened to us. We're so used to being disbelieved and undermined. That's why we suppressed these traumas.'

'Excuse me.' It was the woman on my left. 'Can I introduce myself before we start the discussion?'

'Yes, of course,' said Melanie. 'Go ahead.'

'Hello, my name's Sally,' she said. 'I remembered being abused by my father and a family friend. That's all. Sorry for interrupting, Sylvia.'

There was a moment of awkwardness because Sylvia had actually finished her point. I leapt into the silence.

'I'm sorry, I'm just not ready for this. You're all brave women and the idea of what you must have been through is unbearable, but this is all too recent for me.'

'You don't need to feel sorry for us,' said Carla, a young woman with beautiful hennaed hair wearing a long gorgeously patterned dress. She looked like a dream gypsy. 'The terrible thing is being unable to talk about it. What we've done in this group is to liberate each other. Jane, I don't know much about your circumstances but I would guess that what you are feeling at the moment is doubt about the memories you have recovered and guilt about the effect they have had. Abuse victims get abused all over again when they try to describe what has happened to them. Every person who questions the testimony of an abuse victim is also an abuser. The whole point of our group is to support and strengthen each other. We believe you, Jane, and we trust you.'

'Thank you, I'm sure this group must be very emotionally helpful.'

A little laugh ran round the circle and looks were exchanged. Melanie tapped her pen on her folder and called for silence. Then she spoke:

'This isn't just about emotions. This is a political issue. If you join with us, and we truly hope you do, you'll start to learn that there are networks of abuse, that there are abusers in positions of authority. This is what we're up against.'

'You can't be serious,' I protested.

'What has been your own experience, Jane? You found a murderer and a rapist who had escaped justice for a quarter of a century. What happened? Is your testimony going to be used? Will your revelation be on the record?'

'I gave a statement. But he confessed,' I admitted. 'He's pleading guilty.'

'How convenient,' said Melanie. 'Look, people can't bear to admit that abuse is widespread, that it's not just the evil maniac but the man next door – the man in the next room. It's too terrible to contemplate. So we, the victims, are not supposed to remember – are *blamed* for remembering. Now we are speaking up. Soon other people will speak up as well and the systematic protection of these abusers will be revealed. The police and your family have tried to make you deny your own reality, to alienate you from yourself. We're here to help you.'

After the workshop, Alex had other people he wanted me to see but I told him I wanted to leave. I said I would catch a cab but he insisted on driving me and making sure I was all right. I was silent for several minutes as we moved slowly in the early rush-hour traffic.

'What did you make of Melanie's group?' he asked.

'I don't know what to say. I find it difficult to be rational about so much suffering.'

'Would you be interested in joining?'

'God, I don't know, Alex. I once had to run a bring-and-buy stall at the boys' school fête. That experience put me off joining anything. I can't really cope with crowds.'

There was another long silence. I had two difficult questions to ask.

'Alex,' I said finally, 'you're a recovered memory specialist and it turned out that I had a memory waiting to be recovered. Isn't that strange?'

'No, Jane, it isn't. Don't you remember our first meeting? I didn't think I could do anything for you. You talked about having a black hole somewhere in the middle of your golden childhood. That interested me. I looked for a hidden memory because I was already sure that it was there.'

'You couldn't have been wrong?'

'You found it, didn't you?'

'Yes, I did. I wish I felt happier about it.'

'Remember what Melanie said to you. It's natural to feel guilt about a recovered memory. Life seemed simpler before, didn't it? But it wasn't *you* who killed Natalie.'

'Alex, you didn't tell a journalist about me, did you?'

With startling suddenness, Alex turned the car and brought it to a sudden halt by the kerb. Somebody hooted and shouted something.

'Jane, I'm your doctor. That's a terrible thing to say.'

'It wasn't exactly a secret at the conference.'

'They're a community of sufferers, Jane. They can help you, you can help them. You're a strong and intelligent woman, a survivor. You have an opportunity to do a great deal of good.'

'This is all happening too quickly, Alex. I can't start making commitments to other people. I'm having difficulty looking after myself.'

'You're stronger than you know. If you wanted you could be a witness on behalf of a great cause. You might think of writing about your experience, if only as a form of therapy. Don't say anything, just bear it in mind. If you needed any help, we could do it together.'

I shook my head. I felt the utmost weariness.

'Home, James.'

Thirty-Three

Of all the characters caught up in the ghastly drama, Claud was undoubtedly the hero. For months – years, if I'm honest – he'd hovered in the wings of my life before I'd tried to push him off the stage altogether. Now it was hard for me to imagine my life without him, although I was very careful not to see him too much, nor to lean on him when I did. Kim continually warned me.

'Be kind,' she said, 'but think about what kindness means in this situation.'

There were days when I wanted him back, and couldn't understand why I'd left him in the first place. On those days, I cooked and gardened and drank gin, and I tried to ignore the jittery, fluttery panics high in my stomach.

Claud, of course, had been warned about Alan in advance, but I am not sure that that made the horror any less, or the pain easier. Over the next four months he reacted by taking on the part of the eldest son, the man of the family. I watched with bemused admiration as he dealt with the press, wrote letters, sorted Martha's possessions. He seemed to have stopped sleeping, and was ceaselessly concerned to make everyone's life run more smoothly. He looked younger; the deep lines running down from his mouth, which had given his face a look of middle-aged sorrow, faded; his eyes were brighter. While everyone around him, in one way or another, went to pieces, he seemed to cohere, be a more collected person than he'd been for a long time. He was charged with a sense of purpose; I thought maybe he was heading for a nervous breakdown.

He never blamed me. He seemed to me to be watching my every word and every gesture, always careful not to say anything that would hurt me. His niceness was unnerving, and reminded me of when we first started dating: how he would always hold open doors, arrive carrying flowers, never interrupt my sentences, make sure to compliment me on my clothes. He tried not to disagree with me, and when he did it was in a respectful, cautious kind of way that used to drive me mad. It had taken him a long time – well into our marriage, when we had two sons and a mortgage and a whole network of friends in common – to relax his guard, or take me for granted. I'm not sure that he ever did entirely. He was always too scared of casting me off and losing me. Perhaps he had lost me because he had never quite given himself up to me. He'd offered me his adoration and strength, but not his fears and failures. He had tried too hard. Now, in this reacquired solicitude, he diligently kept me informed about everything: how Theo and Jonah and Alfred were, how their wives and offspring had behaved over the whole business, even what they all said about me, although he was evasively informative about this: I could sense him editing out all the bitterness.

'And Alan?' I asked him on one of his early visits.

'He won't speak,' replied Claud. 'Not to anyone. Not a single word.'

The thought of Alan – who for as long as I'd known him, had never been able to stop himself speaking – retreating into silence, was somehow terrifying. I imagined his mind, like a great fish, thrashing just under the quiet surface.

As the prospect of the trial became more concrete I felt increasingly vulnerable and exposed. One day I was photographed unawares walking to the shops and the photograph was widely published: 'The Memory Woman.' There were legal constraints about what specifically could be said of me but that didn't stop medical correspondents writing about recovered memory in the newspapers, columnists talking about the supposed issues involved and about families and the pressures on a famous writer as he grows old. I had wandered into a zoo and couldn't get out.

Frantic efforts were made to persuade Alan to accept a lawyer but he refused legal representation of any kind. He insisted that he would plead guilty and would make no defence and allow no defence to be made on his behalf. There was some nervousness that this might be a perverse trick and that he might suddenly plead not guilty at the last minute. So I had two interviews in small chambers off Fleet Street in which a formally dressed young man and woman questioned me closely with particular attention to the means by which I had found the diaries and details of my sessions with Alex Dermot-Brown. Almost everything I said provoked whispers and serious expressions.

'Is there a problem?' I asked.

'Admissibility,' the young man said, 'but that's our problem, not yours.'

Claud behaved as if he could, by sheer willpower, make things 'all right' ('It will be all right' was a repeated phrase, mechanically hopeful). He was the only person still seeing all the brothers, and talking to Jerome and Robert, playing squash with Paul, maintaining the fiction that there was still this glorious entity made up of the Cranes and the Martellos. He went to see Dad several times, and I think that they managed to talk together in a way they'd never done while we were still together. Claud even visited Peggy, whom he had never really got on with, and answered her questions. 'Just because she and Paul are divorced, it doesn't mean that she should be excluded. After all, she knows Alan far better than Erica does.'

I wondered what he did when he got home to his small tidy flat, how he managed the times he didn't have tasks to perform. I wondered if there was anyone he talked to about himself. I could picture him grilling a chop, pouring out a single glass of red wine, eating his modest meal in front of the nine o'clock news. Then he'd go round the small flat straightening cushions, drawing curtains, making sure that the door was properly locked and that his clothes were ready for the morning, and that the alarm on his clock was set for radio. He would lie in the centre of his bed waiting for sleep, and I was sure that then the images of recent horror would play, over and over, and he would accommodate them. For all Claud's fastidiousness, his prudence, his love of habit and his attention to detail, he's a brave man: stoical, I suppose.

One evening, I invited him for a meal at my house. It was the first time since we'd parted that I'd cooked for him – except that mushroom dinner. I planned the meal nervously: it mustn't be too special, as if this were a date, but it mustn't be completely casual, as if we were still man and wife. In the end I decided on a simple chicken, with garlic bread and salad, followed by a couple of good cheeses, and fruit. Forty-five minutes before he was due to arrive, I sliced two large red peppers into strips, and fried them with garlic. When they cooled down, I would add balsamic vinegar and a drained tin of tomatoes. I spiked the chicken with rosemary and put it in the oven; then I washed the lettuce and tore it into a salad bowl, with cucumber, fennel, avocado. I wondered briefly whether to change out of my office clothes, but in the end stayed as I was – though I put mascara on my lashes and dabbed rose water behind my ears.

It's satisfying watching Claud eat. He is methodical, putting a little bit of everything onto his fork, then chewing it well and washing it down with a sip of rich chardonnay. I get the same feeling from seeing him eat that I used to have when as a child I watched Dad shaving in the morning. Would Claud and I ever get back together? I wondered, as I watched his thin wrists and his clever long fingers and his air of calm concentration. This evening, it didn't seem so unlikely, although even as that thought flickered through my mind I felt defeated. When he was finished, he put his knife and fork neatly together, wiped his clean mouth with the corner of his napkin, and smiled at me.

'Who is Caspar?'

The question took me by surprise.

'A friend.'

'Just a friend?'

'I don't want to discuss it.'

'At least tell me if it is serious.'

'There's no "it". I haven't seen Caspar for weeks. All right?'

'Don't get ratty with me, Janey.'

'Don't call me Janey.'

He cut himself two wedges of cheese, and took a couple of cheese biscuits from the tin.

'Don't you think I have a right to know?'

'No, I don't.'

This was better – my feeling about the inevitability of our marriage was dissipating; I wished that the evening was over now. I wanted to be drinking tea in bed, with a thriller.

Claud balanced some goat's cheese on a water biscuit and popped it into his mouth. He chewed several times.

'The thing is, I still feel married to you,' he said quite calmly. 'I still feel you're my wife, that I'm your husband.'

'Well, you . . .'

'Let me finish.' He didn't seem to notice that now was not the time; that any possibilities had already dribbled away from the evening. 'I've felt that more strongly since Dad confessed. We've been through terrible times, the worst times it's possible to go through, and we've helped each other. I *have* helped you, haven't I?' I nodded, mute. 'I won't lie to you: one of the reasons I have pulled through this – this horror – is the hope that it might bring us back together. Oh look, we're middle-aged now, Jane; we should be kind to each other, not pull away. We belong together; us and the boys.' I stiffened when he mentioned the boys – that was playing dirty, using them. He didn't notice my withdrawal. 'We should be a family. Don't you feel that too?'

But I had no chance to reply. He stood up, walked round the table and took my face in his hands; he didn't seem excited or upset, just very determined, as if he felt that he'd managed to work everything else out and now he was going to get this settled as well. He was too near me, out of focus, and I could smell his wine-and-garlic breath. I pushed him away.

'No, please Claud. It won't work.' I was shaking. 'It's

319

my fault; it's true that we've been closer recently, and been kind to each other. And then I invited you over here, and of course you thought . . .'

'Stop. Don't say a word more.' Two hectic spots had appeared on his pale face. He grabbed his overcoat. 'Not a word. Not now. Just think about it, will you? I didn't mean to rush things like that. I didn't want to alarm you.' As if I was a shy animal, who needed coaxing. He stood for a moment in the doorway. 'Goodbye.' He hesitated. 'Darling.'

I had felt no desire, I thought, as I cleared away the plates, wrapped the cheeses in their waxy papers. None at all. Instead, I'd felt a kind of dreary panic: I couldn't just go back to my old life, as if I'd suffered a mid-life crisis and then recovered equilibrium. Claud had called us middle-aged and of course it was true. But I didn't feel it.

'I'm sorry I'm late.'

Caspar slid into the seat opposite me; he didn't touch me.

'I've only just arrived myself.'

We were both being warily polite. I held out the wine list, and he took it carefully, so our fingers didn't touch.

'I've ordered a pinot noir,' I said.

'Good,' he said. 'Shall we get something to drink as well?' He looked up and caught my eye. 'Haven't you missed my irresistible humour?'

I shook my head disapprovingly. 'Is that an example of it?'

'Well, I haven't been using it much.'

The wine arrived and we sipped it gravely. I lit a cigarette and found that my hands were gently trembling. Caspar's expression darkened slightly.

'Would you rather that I asked you resentfully why you suddenly dropped me without any explanation and then suddenly rang up again?'

'You can ask. I don't want you to be resentful.'

'How are you, Jane?'

I had forgotten, in the weeks in which I had kept away from Caspar, the quality of his attention. When he looked at me, I felt as if he were really looking; his gaze was a kind of scrutiny. When he asked me how I was, I knew the question wasn't rhetorical, he really wanted to know. I took a deep breath.

'Not at my best, I guess. You know . . .'

He nodded. 'Has the press attention died down?'

'Yes, a bit. But the trial's still to come, so it'll get worse again, I suppose.'

'And will you have to give evidence?'

'Probably not. Unless Alan suddenly changes his mind again and pleads not guilty. Then it all hangs on me.'

'Will you tell me about it?' His question was phrased just right. If he'd said 'Do you *want* to tell me about it?' I'd have felt he was offering to help me and probably would have closed down on him. As it was, I found that I did, very much, want to explain what I had gone through. After all, I hadn't quite explained it to myself, yet. I needed this conversation.

'I'm sorry I didn't call,' I said impulsively.

Caspar smiled. 'I'm glad that you're sorry, but it's all right,' he replied. He studied the menu. 'Let's have some dips and some olives. I've hardly eaten anything since breakfast.'

I told Caspar everything. I described my childhood, our friendship with the Martellos (I skated over Theo) and the disappearance of Natalie. I told him how I'd married Claud young, and how my long marriage had over the years invisibly eroded, like a sandcastle flattening back into the rippled surface of a beach. I told him how I had finally left Claud, and then I described finding Natalie's body. Caspar was a good listener. When I paused to light a cigarette, he ordered another bottle of wine.

I said I had realised that I was profoundly unhappy, and that after a few false starts (I offered up my first aborted attempt at analysis but didn't mention the one-night stand with William), I had started therapy with Alex Dermot-Brown.

'What did you want from therapy?' Caspar enquired.

'Some kind of control over my life, I guess. I felt I was in a mess and didn't really know how to get out of it. Later, it became more of a search for the truth about my past.'

'That's a big thing to search for,' said Caspar mildly.

I tried to tell him about the therapy, but that was more difficult; the illuminations I'd received on the couch slipped away from me, like beads of mercury under the press of a finger.

'He helped me find a narrative to my life,' I said ineptly, echoing what Alex had once said to me.

'I've always thought,' responded Caspar, 'that the great appeal of psychoanalysis is that it enables us to tell the story of our own life.'

I couldn't tell whether he was criticising or complimenting me – probably neither.

'It's hard to talk about it now; it's weirdly hard to remember it as a chronology,' I admitted. 'It's more like a kind of space, where I explored myself. I don't know if I'll continue with it, though – I don't know what it would be for. Also' – the wine bar was filling up now; I had to

322

raise my voice against the hum and chink of a day ending – 'also, it's quite scary. I mean, I never really thought before how much pain people can carry around with them and still cope. And I'm still not sure whether dredging up memories and re-opening wounds is always right. Sometimes, horror should be left buried.' I shuddered. 'Not in my case, of course. But I think some things don't need to be explained. And sometimes damage should be left in sealed containers, like nuclear waste. That's heresy to therapists, of course. Except sceptical ones like Alex.'

'I'm glad you're sceptical too,' said Caspar. 'And I'm glad that you haven't used the word *empower*.'

I laughed. Then I told him about the group I'd been to, and he didn't say anything at all.

'There, that takes us up to now. And now you know about a hundred times more about my life than I know about yours.' I felt suddenly and dazedly self-conscious, as if the lights had gone on in the cinema.

'My time will come,' he said, and beckoned the waiter. 'Can I have the bill, please?' He pulled on his gloves. 'I've got to get home to Fanny now,' he said. 'She talks about you, by the way.'

We left together. 'Will you be all right?' he asked.

'Yes,' I replied, for I thought I probably would be.

'And will you call me?'

'Yes, I will. This time I really will.'

'Goodbye, then.'

'Goodbye, Caspar. Thank you.'

For a moment I thought he would touch me, but he didn't and I was glad.

Thirty-Four

One evening, Claud dropped off my box from the Stead on the way home from work. He hovered a bit on the doorstep. He didn't ask, but I could tell that he wanted to be invited in for a drink or dinner or to live with me again. I held firm on every count. This wasn't an evening for dealing with things like that. I wanted to go through this box on my own. Claud talked about what things were like up at the Stead now that Jonah was getting rid of everything and preparing for the house to be sold. I listened but didn't ask questions and scarcely responded. After a few minutes the conversation slowed and I was still standing resolutely in the quarter-opened door. He looked crestfallen and said he supposed he had better be going and I said thanks for bringing the box round and he looked even more crestfallen and mumbled something. I didn't ask what it was he had said and he looked downright self-pitying and walked off.

The brothers had lived at the Stead, of course, but Paul and I used to go there only at intervals, so we had our boxes. Martha and Alan had given them to us when we were small. They were packing cases with lids and they were for the possessions we had at the Stead, the things we put away at the end of the summer when we returned to the world and the boxes were stowed away in the loft. The first thing we would do when we came back from the world at the end of the following July, would be to run up and retrieve our boxes and extract the things that had got smaller because we had got bigger.

The sight of the box was incongruous, almost indecent. It belonged in the Stead, in my past, and now it had been dumped on my doorstep by my ex-husband. When I tried to pick it up, I almost regretted not asking Claud in. My arms are too short to go around a packing case, so I had to drag it down the hall, making a sound like a fingernail on a window-pane and leaving a dusty white line that I suspected was now a permanent feature. I got it as far as the kitchen and parked it by the table.

This was going to take time. I needed to be prepared, so I fixed myself a gin and tonic, took a fresh packet of cigarettes from a duty-free carton of Marlboro that Duncan had tolerantly bought me the previous week, lit the first and opened the box. It wasn't quite like the boxes that I still have up in my own attic. There weren't the bundles of old letters tied with ribbon, the old reports, the student cards, essays, certificates, school photos. It wasn't a life. These were the fragments of the bits in between my life.

I lifted out some old books, *The Little White Horse*, *Anne of Green Gables*, *Pride and Prejudice*, *Little Women*, *Kim* and some old *Look and Learns*, each of which I wanted to read through immediately but put aside for another evening. There were some utterly useless objects: old pens, batteries, flattened out tubes of glue, single earrings, lipstick tubes without lipstick. Why hadn't I thrown them into the bin? Lots of oddities. A heart-shaped box full of cotton wool. What had it contained? Combs. A heavy painted stone, which I decided I would use as a paperweight. A funny little earthenware dish with a picture of a monkey. I'd forgotten all about that. I could use it for paper-clips, perhaps. Some old cassette tapes. I tossed a couple of pocket guidebooks to Greece and Italy straight into the bin. I'd bought the Greece guidebook and never got around to the actual holiday.

Right at the bottom was a stratum of old notebooks. All of us, but especially Natalie and I, used to write and write, especially in those bits of summers that we suppress in later years, the times when it rained for day after day and we knocked around the echoey house. I took a cursory look through the books, the faded old drawings and stories, games of hangman and ghosts, doodles and letters. And the diaries that I used to keep almost every year. A thought struck me and I rummaged around until I found a dull red exercise book inscribed, 'J. Crane. Journal. 1969'. I flicked through until I reached the last of the biroed pages. It was useless of course. There was no entry for the day after the party or even for the day of the party itself. Life had become too big, too emotional, to be written about in a diary. What had I felt and done in those last golden days? I turned back a couple of pages and read:

24 July

Theo Theodosius!! Natalie is being completely tedious and won't talk to me, Paul is moaning all over the place, don't know what's got into him, Fred and Jonah are totally childish, Claud has been driven round the bend by organising the whole party and he looks ill and he says that he doesn't know where the tent will go and who will put it up and whose idea it was to have the barbecue – on which everything depends – built virtually as the party's about to start, and can anybody get in touch with Alan and Martha if there's an emergency and he (Claud) looks completely ill. And Luke is hanging around looking miserable and Mum and Dad aren't exactly in the pink either. With all this chaos, and everyone having nervous breakdowns, I feel more wonderful than I've ever felt in my whole life. It's all starting, and it's wonderful. As I'm writing this, it's very late at night (Natalie is asleep – she looked really awful this evening but if she's not going to be nice to me then I'm not going to bother about her). I'm holding a torch over the page and I'm so excited I can hardly hold my pen straight.

Lots of Claud's organising during the day – fetching food from Westbury, clearing up, deciding who was sleeping where and I hardly saw Theo at all. Then, after supper, when it was starting to get dark, we caught each other's eye and met outside and took each other's hands without even speaking and walked around the lawn and through the trees almost all the way to Cree's Top. We sat down beside each other and kissed and touched. Theo unfastened some of my clothes and he touched my body through the clothes he hadn't taken off and I touched his body with my trembling hands and I hoped he couldn't feel the trembling and didn't care anyway. I can still feel ripples everywhere and if I close my eyes I can feel just where he touched me, every bit, every spot. We said we loved each other. We lay holding each other and I felt like I wanted to cry but didn't. Then we walked back very slowly and it was the last crescent of the moon, the thinnest sliver you could imagine. Then we kissed very deeply and said good-night and I tiptoed up the stairs and wrote this and I know I won't be able to sleep at all.

July 25
I was almost right. I lay for hours and then slept and

327

was woken early by the birds at half past four and I've felt half asleep and half in a dream all day. Boring boring boring day. Lucky Alan and Martha just getting the party and not having to get it ready. Everybody miserable as per yesterday. With the addition of Mr Weston who came with the marquee and bricks and things for the barbecue and he was in a very bad mood. And Claud was telling Mr Weston what to do and then they were both in a bad mood. I couldn't help giggling. (Natalie a complete misery, natcherly.) First Claud said get the barbecue prepared, then suddenly the tent needs to be put up, then by the end of the day the barbecue hasn't even been done, Claud says first thing tomorrow will be okay, Mr Weston in a complete state et cetera, et cetera. Lots of shouting. Tomorrow is the party and will be total chaos with everybody going all over the place, about ten million people arriving, people staying in different places, the day beginning with all of us sent on errands to every corner of Shropshire by His Highness Claud of Martello. But these are all the boring bits. Theodore and I talked secretly about it and we are not going to go to the party at all (!!!). While Claud is serving hot dogs from the el nouveau barbecudos, Theo and I are going to slip away and go to the woods and I am going to give myself to him completely and I can't bear it, I'm so happy and so scared.

When I had read it, I wasn't exactly crying, I don't know what I was doing, but my cheeks were wet. I didn't feel weak or anything. I had a deliberate five-minute howl, felt better, washed my face and rang up Caspar. When he answered, I was suddenly not entirely sure why I'd rung and I asked him if we could have a drink together, and he

328

said yes, when?, and I said now, and he said that the problem was that he had a child asleep upstairs in bed and I suggested that I come over with a bottle of wine and I promised to be polite and well-behaved, not to make a scene, I didn't want sympathy or advice and he said, stop, don't make any more promises. All right. So I went.

'You're a patient man,' I said to Caspar, when my bicycle was in his hall and my bottle of wine was on his kitchen table.

'I'm patient with *you*,' he said. 'Don't rely on it, though.'

'I've been a trial to you, I know. I'm very sorry.'

'I'm probably attracted to damaged women. It will be interesting to see how I cope with a happy Jane Martello.'

'Happy?' I said. 'Let's not get carried away.'

I told him about my evening and described, in somewhat general and vague terms, my reading of the old diary.

'Are you still looking for something, Jane?'

'No, of course not, I'm putting it all behind me, but I suppose I hoped there would be some amazing confirming detail in there. It still seems so strange. I want something else, I want somebody to tell me it's all right.'

There was a long silence which I half hoped Caspar would fill with reassurances but he didn't. He just smiled in a curious way and toyed with his glass, then took a sip of wine.

'And yet,' he said, 'you turned down the chance to join that recovered memory support group. They were all there to support you. Why did you reject that?'

I laughed and took my cigarettes out of my pocket, thought of Fanny upstairs and put them back.

'A few reasons, I suppose. One of them was something *you* said.'

'Me?' said Caspar, raising his hands in mock alarm.

'When we spoke that time before you came to the public meeting about the hostel . . . You said something about a study that showed that once people had made a public commitment to something, then even evidence that contradicted their stand would only make them more committed to it. That's how it went isn't it?'

'Yes.'

'I want to be reassured but I want to be *right* and reassured.'

'Then I can't reassure you.'

'I don't know about that.'

We both placed our glasses on the table and I don't know who made the first move but we were against each other, kissing each other hard, running our hands over each other. I pushed open the buttons of his shirt, pop, pop, pop, and pulled my mouth from his and ran my lips in the soft down of his chest. He lifted my sweater over my head and pushed my bra up off my breasts without even undoing it.

'Wait,' I gasped. 'Let me undo my boots.'

My boots were fastened like Victorian stays. He shook his head and I felt his hands on my knees and then moving up my legs. No tights, thank God. He reached my knickers, took a double-handed grip and pulled them down, over my boots and off. I fell back on the sofa, my skirt above my waist and he was inside me.

Later, we went to the bedroom and took off our entangled, twisted clothes and examined each other's bodies all over in precise detail and made love again and I felt, almost for the first time, that sex was something I could become really good at. We lay together for hours, talking, until at about five Caspar murmured something about Fanny and

I kissed him deeply and got up and got dressed, then kissed him deeply again and left. As I cycled in the dark early morning, I thought with sweet contempt of all the people who were in bed asleep.

Thirty-Five

The day before the trial, a couple of photographers had lurked outside my house and snapped at me as I'd come out to buy a carton of milk. I'd put my hand over my face, knowing as I did so how that would look in the next day's papers. I could imagine the captions: 'The hidden face of the accuser', 'The defiant daughter-in-law'.

I didn't attend the trial itself, such as it was. I knew that I would be summoned if required. On the morning it began and ended, I left for the office very early – before seven – to avoid any further press attention, but still a journalist managed to collar me. 'Are you going to the trial?' he shouted, and I blundered past him, pushing my bike, saying nothing.

On the way home, I saw it on the news-stand in block capitals: NOVELIST: 'I KILLED MY DAUGHTER'. I braked to a halt, and bought a *Standard*. An old handsome photograph of Alan dominated the front page. Sweat broke out on my forehead and my breath came in short, frantic gulps.

I biked home, fumbled the Chubb lock. A package had been squeezed through my letter-box, and I recognised the handwriting: Paul's. This must be his video. All I needed.

The house was chilly, so I switched the heating on early and made my way to the kitchen. I put on the kettle and placed two slices of bread in the toaster. The answering machine was flashing messages at me but I didn't play them back. I was pretty sure they'd be from journalists, asking for my comment. The paper, still folded in my bag, was like a magnet, but I resisted it at first. I spread bitter marmalade (given to me the year before by Martha) onto toast and poured boiling water over a tea bag. I sat at the table in my coat and took a gulp of weak tea.

My eyes hopped through the text, trying to find the important details. Alan had pleaded guilty, refusing to make any plea in mitigation. The prosecution QC had made a brief evidentiary statement (much of which consisted of Natalie's note, the circumstances of its finding and my memory). He concluded that, in the light of the psychiatrist's report, the prosecution saw no reason to doubt that Alan Martello was sane. There was nothing about him having made Natalie pregnant. I didn't know why. Before the judge passed sentence, Alan had made just one statement: 'I am expiating a horrible crime which has haunted my family for decades.' He refused to elaborate on this or to say anything else at all. The judge described the murder of a daughter by her father as one of the most heinous and primal of crimes and said that Alan's refusal adequately to acknowledge what he had done or to co-operate fully with proceedings had only made matters worse. He was sentenced to life imprisonment with the recommendation that he serve at least fifteen years.

There was a large photograph of the Martello brothers, grim-faced, all present at the trial. They had refused to make any comment to the press and the *Standard* called them 'dignified, almost heroic'. Claud, apparently, had held Fred while he wept. There was a smaller picture of me, hand flung over my face, and a cropped portrait of Natalie which I'd never seen before. She looked younger than sixteen in it and conventionally pretty. Nothing threatening or sinister about that face. There was a two-page story under the heading, NATALIE'S SHORT LIFE AND BRUTAL DEATH. Under a slightly blurred photo of the seven Martellos all together and smiling ran a short piece starting: 'They seemed such a happy family.' There was another story about the police investigation; my own name flared up at me from the first paragraph but that story I didn't read; couldn't.

The phone rang, and I froze, cupping my cooling tea in my hands.

'Jane, it's Kim. Come on, you can pick up the phone.'

'Kim.' I think I'd never been so glad to hear a voice. 'Kim, thank God it's you.'

'Listen, we can talk later. I've booked us a room in a little hotel in Bishop's Castle, on the Welsh Borders. I'm taking you away for the weekend. Can you be ready by half past five? I'll pick you up.'

I didn't protest. 'What would I do without you, Kim? Yes, I can.'

'Right. Pack walking boots and lots of warm clothes. Bye.'

I ran upstairs and threw some long-sleeved T-shirts, jumpers and socks into a large hold-all; dug out my walking boots, still caked with mud from a year before; found my cagoule wrapped up in itself at the back of the cupboard. A quarter to five. I lit a cigarette, and turned on the small TV at the end of the bed. Alan's face again stared at me, all beard and fierce eyes, before the camera switched to the earnest face of an absurdly young reporter. 'Passing sentence, the judge described the murder of a

334

daughter by her father as one of the worst, and most unnatural crimes that could be imagined . . .' I leant forward, in a panic, and shoved Paul's video into the player. The young reporter disappeared abruptly. Through a curl of smoke, the Stead appeared on the screen as the title and credits rolled.

Paul's making of his film about the family had seemed so sporadic and arbitrary that in spite of having seen the final sequence I think I had expected something like a camcorder picture of a holiday. It wasn't like that at all. Paul began by reading an extract from *A Shropshire Lad*:

> *Into my heart an air that kills*
> *From yon far country blows.*
> *What are those blue remembered hills,*
> *What spires, what farms are those?*

The camera moved slowly over the Shropshire landscape around the Stead, skeletal in its winter garb, but still gorgeous. The sun glinted through the bare branches, and the old house sat rosy-stoned and welcoming. It was the house of my childhood and the land of my lost innocence.

I sat entranced while my cigarette burnt down to my fingertips and gazed as Paul spoke intimately to the camera. Memory, he was saying, is intangible, and the memories one has of childhood, which glow so vividly through all of our adult life, are seductive and nostalgic. And if one's childhood is happy, then adulthood is like an exile from its joy. We can never return. More music, and the camera zoomed in on the door of the Stead. Alan walked out. My ash fell onto the duvet cover and I brushed it heedlessly away. He quoted something from Words-worth, and spoke about love. He said, with all the old Alan bravado, that he had been a wild young man who had

335

scorned the concept of family and kicked against its traces. But he had learnt that this – he gestured at the Stead – was where he could be himself. He talked about the family as the place where you could be most tormented, or most at peace. 'For myself, I have found a kind of peace,' he said. He looked, as he stood on the threshold, like a mass-produced wise patriarch that you might buy in a souvenir shop. I watched his broad hands as he gestured, and I shuddered. Martha, thin as a tree branch, came through the doorway carrying a broad basket and some secateurs, smiled strangely at the camera and walked off screen. The camera moved sideways, and came to rest on the site where Natalie's body had been found. Paul stated the facts. Then came a series of stills of Natalie: as a baby, a toddler, a ten-year-old, a teenager; on her own, with her family. Then her tombstone.

Claud appeared and now that I was his audience I saw how handsome he was, how serious. I sat like a coiled spring while I waited for him to talk about me, and our marriage break-up, but all he said was that 'some things had not turned out as he had hoped'. I was shocked by the spasm of pity and love that jolted me. Cut to Robert and Jerome playing frisbee on Hampstead Heath. So young and carefree. Then Jerome, affectionately derisive on how the older generation was obsessed with the past. Fred, at home with his family on their well-tended patio. Alan again, drinking brandy and being expansive on the power of forgiveness. Theo comparing a family to a computer program.

Me, that was me, red-faced in my kitchen. Oh God, Christmas – but the Christmas I watched as I waited for Kim to arrive was one of festive hilarity: laughter boomed out of the television; I smiled a lot and handed round wine (had I smiled a lot that evening? I couldn't remember). Erica and Kim looked like two extravagant birds of paradise in their purple and yellow get-ups. Dad was distinguished Old Age, and my sons fresh Youth. The power of editing – to splice images so that collective trauma becomes a display of boozy unity.

I smoked the last cigarette in the packet. In spite of being revolted by the film's message, smashed as it was into a thousand pieces by Alan's confession, I was half seduced by its melancholy insistence upon the past as a place of innocence and joy, the lost Eden in everyone. The music, the winter greenness of Shropshire, the faces that came and went on the television screen, as familiar as the palm of my hand, the way that Paul, somehow, had made even his most resistant interviewees talk with a kind of inner concentration so that they seemed to be discovering truths about themselves for the first time – these things filled me with rich sorrow.

The film was nearing its end now. Paul was walking along the Col, hands in his pocket. The brown water was swollen with all the recent rain. He stopped and turned towards the camera, held out his hands in a gesture of offering. Oh, God, he was reciting poetry again:

> *That is the land of lost content,*
> *I see it shining plain,*
> *The happy highways where I went*
> *And cannot come again.*

I was getting confused. Was the point of this documentary that you *could* go home again or that you *couldn't*? But Paul was talking again. 'The family,' he said. 'Alan Martello called it torment and peace. Jane Martello, my sister, said that it is where we are our best and our worst selves.' [Oh, Christ.] 'Erica, my wife, calls it a haven and a prison – we can always return to it, but no matter how far we go from it, we can never escape it.' (Which Christmas cracker did she get *that* from?) Paul smiled with the wisdom of the ages and walked on, into the final sequence I had already witnessed, full circle back to the house and the site of the body.

I switched off the television, resolving to sell it. Or maybe a crack addict would break in and steal it while I was away with Kim. It was nearly five thirty. I buckled up my suitcase, then on an impulse I opened it once more and threw in my childhood diary. I quickly punched in Paul's number but was answered by a machine. After the bleep I said:

'Paul, it's me, Jane. I've just watched your film. It's very impressive – honestly, in spite of everything, it holds its own ground. I'm going away for the weekend with Kim, but I'll call you as soon as I get back. Well done.' I was going to replace the receiver but a thought struck me. 'Oh, and Paul – can you just tell me: which side of the river were you walking along at the end?'

As I put the phone down, I heard Kim's horn. I put on my leather jacket, picked up my bag and walked into the weather.

River Arms was a small white inn with low beams and a huge open fire in the bar. We had a double room, with a bathroom. Kim said that when we woke in the morning we'd be able to see the river and the mountains from our window. Now it was dusk and damp. I sat on my bed, feeling too tired to move.

'It's nine o'clock,' said Kim. 'Why don't you have a bath, and I'll meet you in the bar in half an hour. They do wonderful meals here, but we'll wait until tomorrow for that. Let's just have a snack by the fire tonight.'

'Fine.' I yawned and stood up. 'How do you know about this place?'

Kim giggled. 'My romantic past. It comes in useful sometimes.'

I had a deep warm bath, breaking open all the bath gels and foams. I washed my hair and dressed in leggings and a thick baggy cotton shirt. Downstairs, Kim had ordered two large gin and tonics, and had managed to secure a place by the fire. She raised her glass and chinked it against mine.

'Here's to better times,' she said.

My eyes filled with tears, and I took a long swallow of cold clean liquid.

'I've ordered our meal, as well,' Kim continued. 'Cold roast beef sandwiches, and a bottle of red wine. Okay?' I nodded; I was glad, today, of someone to take decisions for me.

'Tomorrow we can go for a long walk, somewhere high up, with thin air and fine views. If it doesn't rain. I've got Ordnance Survey maps in my bag; we can look at them at breakfast.'

We sipped our drinks and said nothing for a bit. There aren't many people you can be happily silent with. Then Kim said:

'Was it worse than you expected?'

'I don't know. I don't know what I expected. Pretty bad, though.'

The sandwiches arrived: thin slices of rare beef, horse-radish sauce on the side; a bottle of shiraz rich and smooth enough to befuddle me into a kind of peace.

'Why did you and Andreas split up? You seemed so happy together.'

'We were. I thought we were.' Kim opened her bread and carefully spread a thin layer of horseradish over the beef. 'One minute he was talking about where we would go on holiday in the summer and what kind of house we would live in together, and the next he was telling me he and his old girlfriend had decided to give it another go. Sorry and thank you and I'll never forget you and you're wonderful and all that crap.' She topped up our wine glasses. 'I was too old. I can't have children. I'm past not future.' She raised her glass once more: 'Here's to growing old disgracefully.'

I leant over and gave her a hug.

'He was mad. He didn't know how lucky he was.'

Kim grinned a little crookedly.

'Life never turns out the way you think, does it? When we were at university together, if you'd asked me what I wanted from life I'd have said I wanted it all: a good lasting relationship, children, lots of children, a career, friends. I've got friends and I've got the career, though nowadays that doesn't seem to count for much with me. I can do it standing on my head. But I don't seem to be doing very well with the lasting relationship. And I'll never have children.'

What could I say? 'Life's cruel. I used to think you made your own luck but that's a very young thing to think, isn't it? Here are you, beautiful and witty and warm – and on your own. And here am I. I've always had more or less what I wanted and suddenly I'm living in a nightmare. Anyway' – I was a bit drunk now, garrulously mournful – 'we'll always have each other.' This time, I raised my glass. 'To us.'

'To us. I'm plastered.'

We ate hungrily.

'Did you know,' I said after a bit, 'that we're really quite near the Stead.'

'Actually,' replied Kim, 'I did know. Is it a problem?'

'Not exactly a problem. Do you mean you chose this place because it's near the Stead?'

'Kind of. I mean, I thought of it as a lovely place to come to, and then I also thought you might want to go there. To lay a few ghosts. Otherwise I thought it might come to hold a hellish power over you.'

I stared at her in astonishment.

'Kim, you're amazing. Ever since we arrived I've been thinking that I've got to go back there. I've got to go to where it happened, not just the Stead but the hillside. I can't explain it, but I feel as if it won't be over until I've revisited it. I've gone back there so many times in my memory; if I close my eyes I could describe the place inch by inch, each ditch and tree. But I've never, not ever, been back to it in person – not since Nat vanished. It became like a forbidden area to me. Well, I know why now, of course, but I also know that I can't escape from what I've done, so I've got to confront it. Walk through it, as it were. You do see, don't you?'

Kim nodded, and drained the last of the bottle into our glasses.

'Certainly. If I were in your shoes, I think I'd feel the same.' I started to speak, but she stopped me. 'Since I'm not in your shoes, I will go for a long walk tomorrow, while you return.'

We relapsed into silence once more, both staring into the flames, blurred by wine and fatigue.

'What are you thinking?' Kim asked.

'It wasn't the Memory Game, you know,' I said.

'What?'

341

'The game we played at Christmas, trying to remember the objects on a tray. It's not called the Memory Game. It's called Kim's Game.'

'*My* game? What on earth are you talking about?'

'I found a copy of *Kim*, you know, Kipling's novel, in a box of my old stuff from the Stead that Claud brought round. I was browsing through it and when Kim is learning to be a spy, his memory is trained by memorising collections of random objects which are then hidden. Kim's game.'

'You want another glass of wine, Jane,' said Kim, smiling.

'The Memory Game is where you have cards face down and you try to pick out pairs. I don't know how I forgot that.'

Kim stood up.

'I forgive you,' she said. 'Come on. Bed-time.'

Thirty-Six

The Stead already looked as if it had been abandoned. As soon as I got out of Kim's car and looked around I could detect the absence of Martha. She once told me that her books got illustrated somehow and the children brought themselves up, but she felt that her garden really needed her. There was a man who used to come from Westbury a couple of times a week but in my days at the Stead she seemed to be out in the garden for almost every minute, on her knees poking at the soil with a trowel, pruning, planting. She had been endlessly resourceful at a craft about which the rest of us knew almost nothing. When we noticed the flowers and the fruit and the vegetables, we adored them, we were glad to have them around, but we paid no attention to all the little battles that had been won and lost in their creation. Had anybody thought about how the garden could function without Martha? She had been absent from it – first in spirit and then in body – for less than six months, but it looked bereft. Canes stood in the beds with nothing attached to them, there were sprigs of dandelion in the lawn dotted among the mangy half-piles of leaves.

The house was closed up and I didn't have a key. I'd never needed one. I peered through a window and saw empty rooms, bare boards, expanses of wallpaper with the pale rectangles recalling absent pictures. It was no longer ours and I took a bleak pleasure in seeing all signs of the Martello family stripped so brutally from the property. It was up for sale. Soon somebody else could move in their memories. My own were still cluttering up the place, like the crisp packets that blew down from the B road at the end of the drive. I turned away from the house. The dismal apology for a hole where Natalie had been found remained, half full of sludgy water. Was nobody ever going to fill it in?

But this was not what I had come to see. There was no point in messing around, there was nobody to bleat to. I just wanted to get this over quickly, see what I had to see. Then I would leave the Stead for ever, rejoin Kim, have a good meal, a good weekend, go back to London, get on with the rest of my life. I walked quickly across the shaggy lawn and felt the damp closing around my toes. Wrong bloody shoes. I reached the wood and to the left I could see Pullam Farm and to my right was the path that led along the wood and then back down and around to the Stead. Not today. Today, for the first time in a quarter of a century, I took the path into the wood that led to Cree's Top and the River Col. It was a damp, misty morning, and I shivered even in my anorak. This wouldn't take long. The path divided as I approached the rising ground which hid the river from sight and I took the right fork, which would bring me around the side of Cree's Top to the path by the river.

The path was rarely used now and branches extended across it. After a few minutes of brushing them out of my face, I reached the edge of the Col and the foot of Cree's Top. I was back. One detail had started it all, attracted Alex's interest, hadn't it? Those funny little pubescent poems screwed up and tossed into the water as I'd sat here with my back to Cree's Top and watched them float away down the Col. Would any of them have reached the sea? Or did they all snag in reeds round the first bend? I felt in my anorak pocket and extracted a menu from a local Indian take-away: Half-Price Madness. I screwed it into a ball and tossed it into the river.

The silliest thing happened, and it almost made me laugh. The river was flowing the wrong way. The scrunched up menu from The Pride of Bengal didn't flow away from me and disappear round the bend. It flowed *back* past me. And, indeed, as I looked up the Col, against the flow, I saw that there was no bend in that direction for several hundred yards. What a stupid thing. I felt disoriented for a moment but it was quickly obvious to me what had happened. I quickly strode up Cree's Top. The trees were thinned out now and when I reached the summit I could see that the mist had lifted and the view of the river and of the path proceeding along the side of it was clear. The Col curved slightly to the right and then back to its previous course, forming a reversed letter C. Fifty yards further on was the bridge from which Natalie had been seen that last time.

The path steepened sharply in front of me and I had to stop myself from trotting down the slope. When I reached the flat I sat down, with my back against the large rock at the foot of Cree's Top. I felt in my pocket and found a credit card slip from a petrol station. If I were efficient I would file it somewhere and set it against something. I screwed it up and tossed it into the water. The sun was out now and the light blue paper was hard to pick out against the sparkling ripples but I focused intently on it as it picked up speed and disappeared round the grassy bend. Like a dream.

Thirty-Seven

We used to play by the copper beech tree, with its thick and grizzled trunk and its vivid flare of leaves. It stood in front of a dry stone wall, and if we stood on the wall the lower branches of the tree were near enough the ground to allow us to scramble up to what now seemed to me like dizzying heights. We could look down through the bronzed foliage at the Stead, watch the adults come and go through the porched front door, but no one could see us. We spent hours up there. We'd take dolls, then, when we were older, books and apples. Natalie and I would sit and talk while dappled light streamed through the leaves. We would watch scudding clouds and exchange secrets and the days seemed to pass slowly, so slowly. I hadn't remembered this peaceful, happy Natalie enough. I hadn't been a loyal enough friend to her after she had disappeared. If it had been me who had gone, suddenly and with no word of explanation, I knew that she would have furiously searched for me. She would have felt betrayed by my desertion and furious with adults who tried to comfort her. She would have been spitting mad. Whereas I – I had been passive and sorrowful, lying night after night in the room that had once been hers, dreaming of her and never once searching for her. Once, when Natalie and I had been playing hide-and-seek in the garden, I'd failed to find her, and after peering dismally behind large bushes and into garden sheds, I'd mooched into the kitchen where Martha had been making rock cakes. As I'd licked out the bowl, Natalie had burst into the room, 'You give up too easily,' she'd shouted at me. 'I don't know why I should bother with you when you just give up. I've *gone off you*, Jane Crane.'

I rubbed the bark with one finger. Martha had loved this tree too. She had planted crocuses and snowdrops around its base. I sat down and leant against the tree trunk, feeling its ridged age through my jacket.

When I was in my early twenties I had spent four months in Florence as an architectural assistant. I had adored the city and spent all my spare time wandering down narrow streets and into dark, incense-filled churches where statues of sightless madonnas stood in niches and old women burned candles for their dead.

I had gone back again ten years later, the map of the city still clear in my head, and soon discovered that I was slightly out of kilter. Roads were shorter than I remembered; where there should have been a view there was a tall building; the café where I'd drunk a daily espresso and eaten little rice cakes had shifted from the centre of the square to its corner. Claud had said calmly that you always had to rediscover places; the joy of travelling was that new meanings were always emerging and old ones altering. But I had felt obscurely cheated: I had wanted to step back into a past that was intact and where each site held its memories for me and instead I entered a city that had somehow grown away from me. Florence was no longer mine.

The same hazy dissatisfactions niggled at me now. On an impulse I zipped up my jacket to my chin, stood up and hoisted myself into the lowest branch of the tree. I clambered from branch to branch until I reached a familiar perch. I gazed through the skein of twigs with their pale green leaves at the Stead. There was the house, bearing its invisible signs of disintegration. How do you recognise, when all the features remain the same, the moment that life passes from the face of a friend, or know, although you can point to nothing that has changed, that a house is abandoned? From where I sat I could not see the front door, although I could clearly remember seeing it from here as a child. I clambered down the branches and jumped clumsily onto the grass; sat down once more with my back against the ancient tree.

I picked up my old diary which I'd picked out of my case as I'd set out that morning and idly started leafing through its later pages. Some entries were like triggers that brought memories easily back: the candle that had set fire to Alan's beard when he'd leant over greedily to scoop up the last of the potatoes; I had laughed so hard that the muscles of my stomach had ached. Sailing in the gravel pit reservoir nearby, being frightened as the boat had keeled and water slopped over the edge but not wanting to admit it – certainly not admitting it to Natalie or to Theo, who were always physically brave and were contemptuous of timidity. Getting up at four in the morning with Alan and the twins to hear the dawn chorus and coming back chilly, ravenous and euphoric.

But there were some entries – an argument with Mum, which I represented with sanctimonious lack of imagination, or a visit to a medieval mansion where Catholics hid under the floorboards during the Reformation – that stubbornly refused to yield their treasures. They were like the graves in Highgate Cemetery, grown over with ivy

348

and nettles, unvisited and quite forgotten. Most of our lives lie underground.

The last entry had always been available to my recall – which wasn't surprising since the day before Natalie's disappearance had been like the defined rim around a black hole. I could summon up the party preparations without much difficulty: I remembered kissing Theo in the square of mud between the newly laid stone tiles where the last pieces of the barbecue would be built in time for the party and jumping up guiltily as we heard Jim Weston approach.

I shut the diary and rubbed my eyes. A few drops of rain fell heavily on the book's cover. I felt as if I were staring at something through thick liquid; all the shapes I was trying to make out were distorting and breaking up. Kissing Theo in the earth made ready for the barbecue. The barbecue.

I stood up, stumbling in my haste, and ran in the increasing rain to where Natalie's body had been found. It was still a livid scar of churned-up mud and rubble and a few shallow-rooting weeds. I jumped down into the mud and sunk my hands into it, digging around messily. I pulled out the leg of a doll, a rusted fork, its tines clogged, a beer bottle with a chipped neck; then a broken tile, a fragment of rusty grating. They were the remains of the barbecue. Natalie had been buried underneath the barbecue.

Heavily, I sat down at the edge of the hole, wiping my muddy hands on my muddy jeans. Rain fell steadily now, obscuring the landscape, and it was as if a curtain was being drawn across the Stead and all its secrets. Something was wrong. I couldn't think straight; it was like trying to remember a dream but losing it in the process. Natalie was buried under the barbecue but the barbecue was built before she died. I spoke out loud:

'So that's why the body was buried there. It was an improbable place because it was an impossible place.'

I buried my face in my hands and stared through my fingers at the muddy hole. Rain slid down the back of my neck. I tried again:

'Natalie was buried before she died.'

Or:

'Natalie was buried underneath the barbecue; Natalie died after the barbecue was completed; therefore . . .' Therefore what? I kicked a few fragments of tiles back into the hole and stood up. Kim would be wondering where I'd got to.

Thirty-Eight

Kim was lying on her bed in our room when I got back, studying a map. She sat up.

'You've been ages. Christ! Look at your face: have you had a mudbath or something? What's the matter?'

'What? Nothing. I don't know.' I went into the bathroom, washed the mud off my grubby face and hands. When I returned to the bedroom, Kim was pulling on her boots.

'Do you want something to eat?' she asked.

'No. Go ahead if you want something.' Then, abruptly: 'Can we go for a walk?'

'Of course; I've found one of nine miles that starts just down the road from here, so we should be able to finish it before it gets too dark. Lots of hills and valleys. I should think in this weather it'll be a bit muddy.'

I looked down at my jeans.

'I think I can cope with that.'

I didn't say anything for the first couple of miles – and anyway we climbed up the narrow rocky path so swiftly that I probably wouldn't have had the breath to walk and talk at the same time. Brambles tore at my clothes, and rain dripped from wet leaves. Eventually the path widened out and we reached the top of a rise. In fine weather there would have been a view.

'It's all jumbled up in my mind,' I began.

'What do you mean, jumbled up?'

'At first it seemed clear, everything was as I'd expected. I mean of course it was – I know the Stead almost as well as my own house. I just mooched around for a bit; you know, all those old memories.' Kim nodded but said nothing. 'Then I went back to where it happened.' It was strange how I still found it difficult to say baldly 'where Alan murdered Natalie'. 'I haven't been there for nearly twenty-six years.' I stepped over a tree that lay across the path, and waited for Kim to draw level with me again. 'I started to walk towards it. But Kim, it was all wrong. I remembered it wrongly.'

'What's so surprising about that? You say yourself that you hadn't been there for years. Of course you didn't remember it.'

'No. I *remembered* it – but I remembered it wrongly. Don't you understand, Kim, I've walked through that landscape so many times in my memory with Alex, but when I actually went there it was all back to front. The wrong way round. Oh shit, I don't know.' I took out a damp packet of cigarettes from my jacket, and lit one as I walked along.

'Let me get this straight, Jane. Are you saying that the walk that you pieced together with Alex was inaccurate?'

'No, no, I'm not. It was accurate, all the details were there if you see what I mean, just the wrong way round.'

'I'm a bit confused. What does it mean?'

'I don't know. I feel completely bemused, Kim. And that's not all.'

'What's not all?' Kim's voice went up one notch more in exasperation.

'It's not just that the walk was the wrong way round, I

worked something else out – I can't think why no one's worked it out before. Now it seems blindingly obvious.'

'What's obvious? Come on Jane, don't be so fucking gnomic with me; spell it out, will you?'

'Okay. Listen then. You know I've been re-reading my diary, the one Claud brought me, which takes us right up to the day before Natalie died?'

'Yes.'

'Well, in the last entry – which was on the day before Natalie was killed – I wrote about the unfinished barbecue; the barbecue that Jim Weston was getting done in time for the party.'

'So?'

'That's where Natalie was buried, Kim. Under that barbecue.'

I watched as very slowly Kim's face turned from blankness to bemusement.

'It's not possible. It means . . .'

'It means that Natalie was buried under bricks that were laid before she died.'

'But . . .'

I counted off the points on my fingers.

'Look, number one: we know that she died the day after the party. She was seen the day after, and by someone trustworthy, who had no involvement with the family. Two: we know that Alan killed her – I remember it and he's confessed. But Alan didn't arrive at the Stead until after the barbecue was finished. Three: Natalie was buried under the barbecue.' I was striding along now, with vigour borne of frustration. Kim had almost to run to catch up with me.

'If what you say is true, you should go to the police, Jane.'

353

I stopped dead.

'What on earth could I say? Why would they accept this new twist to my memory? Anyway, it doesn't make any difference to the result. Alan killed Natalie and he's in prison. I just want to know *how*.'

I kicked a bramble out of my path and dug in my pocket for another cigarette.

'Oh Christ, Jane, can't you stop this?' Kim asked. 'Why is it so important to know? Think about it. You know the big thing about Natalie's death – you know who killed her. And now you want to know all the smaller things as well. And then if you find those out, you'll want to ferret around and fret and smoke dozens more of those cigarettes of yours until you've pieced together all the tiny details. But you'll never know everything about this, Jane. Do you want to hear what I think?'

'Go on then; you're going to tell me anyway.'

I felt damp and cross. A bit of grit in my shoe pressed against the ball of my foot; my scalp itched under my head and my neck itched and my hands sweated and my nose felt cold. Why couldn't she just listen and nod and hold my hand?

'I think you've turned this into a self-consuming obsession. Solve this puzzle, and another one will appear. You want some ultimate, complete meaning to a messy tragedy. You've lost your wit.'

'Wits.'

'*Wit*. You're getting boring. Can't you let it go?'

I climbed over a stile, staining my palms green with slimy lichen.

'I want to. I thought it would all be over, that I was coming here to end the whole foul business and – this'll sound stupid – to find Natalie again. She'd become like a jigsaw puzzle or something, and the only bits of her character I thought about were the bits that made sense of her murder. And then the other day I had this really clear image of her, it was as if I could reach out and touch her. I did love her, you know; she was my first best friend. So I needed to come and say goodbye to the real her, in the place where she last was. But I feel so . . . so strange, somehow. It's as if I know something more, but I can't get at it. It might be boring but . . . oh shit, lateral thinking, that's what I need. I feel like I'm going mad.'

Kim said nothing. We walked down the hill to the car.

'You do still want to stay for the rest of the week-end, don't you?' asked Kim, as we drove back to the hotel.

'Yes, of course.' Then: 'Well, actually, Kim, I don't think I can. I feel all restless now. I'm really sorry, but can we drive back tonight?'

Kim looked grim.

'It was a bit of a long drive for one late night, and a single soggy walk.'

'I know. I just wouldn't be very good company.' I opened a window and lit a cigarette. 'Unfinished business and all that. It's like that mad woman said to me: it's not over yet.'

'As usual today, I haven't the faintest idea what you're talking about. However' – Kim reached out a hand and touched me briefly on the shoulder – 'let's not bicker. I don't mean to be so grouchy.' She grinned ruefully. 'It's just that I'd planned what my evening meal would be: scallops and raw tuna marinaded in lemon juice and herbs, followed by spring lamb. Then I rather fancied the apple strudel and cream.'

'I'll buy sandwiches for the journey,' I said. 'Cheese and salad on brown, with an apple to follow.'

'Whoopee.'

It was still not quite eight o'clock when we left the hotel with our bags and boots. I insisted on paying for the unused second night, and apologised to the perplexed owner.

'They probably think it's a lover's tiff,' said Kim.

'They probably think we're fair-weather walkers from London, fleeing from this rain.'

It was still raining as we drove off in the growing darkness, a horrible June evening. The windscreen wipers slapped down water, and Kim put on some music. Bent jazzy notes of a saxophone filled the car, drowned out the patter of wild weather. We sat in a silence that was not uncomfortable. Gradually the rain ceased, although puddles in the road still sprayed up under our tyres, and Kim had to turn on the wipers every time a lorry thundered by in the opposite direction.

I sat back wearily, and gazed at the countryside flowing past. I could see my face, a hazy blur, in the window. I hadn't been able to stay, but I didn't really know what I was going back for. What should I do now? My life was at an impasse. Maybe the only thing to do was to return to Alex's couch and try to sort out all the ugly, itchy inconsistencies. With Alex, I had managed to illuminate one sickening patch of my past, but everything else lay in shadow. Perhaps I had to illuminate all of that, too. I felt unutterably tired at the very thought, as if my bones ached. When I had begun this journey back into my childhood, I had used the image of a black hole in the visible landscape of my past. Now it seemed as if, like the negative of a photograph, that image had been reversed. The only thing that was visible, dazzlingly visible, was that which had been obscure. Topsy-turvy land ruled over by a dead child.

'Can you turn the light on while I try to find another tape?' asked Kim, scrabbling among the mess of cassette cases in the compartment of her door.

'Sure.' I blinked in the light, and the world outside the car was blotted out. 'You know, Kim, it all feels so inside out. When I walked up Cree's Top this morning, I felt exactly like Alice in the looking-glass garden, where everything is back to front, and in order to get somewhere you have to walk away from it. Strange, isn't it?'

I blinked back unexpected tears, and gazed at the window. A middle-aged woman, her thin face lined with worry, stared back, stuck in her world on the other side of the glass. We looked at each other, eyes wide and appalled. She wasn't a stranger; we knew each other quite well though perhaps not well enough. A cold knife was slicing through my brain. Oh no, oh dear God, please no. What had I done?

I reached up and turned off the light. A flute, haunting, silver, trembled in the air. The woman's face was extinguished. I had been looking at myself. Of course. I was that girl on the hillside, Natalie for an hour; I had seen myself on that hillside, and tracked myself down. I had been in the looking-glass garden and I had followed my own image and when I had found myself I had lost myself most terribly. Most terribly. I felt a scream rising up in me and clapped my hand over my mouth. It had never been Natalie on the hill; it had only ever been me, Natalie's friend, her lookalike. It was me who had been seen all those years ago by an old man on his way to dismantle

357

the marquee, me who had been called Natalie. It was me for whom I had searched among my living nightmares.

'Please Kim. Please can you drop me off at the next tube station.'

We were coming into the suburbs of London and I knew where I had to go next.

Kim looked at me in astonishment but obediently braked.

'I hope you know what you're doing, Jane, because I certainly don't.'

I kissed her on the cheek then gave her a long hug.

'I know what I'm doing; for the first time in a long long while I know what I'm doing. There's something I've got to sort out and I think it's going to be painful.'

'Jane,' said Kim, as I turned to go. 'If you ever get through this you owe me one. More than one.'

Thirty-Nine

'Hello?'

'Hello, is that Dr Thelma Scott?'

'Yes.'

'This is Jane Martello, you may remember we met at . . .'

She interrupted me with a new note of interest in her voice.

'Yes, I remember.'

'I know this will sound stupid but could I come and see you?'

'What? Now?'

'Yes, if that's all right?'

'It's Saturday night, how do you know I'm not having a dinner party or going to a nightclub?'

'I'm sorry, I don't want to interrupt anything.'

'That's all right, I'm reading a novel. Are you sure this is important? You can't just ask me over the phone?'

'If it isn't, you can send me away. Just give me five minutes.'

'All right, where are you?'

'Hanger Lane tube station. Should I get a taxi?'

'No, you're quite close. Just take the tube to Shepherd's Bush.'

She gave me some brief instructions and in a few minutes I was walking out of Shepherd's Bush tube station and around the corner into a quiet residential street by Wood Lane. Knocking at the door, I was greeted by the small woman with the alert expression I remembered from before, but dressed casually in jeans and a very bright sweater. She had a slightly sardonic smile, as if I were acting up to expectations, but her handshake was friendly enough.

'Are you hungry?'

'No, I'm not.'

'Then I'm afraid you'll have to watch me eat. Come through to the kitchen. No smoking, I'm afraid,' she said, noticing the cigarette in my hand. I tossed it back onto the path. In the kitchen she poured herself a glass of chianti and I asked for nothing but tap water.

'Since you're not eating, I'll just nibble a bit,' she said. 'Now what was it you wanted to see me about.'

And as we talked she prepared and ate the most enormous selection of food: pistachios, olives stuffed with anchovies and chillies, tortilla chips dipped in a guacamole from the fridge, focaccia with mozzarella and Parma ham with a large splash of olive oil.

'Are you a psychoanalyst?'

'No, I'm a psychiatrist. Does it matter?'

'You know what happened to me, what I've done, don't you?'

'I think so. But you tell me.'

God, I wanted a cigarette. To help me think. For something to do with my hands. I had to concentrate.

'I've been in therapy with Alex Dermot-Brown since November. I'd had some emotional problems after the body of my dear friend, Natalie, was found. She'd gone missing in the summer of 1969. Alex was particularly interested when I told him that I had been close by when

360

she was last seen alive. We worked over and over that scene, visualising it, and I gradually recovered the memory of seeing her being murdered by her father, my father-in-law, Alan Martello. I confronted him with it and he confessed. He's now . . . well, you've read the papers.'

'Yes, I have.'

'I've got to ask you something, Dr Scott. Two things, really. Is it possible that someone would confess to a crime they hadn't committed? I mean, why would they?'

'Hang on a second,' Dr Scott said. 'This takes concentration.' She was slicing her focaccia construction into sections. 'There we are. Now, why would you want to ask me that?'

'What I really want to ask is, is it possible to remember something that then turns out to be false? I mean a clear, detailed visual memory.' She started to reply but I carried on speaking. 'I felt I was doing something like retrieving a file on my computer that had been accidentally lost. Once I'd got it back I would never doubt that it was the actual file that I'd typed, would I?'

Dr Scott was now seated at the kitchen table with plates of food radiating out from her. When it became clear that an answer was required, her mouth was full of sandwich and she had to chew energetically and then swallow.

'Call me Thelma, by the way. My name's an interesting example of the problems of transmission. It comes from a Marie Corelli novel written in the 1880s. It's the name of the heroine, who is Norwegian. I once went to a conference in Bergen and began my speech by saying that it was appropriate I was there because I had a Norwegian name et cetera et cetera. Afterwards, a man came up to me and told me that actually Thelma wasn't a Norwegian name at all. Corelli must have misheard, or something. Or made it up.'

'So your name is a mistake?'

'Yes, all of us Thelmas ought to be recalled and given authentic names.' She laughed. 'It doesn't matter, as long as one doesn't take ideas about cultural tradition too seriously.

'Your comparison with the computer is interesting. Even neurologists have no precise model for the way that memory works, so we all invent our own rough-and-ready metaphors. Sometimes the memory can be like a filing system. A whole section of it might get lost, perhaps the bit dealing with a class you were in at school. Then, by chance, you meet somebody who was in that class, he provides a few clues and you suddenly recapture a whole lot of memories you didn't know you had.

'The problem is when metaphors take over and start to assume a false reality. The filing system comparison might lead you to believe that everything you have ever experienced can potentially be recaptured and re-experienced, provided you can find the right stimulus. I would compare some memories to a sandcastle on a beach. Once the sea has come in and washed it away, it is gone, and it can't be precisely recreated, even in theory. Is that all you wanted to talk to me about?'

'Of course not. I'm desperate and I don't know whom to talk to.'

'Why don't you talk to Alex Dermot-Brown?'

'I don't think Alex would be very receptive to what I'm about to say.'

'And you think I'm hostile enough to Alex to believe it,' said Thelma, pouring herself a third (or was it a fourth?) large glass of wine.

'Look, at the conference where we met, I also met some good, damaged women who said that they would support me and believe me and not question me. I'm standing on the edge of something terrible but what's important is that I don't want to be supported. I don't want to be believed if I'm wrong. Do you see what I'm saying?'

'Not quite, but go on.'

'Let me give you the important details. The last witness who saw Natalie alive saw her by a river near her home on Sunday 27 July 1969. The work on my memory with Alex was based on the fact that I was there, right by where it had happened at the very same time. I was having a passionate love affair with Natalie's brother at the time and I went down to the River Col, and sat there with my back against the small hill that separated me from Natalie. In an impulsive adolescent gesture I took some poems I had written, screwed them up, threw them into the river and watched them drift away round the bend of the river.'

Thelma raised an eyebrow. 'Is all this relevant?'

'Yes, very. This was the original account I gave Alex, the bit I remembered without any question, the bit there's no doubt about.'

'So?'

'I walked down to the river this morning, for the first time since it happened. When I got to the spot I'd remembered, the river was flowing the wrong way.'

'How do you mean "the wrong way"?'

'It sounds stupid but it's true. I threw a piece of paper and it didn't float away from me, but towards me.'

Thelma looked disappointed. She shrugged. Was this all?

'It was quite simple,' I continued. 'I turned and walked

over the small rise to the other side, and I realised that this was where I had sat and thrown the paper in. In fact, I threw another piece in and it floated away and around the bend, just as I had remembered.'

Thelma's expression had chilled now. She looked distant, a little embarrassed. She wasn't even eating with the same energy. I could see that she was starting to wonder how she could get rid of me without too much fuss.

'I'm sorry,' she said, 'I'm sure I'm being dense but I can't quite see where we're heading. I don't see why it matters that you got things the wrong way round.'

'It wasn't just the wrong way round. The bridge from where the witness saw Natalie was on that side of the hill as well. But bear with me for just one more minute. For reasons I won't go into, I've just received a whole lot of stuff from when I used to spend summers at Natalie's house. It included the diary I kept during that summer. It finished two days before Natalie was last seen, so I didn't pay it much attention. But then when I looked at it today, an interesting detail occurred to me. It always seemed strange that Natalie's body was never found. When she was discovered in October, it seemed – to me, at least – even stranger. It was a brilliant place to bury a body because it was right under our noses, in the garden just a few yards from the house. But how could it be done?'

'I don't know. Tell me,' said Thelma with obvious impatience.

'My diary reminded me that a barbecue was being built in front of the house and it was completed on the very morning of a party that was held on Saturday the twenty-sixth of July, the day before Natalie was last seen. This morning I looked at the hole where Natalie's body was found, and I saw the remains of that barbecue. The barbecue was made of brick installed in clay tiles set in concrete mortar. There are only bits of it now because the barbecue was removed and the clay tiles broken up when Martha – that's my mother-in-law – extended the lawn. But the point is that the murderer buried Natalie's body in the hole knowing that it was about to be covered with concrete, tiles and a heavy brick construction.'

'Wouldn't a hole in the ground be the first place where the police would look?'

'But it wasn't a hole in the ground, don't you see? When Natalie was last seen on the twenty-seventh, the barbecue had already been *in situ* for more than twenty-four hours. It would obviously be impossible to place a corpse under a brick barbecue that had already been constructed.'

'Well, yes, so aren't you answering your own question?'

'You're not following me. Natalie couldn't have died on the twenty-seventh, let alone the twenty-eighth, when she was reported missing. She was already dead and buried by the morning of the party on the twenty-sixth.'

Thelma looked puzzled, but she was alert now.

'But you said that she was actually seen on the twenty-seventh?'

'Yes. But what if I told you that Natalie and I were the same age, we had the same complexions, dressed in the same clothes. And also that she was well known in the neighbourhood and I was only there in the summer, so that there were plenty of local people who had never met me? And if I now seem to have discovered that I was in the same place at the same time where Natalie was last seen alive. What then?'

A very slow smile spread across Thelma's face like

flame through a newspaper. She was thinking hard now.

'Are you sure about this barbecue?' she demanded.

'Absolutely. I found fragments of tile on every side of the spot where she was found. She was definitely underneath it.'

'And are you positive that it wasn't completed a few days later? Maybe it wasn't finished in time for the party.'

'It was the centrepiece of the party. I've got photographs of people queuing up for their spare ribs and hot dogs.'

Another objection occurred to Thelma. 'But does any of this really matter? Alan confessed. The police would say that you just got the date wrong.'

'But Alan wasn't there. My father met Alan and Martha off the boat at Southampton on the morning of the party. They'd just come by steamer from the West Indies. They didn't arrive at the Stead until early evening, just when the party was starting. Alan couldn't have murdered Natalie. There's just one problem.'

'What's that?'

I threw up my hands in despair. 'I saw him do it. And he confessed.'

Thelma laughed out loud. 'Oh is *that* all?'

'Yes,' I said.

'I never believed any of that.'

'Are you saying I imagined it all?'

I may have been shouting.

'Jane, I'm going to have a whisky and you're going to have one too and I'm going to allow you to smoke your awful cigarettes and we're going to have a serious talk. All right?'

'Yes, all right.'

She produced two inordinately chunky tumblers, and

then an equally chunky glass ashtray. I wouldn't have allowed any of them in my house.

'Here,' she said, slurping what looked like a quintuple scotch into each one. 'None of your trendy single-malt rubbish. This is good blended whisky, the way it was meant to be drunk. Cheers.'

I took a gulp and a blissful drag on a cigarette.

'So?' I said.

'Tell me about your sessions with Alex Dermot-Brown.'

'How do you mean?'

'The process by which you recovered this memory. How did it work?'

I gave a brief account of the little ritual that Alex and I had gone through, each time I'd placed myself back there by the Col. As I spoke, Thelma first frowned and then her frown became a smile.

'I'm sorry,' I said, 'is something funny?'

'No. Carry on.'

'That's it. So what do you think?'

'Did the prosecution lawyers show any willingness to put you in the witness box?'

'There was no need. Alan confessed.'

'Yes, of course. But did they seem eager about the prospect of your testimony?'

'I don't know. A couple of the lawyers seemed a bit uneasy.'

'Let me tell you that Alan Martello would never have been convicted solely on your testimony. It might not even have been admissible.'

'Why?'

'Because hypnosis alters memory, and you were hypnotised.'

'Don't be ridiculous, I know what I did and I just lay on the couch and tried to remember. I'd know if I had been hypnotised.'

'I don't think you would. There's no hocus pocus about this. It's my guess that you are a highly receptive subject. I could put you in a trance now and tell you that, oh, I don't know, that you saw somebody run over by a car when you walked here from Shepherd's Bush. When I woke you up, you would be convinced that it was true.'

'Even if that's true, Alex didn't tell me what to remember.'

'I know, but with all the repetition and reinforcement, you were going through an accretion of memorial reconstruction. Each time you added a little more to the story and then the following time you were remembering that detail you had added the previous time and adding a bit more. Your memory is real in a way, but it's a memory of memories.'

'But what about the final terrible crime? I saw it in so much detail.'

'The whole process was leading up to something like that. Alex Dermot-Brown was preparing you for it, he was assuring you that everything you remembered was genuine and he used his professional status and the analytical authority he had over you to convince you that you were witnessing rather than constructing.'

'Is that *possible*?'

'Yes, it's possible.'

'Was Alex doing it deliberately? Was he trying to implant a false memory?'

'Definitely not. But sometimes you can create what you're looking for. I know that Dr Dermot-Brown believes passionately in the phenomenon of recovered memory. I am convinced he wants to help these sufferers and now he has hitched his entire career to it.'

'Are you saying that he is definitely wrong?'

'What other explanation have *you* got, Jane?'

'But what about the women who said they were abused as children? Are you saying that that's all fantasy, the way that Freud did?'

Thelma took a large gulp of whisky. 'No. I'm treating half a dozen abuse victims at the moment. Two of them are sisters who each had two children by their father before they were sixteen years old. I gave evidence at the trial that helped, I hope, to convict him. I also know that abuse is sometimes difficult to prove. I know of specific abusers who are currently getting away with it and it fills me with despair. Perhaps that's why I drink more of this than I should.' She gave her whisky glass a little shake. There wasn't much left in the tumbler. 'But I don't believe that abuse exists in a universe of its own in which normal rules – and I mean rules of law or of science – cease to apply. Just because abuse is exceptionally difficult to prove, that doesn't mean we should try to convict people accused of abuse without proof.'

'But these cases *aren't* without proof. Those women I met at the workshop. They remember being abused.'

'Do they? All of them? I've seen reports of young women, from apparently loving, functional families, entering analysis and emerging a year or two later with accounts of obscene abuse throughout their entire child-hood. They give accounts of repeated ritual rape, sodomy, torture, the ingestion of faeces, satanic ritual. Some of us might say that unprecedented claims require a particular rigour of proof, but the supporters of these sad women say that we must demand no proof at all beyond their own

369

testimony. Anything less is collaboration with the abuser. There isn't even a neurological model to explain the process. We all know about memory loss after a single blow on the head in a traffic accident. But there is no precedent for the systematic amnesia of regular, separate incidents occurring over many years. Your own supposed witnessing of your father-in-law murdering your cousin is trivial by comparison.'

'But why did it happen to be *Alan* that I saw?'

Thelma shrugged. 'Don't ask me. You're the one who knows him. It may be that he was the focus for particular strong feelings during the period of your analysis. At a time when your creative mind was searching for a villain, he seemed like somebody who could be violent to a woman. The imagined murder was the moment when your inner and outer worlds coincided. In a perverse way, it was something of a triumph for the psychoanalytic method. It's unfortunate that reality has intervened so stubbornly.'

'But why on earth did he confess?'

'People do, you know. They have their reasons.'

'Oh, God,' I said, and my head slumped into my hands. 'You're asking if Alan Martello is the sort of man who might deal with feelings of guilt and despair by making a wild, self-destructive, theatrical gesture? You're fucking right he is.'

Thelma drained her glass. 'So there you are then.'

I looked at my own glass. No chance of draining that. There was at least a triple scotch left and I already felt drunk. I stood up, a little unsteadily. 'I think I'd better go,' I said.

'I'll call you a taxi.' She did so and it was barely a couple of minutes before the doorbell rang.

'I suppose you'll be wanting to use me as an exhibit in the crusade against recovered memory,' I said as I stood in the doorway.

She gave a sad smile. 'No, don't worry. Your experience will have no effect whatsoever on their certainties.'

'That can't be true.'

'No? What about you? What would you have thought if you had arrived at your river and found it flowing the *right* way?'

'I don't know.'

'Look after yourself on the way home,' she said, as I got into the cab. 'You'll have to phone the police tomorrow morning. They'll need a whole new murder inquiry.'

'Oh no they won't,' I said.

Thelma looked puzzled but the cab was moving off and I was already too far away to say anything.

Forty

We drove out of London on the A12, against the commuter traffic, and were quickly in the pseudo-countryside between the fringes of London and the Essex flats beyond. I had the road atlas open on my lap. Except for my directions, nobody spoke. We left the main road and entered the mess of roundabouts, corridor villages, industrial estates. A bypass was being constructed, and we sat for half an hour in a single line of traffic, looking at a man rotate a sign. Stop, go. Stop, go. I looked at my watch repeatedly.

For the last stages of the journey, the map was unnecessary. We followed the blue signs to Wivendon. We parked outside a neo-classical building that could have been a supermarket or a tourist centre. But it was a prison.

The others stayed in the car park. I walked up the path, between low privet hedges, to the security gate. My identity was checked, driving licence inspected, bag removed from me. A woman in a navy blue uniform smiled but prodded me through my arms and under my dress. I was led through relatively small doors, much as if I were being led through the staff entrance at a municipal swimming baths.

I sat in a waiting room, where a flowerless pot plant and old magazines stood on a central table. On the wall was a poster advertising a fireworks display. The door opened and a man came in. He was dressed in brown corduroy trousers and a rough checked shirt, unbuttoned at the neck. His thick, reddish-brown hair hung down over his collar. He was heavy-set, about my age. He held several thick brown folders under his left arm.

'Mrs Martello?' He came and sat down beside me, and held out his hand. 'I'm Griffith Singer.'

'Hello.'

'You look surprised.'

'I suppose I'd expected a warder.'

'We try to be a bit more informal than that.'

'How long have I got?'

He raised his eyebrows: 'As long as you like. I'm sorry, you've caught me on a busy day. Is it all right if we talk on the move?'

We got up and he ushered me through the door and along a corridor which ended at two consecutive barred double doors.

'This takes us into the unit,' Griffith said, pressing a simple plastic doorbell which was glued to the wall beside the first door. A uniformed man came out of a glass-walled office between the two doors. Griffith showed a pass and my name was checked on a clipboard. It wasn't there and we had to wait for several minutes for someone to come along from the main entrance with a docket.

'How is he doing?' I asked.

'He's one of our stars,' Singer said. 'We're very pleased indeed. This is a new unit, you know. I – we – only set it up shortly before he arrived and he has been one of the people who has made it work. Do you know anything about us?'

'We've all written. He hasn't replied.'

373

'The residents here all have long parole dates. Instead of letting them rot, we're putting them together in an environment where they can help each other and also, we hope, spend their time creatively.'

'Swap memories,' I said.

'It's not like you think,' Singer said. 'He's doing terribly well. He's formed a seminar, got everybody involved. He's . . . oh, good, here's Riggs now.'

Another man in a uniform clattered along the corridor. He panted an apology. I had to sign a slip, insert it into a transparent plastic tag which was clipped onto my lapel. The first door was opened and locked. Then the second door. A warder with a name tag identifying him as Barry Skelton followed us through.

'Am I safe?'

Singer smiled in amusement. 'You're safer here than you are out in the car park. Anyway, Barry will be nearby the whole time.'

A corridor with a soft felt carpet and whitewashed walls went in each direction. Singer took my arm.

'I'll try to find you somewhere quiet. There's a store-room along here that should be free.'

We passed a couple of rooms. I glimpsed some men watching a television set. Nobody looked round. Something – I couldn't see what – was going on in the storeroom, so we walked on until we reached a seminar room which was empty.

'You go in with Barry,' said Singer and carried on down the corridor. A thought occurred to him and he turned round. 'He's writing a novel, you know. It's rather promising.'

It was a medium-sized room with large windows at the far end overlooking a deserted recreation area. In the centre of the room was a circle of eight orange moulded-plastic chairs. Everything was bright under the strip lighting. Barry stepped forward and lifted one of the chairs and put it down just inside the door.

'I'll stay here,' he said. He spoke in a light Ulster accent. He was a very tall man with pale skin and straight black hair. 'You sit facing me. We're relaxed about the rules here, but you're not allowed to pass any object between you. If you want to end the interview, for whatever reason, you don't need to say anything. Just touch your identification tag and I'll come forward and escort you out.'

I nodded. I sat in the chair as instructed. I let my face fall into my hands. I needed to gather my thoughts.

'Hello, Jane.'

I looked up.

'Hello, Claud.'

Claud had lost at least a stone in weight. He looked leaner, sharper, with a touch more grey in his cropped hair. He wore a faded blue sweatshirt, black jeans and training shoes. He half looked round at where Griffith Singer was hovering in the doorway.

'So, I'll leave you two together,' Singer said awkwardly, as if he had brought us together on a blind date and wasn't sure how we would get on.

Claud nodded.

'Shall I sit here, Barry?' he asked, gesturing at the chair opposite mine in the circle. Barry nodded. He sat down and we scrutinised each other.

'You're looking well, Claud,' I said.

He *was* looking well, better than I'd ever seen him. He gave a slight nod, acknowledging the compliment. He reached into his trouser pocket and removed a crumpled cigarette packet and a grey metal lighter. He offered me a cigarette and I shook my head. He lit one for himself and drew deeply on it.

'This is a stimulating environment,' he said. 'There are interesting ideas being developed here. In various respects, I think it's an improvement on the Barlinnie model. And as for me personally . . .' He gave a modest shrug. 'It's a remarkably healthy existence. But how are you?'

'Have you heard about Alan?'

'I don't look at television or read the newspapers.'

'He's become a literary star again.'

'How so?'

'He's written a prison memoir. It's called *A Hundred and Seventy-Seven Days*. The publishers rushed it out this month. It's been a sensation. The *New Yorker* devoted an entire issue to publishing it complete. The reviews compared it favourably to *One Day in the Life of Ivan Denisovich*. Alan told me that Anthony Hopkins is going to play him in the film version. I think Alan's only uncertainty at the moment is whether he's going to get the Nobel Prize for literature or for peace.'

Claud smiled. He tapped his cigarette and the ash fell on the floor by his right foot.

'So you're on speaking terms?' he said.

'Very much so. Alan took me in his arms and forgave me. I was very moved, even though it was in a TV studio on live television.'

'What happened to your therapist?'

I shrugged.

'How are the boys, Jane?'

'Paul's fine as well. He did a completely re-edited version of his film. It's been sold all over the world. He's at a television festival in Seoul as we speak.'

376

'Good. I thought the original was rather superficial, myself.'

'It must have seemed so to you, Claud.'

'What about your hostel, Jane? Is it functioning?'

'Not exactly, but we do have our third official opening date and we've got closer to it without it being cancelled than ever before. I'm hopeful.'

'I'm glad to hear it, Jane. That's a good sign. It's a wonderful project. I'm happy for you.'

A pain was gathering strength behind my eyes.

'And what about your own *magnum opus*? I hear you're writing a novel.'

Claud laughed. 'Has Griff been blabbing about it? I know that one should never show people one's work until it's finished, but he wouldn't be denied.'

'What's it about?'

'I'm writing a sort of crime story, almost as an intellectual exercise. I must say that I've found it quite satisfying.'

'What's the plot?'

'It's about the murder of a teenage girl.'

'Who kills her?'

'That's the interesting part. I'm trying to get away from the old hackneyed image of young girls as sweet, passive creatures. The murder victim is a manipulative adolescent, conscious of her awakening sexual powers. She is beautiful and charming, but she uses these qualities as tools to damage all those around her. She finds out their secrets and blackmails them.'

'Is that why she's killed?'

'Not quite. She can't resist using her physical attractions even on the men in her own family. Unknown to everybody else, she starts to lead her own eldest brother on.'

'How does she do that?'

'You know the sort of thing, a look here, a touch there, an air of complicity, moments of flirtatiousness. One of the things I'm trying to capture is the transition in a family from the stage where the relationships are innocent to the stage where similar behaviour becomes sexually charged, because the girl has become a sexual being and she is aware of the power she exercises.'

'What happens?'

'She gets more than she bargains for. She is leading him on, so he makes her go the whole way. He makes her see the logical result of her own behaviour. But this is the twist, you see. Even here, she uses her sexuality as a form of power over her brother, taunting him with it, humiliating him. What is meant to be her punishment becomes a pleasure to her.'

'What happens?'

'It's one of those things that might have fizzled out, but she becomes pregnant.'

'Couldn't she have an abortion?'

'That doesn't arise between them. She threatens her brother with it. He receives a note from her saying that she will expose him to the family.'

'You sound as if you're on the murderer's side.'

'You always have to see every side of a story. It's what makes us human, isn't it, our imagination? That's what you used to say, anyway.'

'Do you think you will be able to persuade readers that a young girl deserves to be murdered by the brother who made her pregnant?'

Claud allowed himself a small smile and a shrug. 'It's an artistic challenge.'

'How does he set about it?'

'Yes, that's interesting, isn't it?' Claud's face was quite

calm, reflective. 'Easy to kill, difficult to avoid detection. The brother considers two contrasting methods. The first is to kill her openly, as if by accident in a quarrel. At worst the killer might receive a short prison sentence; if he's lucky he might not even be charged. But it's an unattractive solution. I needed to . . .' Claud paused, suddenly at a loss. He stubbed his cigarette out on the sole of his shoe and lit another. 'I want to create a character who kills his sister almost as a matter of decorum. Obviously she has provoked him, but she is also poisoning the entire family. She is a girl who ferrets out secrets and then uses those secrets. Families need their secrets, the little subterfuges that hold them together. This girl is going to destroy a good family, a fine family. Many people might agree that it is better to lose a girl than to lose an entire family.'

'We don't seem to be hearing much of the girl's point of view in your story.'

'Her point of view is perfectly clear: to follow her own immediate desires, whatever damage that does to anybody else.'

'How does he actually carry out the murder?'

'It's quite straightforward. There is going to be a large summer party at the country house where the family live. People will be staying all over the place. A disappearance will not be noticed. The brother is organising the party and he has an inspiration. He arranges for a barbecue to be constructed at the last minute, and orders matters with the builders so that it is only half finished on the evening before the party. He summons his sister to a meeting late that night. She has been involved in a flirtation with a local boy and he suggests she tell her roommate that she is going to see this new flame. He strangles her and buries her at a relatively shallow depth in the site where the barbecue will be tiled and constructed the following morning.'

'Wouldn't the barbecue be an obvious place to look?'

'The beauty of the plan is that there are various other factors at work. The novel is set in 1969. At that time, if a restless, difficult sixteen-year-old girl disappears, it will be assumed that she has run away. By the time grimmer possibilities are being considered, it is much later and in the chaos of the party it is difficult to establish exactly when she disappeared. But people have a vague impression that they saw her at the party. The brother has told various local artisans and some friends that the sister will be fulfilling various functions at the party. Of course, when the party begins she is already dead and buried. But the sister had a close friend of the same age. A sweet girl. They look alike, they dress alike. The friend isn't much known in the locality because she lives in London. All that I needed – all that the story needs – is for one or two people to mistake one for the other at the party and the hiding place becomes not just very good but perfect.'

I looked over Claud's shoulder at Barry who was looking bored. Obviously not a book lover.

'But I wasn't *at* the party, Claud.'

'Yes, I know. Theo told me all about it when I came back from India. This is the bit that isn't in the novel. It's just too serendipitous to be credible in the tightly organised structure of the book I'm writing. As you say, you were not on hand at the party in order to provide the crucial alibi. Yet when Gerald Docherty walked across the bridge over the Col on Sunday the twenty-seventh of July on his way to help dismantle the marquee, you *were* there, resembling Natalie. Not only had you provided an even more effective distraction from Natalie's resting place, you had given me an alibi so perfect that I could never have constructed it for myself. You were, quite unconsciously, my fellow-artist in creating a perfect deception.'

'Why did you marry me, Claud? Why did you marry me and have children with me?'

For the first time Claud looked surprised.

'Because I fell in love with you, my darling. I've never ever loved anyone else. I'll always love you. You're the one. And I wanted to make you love me. The only flaw in the plan was my inability to keep you in love with me. Everything proceeded from that failure.'

'And you were prepared to sacrifice Alan for your own survival. Was the note you planted really by Natalie or did you fake it?'

'It was a note Natalie sent *me*. I only had to tear the paper to remove the "Dear Claud" or words to that effect at the beginning. I wasn't sacrificing Alan. You've always talked about his theatrical nature. I saw the way events were moving and gave them a small nudge. He embraced the role by confessing. And from what you tell me, I assume he has never been happier. I'm not proud of it, though, if that's what you mean. I'm afraid I saw it as a way of getting you back and that may have blunted my powers of reasoning. That was the flaw, wasn't it? You realised that if Alan was innocent then I must have planted Natalie's note in his diary.'

Claud leant forward and his voice dropped to little more than a whisper.

'Do you want to hear my one regret, Jane?' I didn't reply and made no movement. 'If you had discovered this when we were still married . . .' Claud frowned and shook his head. 'I don't mean married, I mean when we were together, really together, then you would have understood.

No, don't say anything. I know that you would. There's just one more thing I want to say to you, because I know that you'll never come to see me again. That's all right, Jane. I don't mind any of this. All that matters is that I still love you. You haven't said what you think of me, and maybe that's the best I can hope for from you. Just remember, Jane, the family and our two boys, that's my gift to you. You will always live in the world I made for you.'

I touched my name tag. As Barry led me out, I avoided catching Claud's eye. Neither of us spoke.

Griffith led me back through the corridors to the front door. He held out his broad hand.

'Goodbye Mrs Martello. If it's of any consolation to you, I . . .'

'Goodbye. Thank you.'

I stepped outside, and the door swung shut behind me, closing with a muffled click. While I had been inside, the day had changed. The sun shone in a sky that between its strips of clouds was almost turquoise. The few dry leaves that still hung on the small trees fringing the path gleamed. I pushed my hair back with both hands, and tipped my face towards the light, and stood with my eyes closed in the warm air. After a few seconds the roaring in my head quietened. 'That's it, Natalie,' I said out loud. 'That's finished.' Then, 'I wish you were still here with us. My sister. My friend.'

Slowly, I walked down the shallow paved steps, between the low hedges and neat, empty flowerbeds, then stopped again. In the car park a tiny figure in a bulky dufflecoat, with a pointed hood like a pixie's, was twirling in a shaft of sunlight. She stopped, tipped, then sat down abruptly while her world went on spinning. A young man with shaggy blond hair and a thick sweater hanging down under his beaten-up leather jacket ran towards her, picked her up, and threw her high into the air. Fanny squealed with laughter, her hood falling back and a cloud of bright hair flying loose. Robert threw her up again, then lowered her gently onto the tarmac, and stood holding her by the shoulders.

Caspar and Jerome walked towards them; they were talking earnestly, and at one point Caspar stopped and put his hand on Jerome's arm. They joined the other two, and Fanny slipped her hand into Caspar's, tilting her pale solemn triangle of a face up to his, saying something. Jerome pulled her hood back over her wild hair.

Then they saw me and stopped talking. They turned towards me and waited: three tall men and a little girl. I took a deep breath, and I walked down the steps to join them.

Read on for a taste of

The Safe House

by
Nicci French

(Penguin, £7.99)

One

The door was the first thing. The door was open. The front door was never open, even in the wonderful heat of the previous summer that had been so like home, but there it was, teetering inwards, on a morning so cold that the moisture hanging in the air stung Mrs Ferrer's pocked cheeks. She pushed her gloved hand against the white painted surface, testing the evidence of her eyes.

'Mrs Mackenzie?'

Silence. Mrs Ferrer raised her voice and called for her employer once more and felt embarrassed as the words echoed, high and wavering, in the large hallway. She stepped inside and wiped her feet on the mat too many times, as she always did. She removed her gloves and clutched them in her left hand. There was a smell, now. It was heavy and sweet. It reminded her of something. The smell of a barnyard. No, inside. A barn maybe.

Each morning at eight-thirty precisely Mrs Ferrer would nod a good-morning at Mrs Mackenzie, click past her across the polished wood of the Mackenzies' hallway, turn right down the stairs into the basement, remove her coat, collect her vacuum cleaner from the utility room and spend an hour in an anaesthetized fog of noise. Up the large staircase at the front of the house, along the passageways on the first floor, the passageways on the second floor, then down the small back staircase. But where was Mrs Mackenzie? Mrs Ferrer stood uncertainly by the door in her tightly buttoned porridge-meal-tweed coat, shifting her weight from one foot to another. She could hear a television. The television was never on. She carefully rubbed the sole of each shoe on the mat. She looked down. She had already done that, hadn't she?

'Mrs Mackenzie?'

She stepped off the mat on to the hard wood – beeswax, vinegar and paraffin. She walked across to the front room, which was never used for anything and hardly ever needed vacuuming, though she did it anyway. There was nobody, of course. The curtains were all closed, the light on. She walked across to the foot of the staircase to the other front room. She rested her hand on the newel, which was topped by an ornate carving like a beaked pineapple of dark wood. Afrormosia – linseed oil, it needed, boiled, not raw. There was nobody. She knew that the television was in the sitting room. She took a step forward, her hand brushing the wall as if for safety. A bookcase. Leather bindings, which required lanolin and neat's-foot in equal quantities. It was possible, she reflected, that whoever was watching television had not heard her call. And as for the door, perhaps something was being delivered, or the window cleaner may have left it open on his way in. Thus fortified she walked to the rear of the house and into the main sitting room. Very quickly, within a few seconds of entering the room, she had vomited profusely on to the carpet that she had vacuumed every weekday for eighteen months.

She leaned towards the ground, bent double, gasping. She felt in her coat pocket, found a tissue and wiped her mouth. She was surprised at herself, embarrassed almost. When she was a child, her uncle had led her through a slaughterhouse outside Fuenteobejuna and had smiled down at her as she refused to faint in the face of the blood and dismemberment and above all the steam rising from the cold stone floor. That was the smell she had remembered. It wasn't a barn at all.

There were splashes of blood across such a wide area, even on the ceiling, on the far wall, that Mr Mackenzie might have exploded. Mostly, though, it was in dark pools on his lap and on the sofa. There was so much of it. Could it be from just one man? What had made her sick, perhaps, was the ordinariness of his pyjamas, so English, even the top button done up. Mr Mackenzie's head now lolled back stupidly at an impossible angle. His neck was cut almost through and there was nothing to hold it up except the back of the sofa. She saw bone and sinew and the improbable spectacles, still uselessly over his eyes. The face was very white. And a horrible unexpected blue as well.

Mrs Ferrer knew where the phone was but had forgotten and had to look for it. She found it on a small table, on the other side of the room away from all the blood. She knew the number from a television programme. Nine nine nine. A female voice answered.

'*Hello. There has been a terrible murder.*'

'Excuse me?'

'*There has been a murder.*'

'It's all right. Calm down, don't cry. Can you speak English?'

'*Yes, yes.* I am sorry. Mr Mackenzie is dead. Killed.'

It was only when she had replaced the receiver that she thought of Mrs Mackenzie and walked upstairs. It took only a second for Mrs Ferrer to see what she had feared. Her employer was tied to her own bed. She seemed almost submerged in her blood, her nightie glossy with it against her gaunt body. Too thin, Mrs Ferrer had always thought privately. And the girl? She felt a weight in her chest as she walked up another flight of stairs. She pushed open the door of the one room in the house she wasn't allowed to clean. She could hardly see anything of the person tied to the bedstead. What had they done to her? Brown shiny tape around the face. Arms outstretched, wrists tied to the corners of the metal grille, thin streaks of red across the front of the nightgown.

Mrs Ferrer looked around Finn Mackenzie's bedroom. Bottles were scattered across the dresser and the floor. Photographs were torn and mutilated; faces gouged out. On one wall, a word she didn't understand was written in a smeary dark pink: piggies. She turned suddenly. There had been a sound from the bed. A gurgle. She ran forward. She touched the forehead, above the neat obscuring tape. It was warm. She heard a car outside and heavy footsteps in the hall. She ran down the stairs and saw men in uniform. One of them looked up at her.

'Alive,' Mrs Ferrer gasped. 'Alive.'

Nicci French

author photo © Mark Read

Nicci Gerrard was born in June 1958 in Worcestershire. After graduating with a first class honours degree in English Literature from Oxford University, she began her first job, working with emotionally disturbed children in Sheffield.

In the early eighties she taught English Literature in Sheffield, London and Los Angeles, but moved into publishing in 1985 with the launch of *Women's Review*, a magazine for women on art, literature and female issues. In 1987 Nicci had a son, Edgar, followed by a daughter, Anna, but by the time she became acting literary editor at the *New Statesman* her marriage had ended. She moved to the *Observer* in 1990, where she was deputy literary editor for five years, and then a feature writer and executive editor. It was while she was at the *New Statesman* that she met Sean French.

Sean French was born in May 1959 in Bristol, to a British father and Swedish mother. He too studied English Literature at Oxford University at the same time as Nicci, also graduating with a first class degree, but their paths didn't cross until 1990. In 1981 he won *Vogue* magazine's Writing Talent Contest, and from 1981 to 1986 he was their theatre critic. During that time he also worked at the *Sunday Times* as their deputy literary editor and television critic, and was the film critic for *Marie Claire* and deputy editor of *New Society*.

Sean and Nicci were married in Hackney in October 1990. Their daughters, Hadley and Molly, were born in 1991 and 1993.

By the mid nineties Sean had had two novels published, *The Imaginary Monkey* and *The Dreamer of Dreams*, as well as numerous non-fiction books, including biographies of Jane Fonda and Brigitte Bardot.

In 1995 Nicci and Sean began work on their first joint novel and adopted the pseudonym of Nicci French. The novel, *The Memory Game*, was published to great acclaim in 1997. *The Safe House*, *Killing Me Softly*, *Beneath the Skin*, *The Red Room*, *Land of the Living*, *Secret Smile*, *Catch Me When I Fall*, *Losing You* and *Until It's Over* have since been added to the Nicci French CV. *The Safe House*, *Beneath the Skin* and *Secret Smile* have all been adapted for TV, and *Killing Me Softly* for the big screen.

But Nicci and Sean also continue to write separately. Nicci still works as a journalist for the *Observer*, covering high-profile trials including those of Fred and Rose West, and Ian Huntley and Maxine Carr. Her novels *Things We Knew Were True*, *Solace* and *The Moment You Were Gone* are also published by Penguin. Sean's novel *Start From Here* came out in spring 2004.

This was your first book as a team. Why did you decide to write together?

Nicci: It's hard to say now (hard to remember) how something that for a long time had been a vague and slightly mad idea became a reality. Because when we met we were already writers – and obsessive readers – we had talked about what made a 'voice' in a book, and wondered whether it would be possible for two people to create one, seamless voice. We used to say that one day, when we had time, we would try to write a book together, to see if it was possible. And then one day – when we had no time, no money, four tiny children, a life of clutter and chaos – we came across this idea for a book that seemed new and exciting. And we just thought that if we were ever going to do it, now was the time. It began almost like a literary experiment, and then quite soon it took us over.

So how did you actually go about it?

Sean: We spent weeks and months around the kitchen table with glasses of wine and gin and tonics sketching out the story and even, in the case of *The Memory Game*, drawing a detailed map of the Martello property. But when it came to writing the book, we wrote separately. One of us would write a section, then hand it to the other who was permitted – in theory, at least – to cut, add, rewrite without fear of retribution.

Nicci: It sounds simpler than it is, less messy and quarrelsome. We're often asked if we argue and the answer is that of course we do. We argue quite a lot (actually, I argue and Sean doesn't, which is extremely irritating). But it's not over the things you'd expect – not over large ideas, or over the changing of words. It's more like a version of marital bickering: couples rarely argue over big issues, but over things like who does the washing up. More than arguing, however, we struggle and disagree with each other, and I've come to think that our novels are born out of those disagreements: we often want to write about the things we can't quite settle on, the things that bother and disquiet us and we can't let go of, but come back to over and again.

We thought, after *The Memory Game*, that we'd found a way of doing it, but that turned out to be nonsense. Maybe writing can never be easy and maybe it never should be. There are days when things go right, and then there's a kind of magic about the way that writing leads you, and you follow it in order to find out what you are thinking — and then there are days when it's painful and slow and your head feels like glue. We have very few rules together. One is that we never tell anyone – not even our family, not our children who are always asking, who wrote which bit (people try and guess and they're right about fifty per cent of the time). The other is that we'll change each other's words privately, not face to face, otherwise it's brutal.

Did you decide in advance who would write which bit – for instance, who would write about recovered memory and the therapy sessions?

Nicci: Absolutely not. We both do all the research (in this novel, and in all the subsequent ones), and then whoever's turn it is to write will do so. It's imperative that we each own every bit of the book – every piece of research, every word that's written.

Why did you choose the name Nicci French?

Sean: We were always felt the book should be published under a single name. We felt that two names on the cover are a distraction – when you read fiction, you want to hear a single voice talking to you. *The Memory Game* had a female narrator, so it seemed natural to choose a female name. We played around with lots of possibilities but in the end we just gave up and contributed a name each. The only other name I remember, which we quite liked and everybody else hated, was 'Alice London'. As a private joke, we reversed one of the 'n's and made Alice Loudon the heroine of our third book, *Killing Me Softly*.

There's a lot in *The Memory Game* about families – is any of that autobiographical?

Sean: Since this is a family history featuring crimes varying from murder to incest and culminating in two prison sentences, we were rather alarmed that our families claimed to recognize themselves in the book.
Nicci: When our families first read it, Sean's thought it was based on them

read more
www.penguin.co.uk

and on his crowded summers in Sweden with all his cousins, and my family thought it was based on them. Both of them, for instance, recognised the mushroom hunt at the start of the novel – because both Sean and I had experienced that. Part of the impulse behind the novel was our shared sense that every close, happy family is also unhappy and full of secrets, and that memory is unreliable, slippery and seductive. The past is a shadowy country; you can get lost there.

In the early 1990s reports began to emerge in the United States of horrific crimes. Patients undergoing analysis were recovering memories of horrific abuse committed against them years earlier in childhood. These ranged from sexual abuse by close relatives to baroque accusations of satanic rituals and human sacrifices. Families were torn apart by the revelations and there were even arrests, convictions and long jail sentences based solely on the evidence of these recovered memories. There then ensued a ferocious battle between those – mainly therapists – who insisted that the victims must be believed and those who doubted the basic trustworthiness of recovered memory.

We came across the controversy in 1994 and we had the dual reaction that is perhaps characteristic of writers. We were shocked by the suffering involved and also saw it as compelling material for a thriller. We had a feeling of urgency also, because we thought we had better get a move on, because other people might have the same idea.

As it turned out, the part of the subject that most engaged us was not the subject of sexual abuse but the possible manipulation of the relationship between patient and therapist.

The controversy seems to have passed into history now. The decisive weapons against the therapists who specialized in recovering memories proved to be not dissenting arguments but, as so often, the financial penalties. These took the form of litigation from their damaged patients and the refusal of the medical insurance companies to pay for the therapy.

Even so, some of the factual books on the subject are still well worth reading. *Remembering Satan* by Lawrence Wright, an account of satanic abuse accusations in a small American town, reads like a thriller in its own right. *Victims of Memory* by Mark Pendergast is a brilliant, intensely painful account of the subject by a writer who was himself the subject of unfounded accusations. *Making Monsters: False Memories, Psychotherapy and Sexual Hysteria* by Richard Ofshe and Ethan Waters gives a lucid account of the controversy. *The Memory Wars* by Frederick Crews joins his analysis of the subject with a devastating critique of the legacy of Sigmund Freud.

TEN FAVOURITE BOOKS ABOUT MEMORY

Funes the Memorious by Jorge Luis Borges. The great story of a man cursed by an inability to forget.

The Go-Between by L. P. Hartley. 'The past is a foreign country. They do things differently there ...'

In Memoriam by Alfred, Lord Tennyson. The greatest work of poetic mourning in the language?

In Search of Lost Time by Marcel Proust. Is the meaning of life to be found not outside, but in our own memories? About ten times as long as any other novel and about a hundred times as good.

The Man Who Mistook His Wife for a Hat by Oliver Sacks. Understanding the brain through the extraordinary ways it can go wrong – including the 'lost mariner', whose short-term memory has been destroyed, trapping him in an eternal, ephemeral present.

Atonement by Ian McEwan. Memory as apology, memory as fiction.

The Memory Wars by Frederick Crews. A polemic about Freud, therapy and recovered memory. Wonderful knockabout stuff, with Crews the last man standing.

The Prelude by William Wordsworth. The great epic of memory as redemption.

The Rime of the Ancient Mariner by Samuel Taylor Coleridge. The great romance of memory as curse.

Speak, Memory by Vladimir Nabokov. Is memory the new religion? Read this, Proust and *The Prelude*, and you might start to think so.

TEN FAVOURITE FILMS ABOUT MEMORY

Bad Day at Black Rock (1955). A whole town has forgotten its terrible secret, until Spencer Tracy gets off the train one day ...

The Bourne Identity (2002)/The Bourne Conspiracy (2004). A man is washed up on a beach, having forgotten he is an elite secret agent. And then he starts to remember. Oliver Sacks meets James Bond.

Citizen Kane (1941). Why, at the moment of his death, did Charles Foster Kane remember his sled?

Dead of Night (1945). A terrifying film about the hazards of forgetting your dreams when you wake up.

Eternal Sunshine of the Spotless Mind (2004). If you could wipe away the memory of a painful love affair, would you ...?

Groundhog Day (1993). Everyone in the world has amnesia, except Bill Murray. Originally written by a Zen Buddhist, this tale was rewritten by Harold Ramis as one of the funniest films ever made. Touching too.

Memento (2000). A detective's investigation is hampered by the fact that he has no short-term memory and must tattoo the clues on his body. And the film unfolds backwards. And it's fantastic.

Shoah (1985). A documentary about the Holocaust with no historical footage, no photographs, no commentary, just witnesses describing what they remember.

The 39 Steps (1935). One of the most entertaining of all cinematic thrillers, in which the secret plans are stolen and learned by the music hall star, 'Mr Memory', in order to be smuggled abroad. Nowadays they would just email it.

Wild Strawberries (1957). A road movie in which an old man drives across Sweden to receive an honorary degree and through his own memories in search of what he has lost in his life. Ingmar Bergman's most moving film.

Jane Martello's Bloody Mary

Pour a half litre of tomato juice into a jug with a handful of ice cubes. Add a few good shakes of Worcestershire sauce, several drops of Tabasco, three twists of black pepper, three pinches of celery salt, half a wine glass of Russian vodka and a quarter of a wine glass of dry sherry. Stir and serve.

Wild Mushroom Risotto

Assuming you haven't just gone and picked your own in the woods, take a couple of generous handfuls of dried wild mushrooms (particularly porcini) and soak them in warm water for at least an hour. Finely chop a large onion and fry with garlic and seasoning in olive oil until translucent. Squeeze out the mushrooms gently (do not throw away the water), and add to the pan. Cook for a minute or two, then pour in a cup and a half (or thereabouts) of risotto rice. Fry briefly, and add a splash of red wine or vermouth, and then the water (now a deep, brackish brown) in which the dried mushrooms were soaked. Cook slowly until the rice is cooked, adding more water or stock as needed. At the last minute, drop in a knob of butter and then as much grated parmesan as you wish. Eat with robust red wine.

THE SAFE HOUSE

You let a traumatized young woman into your home.
And into your heart.
You want to protect her like a member of your own family.
To save her from the darkness that's pursuing her ...

Samantha Laschen is a doctor specializing in post-traumatic stress disorder. She's moved to the coast to escape her problems and to be alone with her young daughter. But now the police want her to take in Fiona Mackenzie, a girl whose parents have been savagely murdered. Yet by allowing Fiona in, Sam is exposing herself – and her daughter – to risks she couldn't possibly have imagined.

'A superior psychological thriller' *The Times*

'Emotionally acute' *Mail on Sunday*

BENEATH THE SKIN

Someone's watching you.
You don't know who and you don't know why.
But *he* knows you ...

Zoë, Jennifer and Nadia are three women with nothing in common except the letters they receive, each one full of intimate details about every aspect of their lives – from the clothes they wear to the way they act when they think they're alone. And if that isn't terrifying enough, the letters also contain a shocking promise: that soon each life will come to a sudden, violent end. Can Zoë, Jennifer and Nadia discover who their tormentor is? And if so, will any of them live long enough to do anything about it?

'A nail-biting, can't-put-it-down read' *Marie Claire*

'Chilling, startling' *Daily Mail*

'Brilliant' *Evening Standard*

read more
www.penguin.co.uk

KILLING ME SOFTLY

You have it all: the boyfriend, the friends, the career.
Then you meet a stranger and on impulse, you sacrifice everything.
You're in passionate love.
And grave danger ...

Alice Loudon couldn't resist abandoning her old, safe life for a wild affair. And in Adam Tallis, a rugged mountaineer with a murky past, she finds a man who can teach her things about herself that she never even suspected. But sexual obsession has its dark side – and so does Adam. Soon both are threatening all that Alice has left. First her sanity. Then her life.

'Compulsive, sexy, scary' *Elle*

'Cancel all appointments and unplug the phone. Once started you will do nothing until you finish this thriller' *Harpers & Queen*

'A real frightener' *Guardian*

THE RED ROOM

The man who almost killed you has been accused of murder.
And you hold the key to his future ...

After psychologist Kit Quinn is brutally attacked by a prisoner, she is determined to get straight back to work. When the police want her help in linking the man who attacked her to a series of murders, she refuses to simply accept the obvious. But the closer her investigation takes her to the truth behind the savage crimes, the nearer Kit gets to the dark heart of her own terror.

'Gripping, chilling, moving' *Observer*

'Absorbing, highly addictive' *Evening Standard*

'French is excellent at building up suspense and elegantly exploiting all our worst fears' *Daily Mail*

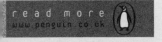

SECRET SMILE

**You have an affair.
You finish it.
You think it's over.
You're dead wrong . . .**

Miranda Cotton thinks she's put boyfriend Brendan out of her life for good. But two weeks later, he's intimately involved with her sister. Soon what began as an embarrassment becomes threatening – then even more terrifying than a girl's worst nightmare. Because this time Brendan will stop at nothing to be part of Miranda's life – even if it means taking it from her . . .

'Creepy, genuinely gripping' *Heat*

'A must read' *Cosmopolitan*

'Nicci French at the top of her game' *Woman & Home*

LAND OF THE LIVING

**You wake in the dark, gagged and bound.
He says he will kill you – just like all the rest.**

Abbie Devereaux is being held against her will. She doesn't know where she is or how she got there. She's so terrified she can barely remember her own name – and she's sure of just one thing: that she will survive this nightmare. But even if she does make it back to the land of the living, Abbie knows that he'll still be out there, looking for her.

And next time, there may be no escape.

'Shocking, uncomfortable, exhilarating' *Independent on Sunday*

'Dark, gripping' *Heat*

CATCH ME WHEN I FALL

You're a whirlwind. You're a success. You live life on the edge. But who'll catch you when you fall?

Holly Krauss lives life in the fast lane. A successful young businesswoman with a stable home life, she is loved and admired by all who meet her. But that's only one side of Holly. The other sees her take regular walks on the wild side – where she makes evermore reckless mistakes.

And when those mistakes start mounting up, the two sides of Holly blur together and her life quickly spirals out of control. She thinks she's being stalked, someone is demanding money from her – threats lurk around every corner and those closest to Holly are running out of patience.

But is she alone responsible for what's happening? Are her fears just the paranoia of an illness – or intimations of *very real* danger? And if she can no longer rely on her own judgement, who can she trust to catch her when she falls?

LOSING YOU

What is worse than your child going missing? Your child going missing and nobody believing you ...

Nina Landry has given up city life for the isolated community of Sandling Island, lying off the bleak east coast of England. At night the wind howls. Sometimes they are cut off by the incoming tide. For Nina though it is home. It is safe.

But when Nina's teenage daughter Charlie fails to return from a sleepover on the day they're due to go on holiday, the island becomes a different place altogether. A place of secrets and suspicions. Where no one – friends, neighbours or the police – believes Nina's instinctive fear that her daughter is in terrible danger. Alone, she undergoes a frantic search for Charlie. And as day turns to night, she begins to doubt not just whether they'll leave the island for their holiday – but whether they will ever leave it again.

UNTIL IT'S OVER (available in hardback)

Dead. Unlucky.

Young and athletic, London cycle courier Astrid Bell is bad luck – for other people. First Astrid's neighbour Peggy Farrell accidentally knocks her off her bike – and not long after is found bludgeoned to death in an alley. Then a few days later, Astrid is asked to pick up a package from a wealthy woman called Ingrid de Soto, only to find the client murdered in the hall of her luxurious home.

For the police it's more than coincidence. For Astrid and her six housemates it's the beginning of a nightmare: suspicious glances, bitter accusations, fallings out and a growing fear that the worst is yet to come …

Because if it's true that bad luck comes in threes – who will be the next to die?

TO FIND OUT MORE ABOUT NICCI FRENCH, VISIT
www.niccifrench.co.uk

Get the inside story behind all the novels.

Read fascinating interviews with Nicci Gerrard and Sean French. Learn more about the authors individually and how they write their novels together.

Extras include a piece from Nicci French's UK editor on the publishing process, and an article from Professor Sue Black on what life is really ike for a forensic anthropologist.

Take Nicci and Sean's (not too serious) test and find out if you are a sociopath!

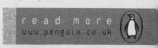

He just wanted a decent book to read ...

Not too much to ask, is it? It was in 1935 when Allen Lane, Managing Director of Bodley Head Publishers, stood on a platform at Exeter railway station looking for something good to read on his journey back to London. His choice was limited to popular magazines and poor-quality paperbacks – the same choice faced every day by the vast majority of readers, few of whom could afford hardbacks. Lane's disappointment and subsequent anger at the range of books generally available led him to found a company – and change the world.

'We believed in the existence in this country of a vast reading public for intelligent books at a low price, and staked everything on it'
Sir Allen Lane, 1902–1970, founder of Penguin Books

The quality paperback had arrived – and not just in bookshops. Lane was adamant that his Penguins should appear in chain stores and tobacconists, and should cost no more than a packet of cigarettes.

Reading habits (and cigarette prices) have changed since 1935, but Penguin still believes in publishing the best books for everybody to enjoy. We still believe that good design costs no more than bad design, and we still believe that quality books published passionately and responsibly make the world a better place.

So wherever you see the little bird – whether it's on a piece of prize-winning literary fiction or a celebrity autobiography, political tour de force or historical masterpiece, a serial-killer thriller, reference book, world classic or a piece of pure escapism – you can bet that it represents the very best that the genre has to offer.

Whatever you like to read – trust Penguin.